IDENTITY PAPERS

IDENTITY PAPERS

Literacy and Power in Higher Education

edited by

BRONWYN T. WILLIAMS

UTAH STATE UNIVERSITY PRESS
Logan, UT

Utah State University Press
Logan, Utah 84322-7800

Manufactured in the United States of America
Cover design by USU Press

Library of Congress Cataloging-in-Publication Data

Identity papers : literacy and power in higher education / edited by Bronwyn T. Williams.
    p. cm.
  Includes bibliographical references.
  ISBN-13: 978-0-87421-649-3 (pbk. : alk. paper)
  ISBN-10: 0-87421-649-4 (pbk. : alk. paper)
  1. Literacy–Social aspects–United States. 2. Education, Higher–United States. I. Williams, Bronwyn
T.
  LC151.I34 2006
  808'.042–dc22
                        2006021376

CONTENTS

1

INTRODUCTION
Literacy, Power, and the Shaping of Identity

Bronwyn T. Williams

We've all seen them on college and university catalogues, brochures, posters, and viewbooks. They are the obligatory photographs of happy, attractive students in classrooms, laboratories, libraries, and fresh green lawns, reading and writing under the thoughtful and attentive guidance of their professors. Though the clothing and the faces may have transformed over the years—the photos are no longer only of white men, but now reflect a carefully chosen mix of race, culture, and sex—and today's students may be shown writing on computers rather than by hand, the message of such photos is remarkably unchanged. What these images imply about the identities of college students and literacy remains much as it did twenty or even forty years ago. The students look comfortable in their literacy practices, no one seems to be struggling, and the professors seem to be offering useful advice. The message seems clear: Come to this college and you will be welcomed into the community of scholarly readers and writers.

Yet for many arriving on college campuses, these images do not reflect reality. For both students, and for many teachers, there is a feeling of alienation, isolation, and frustration. They feel they do not fit the images or identities they have seen portrayed, and they feel their literacy practices are not what they should be even if they are not entirely sure why. Too often they blame themselves when the real conflict centers on questions of identity and institutional power.

As Donna Alvermann (2001) has noted, the goals and interests of educational institutions often create narrowly defined identities for us, whether as scholars, teachers, or students, that we feel compelled to accept to remain a part of the institution. Yet the literacy identities that are regarded as legitimate in the academy can often run counter to our other identities outside the classroom, leaving us feeling isolated and powerless. At such moments we must decide whether to accept the institutional and cultural definitions of ourselves, or to try to find some way to resist or negotiate a professional identity that allows us to live with ourselves while continuing to do the work we value.

The purpose of the book is to focus on how definitions of literacy in the academy, and the pedagogies that reinforce such definitions, influence and shape our identities as teachers, scholars, and students. The chapters reflect those moments in higher education when the dominant cultural and institutional definitions of our identities conflict with other identities, shaped by class, race, gender, sexual orientation, location, or other cultural factors. The strength of this book is that the writers are willing to explore that struggle, identify the sources of conflict, and discuss how they respond to such tensions in their scholarship, teaching, and administration. The authors, in their narratives, theory, and research also illustrate how writing helps them and their students compose alternative identities that may allow the connection of professional identities with internal desires and senses of self. The essays emphasize the necessity for reflection in considering how we negotiate the tensions between our personal and professional identities and then bring those to the classroom.

The essays in this book address key questions about how we compose identities in several important contexts. First, they emphasize how identity comes into play in terms of education and literacy and how institutional and cultural power is reinforced in the pedagogies and values of the writing classroom and writing profession. If we in Composition and Rhetoric are to teach writing and conduct research about writing we need to consider how institutional definitions of literacy shape the identities of ourselves and our students. Who, in the eyes of the institution, is a "reader" or a "writer"? What are the consequences of our definitions of these terms in the academy? How can we as teachers and administrators make definitions of literacy more flexible for student identities? How can we as scholars respond to the inevitable conflicts between the literacy goals and values of our institutions and profession and our identities outside of the academy? The chapters in this book raise and address such questions.

Also, understanding more about institutional definitions of literacy and identity and how students respond to them—how we did as students and how current students do—will make us better teachers. The chapters in the book make these conflicts more visible and suggest ways we might address them in and out of the classroom in pedagogy and research. A number of the essays draw in some way on the student experiences of the writer and the effect those had on the future faculty member, scholar, and teacher. The narratives remind us that our identities are more fluid and overlapping than we sometimes think and that our student identities form the foundation for who we become as professionals. Several of the essays also address how we can engage students in similar kinds of critical reflection in writing that helps them explore their identities and how they negotiate and adapt them according to the influence and expectations of the dominant culture.

Finally, as a graduate student I was often urged to think about my "professional identity" and how I would form it during graduate school. I know I was not alone in feeling sometimes troubled or mystified by what this meant and the feeling that it meant I must give something up about my identity to become a professional in the academy. This book helps articulate these issues and I hope will help graduate students consider how they want to approach such tensions, where to compromise, to resist, and what it will mean for them to compose new professional identities in writing. The narratives about literacy that are reproduced in higher education have a substantial impact on how we construct our identities in our professional lives. The chapters in this book reflect how our identities as scholars, professionals, teachers, and students are shaped by the goals and power of these dominant cultural institutions. The writers integrate narrative, theory, research, and pedagogy in ways that illustrate the need for flexibility in intellectual writing about identity and culture.

LITERACY AND INSTITUTIONS

Recent scholarship in New Literacy Studies has challenged the idea of literacy as an autonomous set of skills and has argued instead that concepts of literacy are always contextual and shaped by cultural expectations and goals. As Brian Street (2001) maintains, such an approach argues that

> [l]iteracy is a social practice, not simply a technical and neutral skill; that it is always embedded in socially constructed epistemological principles. It is about knowledge: the ways in which people address reading and writing are themselves rooted in conceptions of knowledge, identity, being. (7)

Reading and writing in any context, then, is not simply a matter of decoding symbols, but is always inextricable from cultural forces in the context in which the act takes place. Those cultural forces make literacy a powerful element of the dominant ideology of a culture. Though there are multiple literacy practices in different domains of life, the literacy practices that are valued in a culture are based not on an objective concept of utility, but on how such practices reinforce and reproduce dominant cultural norms and power relationships.

Schools at every level are, of course, key institutions in maintaining and reproducing such hierarchies of cultural power. David Barton and Mary Hamilton (1998) argue that dominant literacy practices supported in education "can be seen as a part of whole discourse formations, institutionalized configurations of power and knowledge, which are embodied in social relationships" (10). Such a model of culturally constructed literacies challenges the narrative often embraced by writing teachers that literacy skills will inevitably enable students outside of the dominant culture to become empowered individuals able to change their circumstances. Just as possible is that the writing classroom will "do just the opposite, to embed pupils deeply in the ideology and social control of the teacher's social class and deliberately prevent them from arriving at a detached and critical appraisal of their own situation" (Street 1995, 79). Lynn Bloom (1996) has made a similar argument in identifying composition as a "middle-class enterprise" that devalues certain literacy practices that students engage in outside the classroom while emphasizing the importance of practices and texts that reinforce middle-class values such as decorum, moderation, order, cleanliness, and delayed gratification. Whether the focus of composition course is classical rhetoric or critical pedagogy, students often find that their previous literacy practices, and the identities they supported, are dismissed or ignored and that their work must conform to not just a set of skills, but a set of cultural expectations. Those who enter the academy from backgrounds that are not middle class, white, male, heterosexual, often find that adopting the culturally constructed literacies that dominate higher education challenges important identities that have shaped their lives. Though the students shown in college recruitment photos may seem to have just picked up a book and started to read and interpret the material effortlessly and with smiles on their faces, in fact they can do so only when they have decoded and adapted to identities that fit dominant cultures expectations and values.

IDENTITIES AND PERFORMANCE

At the same time that definitions of literacy have become more complex and situated in cultural contexts, conceptions of identity have undergone similar transformations. Increasingly identity, as opposed to an internal somewhat stable sense of "self," has been recognized as a construction, influenced by culture and ideology and changeable depending on the social context. Indeed the concept of "performing" identity, depending on the context, has influenced much of the discussion on the issue in recent years. The idea of performance emphasizes that, rather than having a single stable identity that I present to the rest of the world, my sense of identity is external and socially contingent. Depending on the social context I find myself in and the social script I believe I should follow, I negotiate and adjust my identity. Sometimes these constructions of identity are conscious and calculated, other times they are so deeply learned that they seem spontaneous and natural. When I enter a classroom I am conscious of constructing my identity for my performance as a teacher. And I am certain that my students are engaged in identity construction of their own to fit the classroom context. When I am talking to a friend I believe I am being "myself" but if I am honest I know that I perform different identities for different friends, not always being the same identity for my friends from childhood as I am for the people I met last year. Consequently I have not a single identity, but multiple shifting identities, determined by culture and context, and sometimes in conflict with one another.

The ways in which we perform identities only seem natural, however, when we are confident of our understanding of the cultural context we are inhabiting. Tensions emerge when we cannot read the cultural context or construct an identity that fits the expectations of others. Cultural theorist Stuart Hall (1994) notes that "identities are the names we give to the different ways we are positioned by, and position ourselves within, the narratives of the past" (394). It is the narratives of the dominant culture that are most often accepted and reproduced as the only relevant narratives. Most people within a culture position their identities within those dominant narratives, and as such are able to perceive identity as singular and stable, as the person you are in the culture that surrounds you. In U.S. culture this seemed a comfortable and rational perspective to a middle-to-upper-class, white, Western, heterosexual, male; but was more problematic and troubling if the identities you wanted to construct did not fit comfortably within the dominant culture's narratives. We all position ourselves within the narratives of the past as a way of constructing and "performing" identities. Yet if the dominant culture rejects or dismisses narratives by "others," those individuals are left feeling as if their identities are misunderstood, devalued, or ignored.

In recent years marginalized groups have succeeded in questioning which cultural narratives should be privileged. Such questioning has included critiques of the concept of stable, unified "truth" and the credibility of the institutions, structures, and processes, such as religion, science, education, and politics, that defined "truth." Through the questioning of such concepts and institutions there has also been a growing conversation about how we construct and perform our identities and what role different social structures and cultural forces play in those processes. We have all heard discussions about the influence on our identities of cultural aspects such as gender, race, class, religion, sexual orientation, location, age, ethnicity, profession, and education. Although some of these discussions have devolved into crude identity politics from both right and left, there are important issues involved in thinking carefully, and without hyperbole or inflammatory language, about how such cultural forces influence our identities and how we can use such issues as important lenses through which to consider who we are and when and why.

The ways in which we read others, how they read us, and how we try to communicate our identities in different cultural contexts are particularly important in the context of literacy. Writing is a deliberate construction and expression of identity on a page (or today, often on a screen). Even if we try not to reveal anything personal in our writing, we are taking on a particular identity, that of the detached, scientific observer—or to put it another way, the white male in the lab coat—in our attempted voicelessness. The way we arrange words, choose to disclose or not, assume our audience, construct our sense of credibility through language are all inextricably bound up with issues of identity (Williams 2003). What James Gee (1990) says about Discourse is also appropriate to questions of literacy in that we use language in such situations as "a sort of 'identity kit' which comes with the appropriate costume and instructions on how to act, talk, and often write so as to take on a particular social role that others will recognize"(142). And if we misread or misjudge, if we get the discourse and literacy conventions wrong as reader or writer, we risk more than misinterpreting the meaning, we also misread identities. Such concerns are directly related to both our work as teachers and researchers in and out of the classroom as well as the work our students do when they enter our classes. Issues of identity influence our work in teaching writing; our decision is whether we acknowledge such influences and what we do to address them in our work.

IDENTITY IN COMPOSITION AND RHETORIC

Exploring the definitions of literacy and identity, of who is literate, and what writing counts as creating a literate identity in higher education, are central to the concerns of the field of Composition and Rhetoric. And in recent years in Composition and Rhetoric there has been a resurgence of interest in how identities are performed in writing by scholars (Freedman, Frey, and Zauhar 1993; Bleich and Holdstein 2001), teachers (Bishop 1997; Tobin 1993), and students (Newkirk 1997). These writers, though accepting that there may not be a single authentic "self" in a given piece of writing, maintain that it is important to acknowledge and examine the identities a writer does present through language. Whether the writing is personal narrative or cultural critique, the argument of these and other writers has been that when a writer writes, an identity is performed and it is important to consider the possibilities and effects of such performances. These works have challenged and enlarged our understanding of identities and writing beyond the well-known cultural critique about the "authentic" self. Included in these challenges are the ways in which contemporary critical theory and identity politics have complicated and enriched our thinking about composing identities. The authors in this volume build on these previous works by now examining issues of identity in the context of the literacy expectations of institutions of higher education.

The question today, then, is not whether identity and the cultural and institutional forces that shape it influence what we write and how we teach, but how it does so. And from this question arise others:

- What identities are we expected to perform in writing and how do those interact or conflict with the identities we perform in other parts of our lives? Which of us are able to display our identities in writing? Which of these displays have the necessary cultural capital to be valued in academic fields and possibly beyond?

- How does the cultural maelstrom of forces such as class, gender, sexual orientation, location, and race influence who we perceive ourselves to be and how we confront them when we compose in writing? How do teachers and institutions that represent and reproduce the dominant culture respond to other identities performed in writing?

- What narratives and positions are available to us as writers and how do they shape our identities on the page? Has the display of identity in writing in fact become an expected rhetorical move that has made personal stories or revelations mere commodities to be consumed by the dominant culture in forms that reproduce that culture?

- And how, when we bring our pedagogies into the writing classroom do we encounter the same forces and experiences in our students? Has the overt display of the writer's identity become, in fact, a move that can limit discussion rather than engage it? Can we respond to the personal in a critical manner? Is that our only available response as teachers?

Alongside these questions, however, there are also new explorations of the creative and critical potential of how we create and communicate identity through writing. Such work, as this book illustrates, does allow for the possibility of bringing into sharp relief the gaps and chasms that often separate our senses of self from the professional identities we must perform as scholars and students. This requires that we engage our personal writing, our lived experiences, with our theoretical inquiries, and bring all of them together in our work with students. We must, as many have said but fewer have accomplished, turn from the false binaries that pit the personal against the academic and instead "continue to refigure our notions of voice and autobiography, separate the notion of authenticity from writing about the self (or at least as the exclusive property of writing about the self), separate writing about the self from hierarchical notions of genres" (Villanueva in Brandt et al. 2001, 52).

At the same time we also have to reconsider how our intellectual theorizing about identity and the performance of self often falls short of capturing the daily human consequences of the identities through which we engage the world. We can talk all we want about multiple selves, but that doesn't stop people from often engaging in particular readings of our identities, or in our responses to those readings. Keith Gilyard (2000), for example, writes that his lived experience as an African American male cannot adequately be addressed through the kind of academic postmodernism that "often gets stuck in passive relativism, just a classroom full of perceived instability. It's useful to complicate notions of identity, but primary identities operate powerfully in the world and have to be productively engaged" (270). Recent work in Composition and Rhetoric has examined particular cultural aspects of identity such as race (Gilyard 1999), gender (Jarratt and Worsham 1998), class (Shepard, McMillan, and Tate 1998), or sexual orientation (Malinowitz 1995), or on aspects of our professional lives such as scholarship (Bleich and Holdstein 2001), administration (George 1994), or teaching (Mayberry 1996). This book draws from the important work done in such books to offer a more integrated perspective of these various cultural forces. Though the chapters in this book often address issues of class, race, gender, and sexual orientation, the book is not an attempt at an exhaustive exploration of any single factor of identity, instead focusing on institutional impositions of identity and literacy and how teachers, scholars, and students respond to such situations.

THE ORGANIZATION OF THIS BOOK

The book is organized into three sections that are broadly chronological in the experiences of people entering and working as reading and writing teachers and scholars in institutions of higher education.

In the first section, *Institutions and Struggles for Identity*, the chapters draw on experiences of coming to the academy as a student or young scholar or administrator, and having one's identity challenged by the institutional goals and identities that one is expected to adopt. The essays in this section focus on how institutions of higher education construct identities of Composition and Rhetoric professionals as faculty and administrators and how the authors resist or negotiate these identities.

James Zebroski in "Social Class as Discourse: The Construction of Subjectivities in English" examines how issues of social class influence our collective and individual identities when working-class students enter colleges and universities and are faced with often conflicting definitions of identity and literacy. These same issues have shaped the field of Composition and Rhetoric and he proposes how we might alter our responses as composition teachers. Patricia Harkin's chapter also focuses on how institutional structures of higher education have shaped the field of Composition and Rhetoric. Her essay "Excellence is the Name of the (Ideological) Game" discusses how the arrival of Composition and Rhetoric as a recognized field in an academic world increasingly influenced by market models of competition influences our sense of identity as professors and teachers.

The other chapters in the first section explore the tensions among faculty when our different identities in and out of the academy collide and conflict. Shannon Carter's chapter "The Feminist WPA Project: Fear and Possibility in the Feminist 'Home'" explores the ambivalence she experienced when her identities as a tenure-track faculty member, writing program administrator, and feminist scholar created tensions for her and for those with whom she worked. She both raises questions and provides possible answers for how writing program administrators can negotiate their multiple identities with the different groups, including those with less institutional power.

Tara Pauliny's essay "When 'Ms. Mentor' Misses the Mark: Literacy and Lesbian Identity in the Academy" explores the unexpected tensions and challenges of identity performance facing scholars as they move from the role of graduate students to faculty members. She specifically addresses how sexuality is often constructed by the academy as an essential, but often ignored, component of identity. She argues that the experiences of lesbian and gay academics remain invisible in the advice literature for new faculty, but require a particular set of negotiations and performances for students, faculty, and scholars.

The chapters in the second section, *Identity in the Composition Classroom,* focus on how cultural and institutional goals pattern and shape the literacy identities of teachers and students and the tensions that can arise when such patterns conflict with other identities they bring into the classroom from their lives outside the academy. The chapters also offer pedagogical strategies for how to acknowledge, address, and particularly reshape identity through narrative and reflection.

Mary Hallet considers the cultural and academic perceptions of nontraditional female students. Her chapter "She Toiled for a Living: Writing Lives and Identities of Older Female Students" explores the positions of older female students in the academy and how their identities are often devalued by traditional colleges and universities. She offers an approach to writing assignments that help them find ways to construct identities in the classroom that allow them to flourish as students and writers. William Carpenter and Bianca Falbo, on the other hand, discuss the struggle with identity the successful writers often confront when moving from high school to college. In "Literacy, Identity, and the 'Successful' Student Writer" they demonstrate how helping such students reflect explicitly on their identities as writers allows them to engage in more nuanced considerations of how such identities are constructed and influenced by cultural norms and institutions.

The final two chapters in this section reveal how working with students' narratives about literacy opens opportunities to help them understand more clearly the challenges of constructing identities in literacy situations where they consider themselves outsiders. Janet Alsup's "Speaking from the Borderlands: Exploring Narratives of Teacher Identity" focuses on preservice teachers and the variety of discourse genres they engaged in as they confronted, struggled with, and eventually negotiated their entrance into the professional discourse community of high school teachers. James R. Ottery in "'Who Are *They* and What Do They Have to Do with What I want to Be?' The Writing of Multicultural Identity and College Success Stories for First-Year Writers" discusses how students from outside the dominant culture can use their literacy narratives to understand more clearly how writing is shaped by cultural forces and different possibilities for response. Ottery discusses how his own identity as a person outside the dominant culture influences his work with students in multicultural settings.

What happens to Composition and Rhetoric scholars when they take their professional identities outside of the academy is the focus of the third section, *Our Identities Outside the Institutional Walls.* Once we have formed professional identities, what happens when they come into contact and conflict with the world outside the classroom? If the first two sections focus on the identities we bring to the academy and the tensions that can emerge, this final section is concerned with what happens when the professional identities we have developed and become comfortable with over the years must engage and adapt with the expectations of others in the larger world.

Robert Brooke in "Migratory and Regional Identity" examines physical location as an important influence on conceptions of identity and literacy. He argues that traditional academic literacies seem to assume "a placeless, migratory self" that can conflict with local identities of those outside of the academy.

How students' representation of their identities in writing is shaped by forces outside of the classroom is the concern of the next two chapters. Sally Chandler focuses her chapter on the ways in which writing teachers shape what students perceive as the possible identities they can adopt in writing. In "Some Trouble with Discourses: What Conflicts Between Subjects and Ethnographers Tell Us About What Students Don't/Won't/Can't Say" she uses scholarship about conflicts over ethnographic representation to look at similar relationships between students and writing teachers in terms of power, academic discourses, and authority and how students' representations of identity are shaped by their teachers' responses. Lynn Worsham's "Composing (Identity) in a Posttraumatic Age" focuses on how events outside of the writing classroom, in particular the events of September 11 and its aftermath, influence the formation of identity in a "posttraumatic culture." Such a response to this cultural shift has implications for how we teach and respond to students' representations of traumatized experience.

Min-Zhan Lu, in her concluding chapter, draws together and responds to the ideas and themes raised in the previous essays. She notes in the volume a common effort to explore the ways that the standardized literacy practices in higher education act as material constraints on how students and teachers go about their work, including their senses of identity and there relations with others and the world.

In terms of how we write, and how we teach and respond to student writing, this book argues for an engagement with issues of identity, rather than treating student writing and our work as if identity could be hidden in the "academic" cloak of a pseudodisembodied objectivity. Instead, taking our cue from the authors in this book, we should work with students to reflect on the identities we all bring to the academy from our lives outside and to understand where those identities connect or conflict with the literate identities recognized by the institution. As scholars, teachers, administrators, and students, we must approach the teaching of writing in ways that recognizes the multiple and overlapping nature of both literacy and identity. It is only then that we can explore the most fulfilling and creative possibilities for composing our identities.

ACKNOWLEDGMENTS

There are a number of people I would like to thank in helping bring this book together for publication. First, I want to thank the contributors for their fine work and great patience in seeing this book through to publication. I want to thank Michael Spooner at Utah State University Press for his guidance and support. And I also thank the anonymous peer reviewers for their thoughtful comments in reviewing the manuscript. I am also grateful for the help of Kyle Sessions in production support and Aarti Asnani for thorough and careful copyediting.

This book developed out of the 2002 Thomas R. Watson Conference on Rhetoric and Composition at the University of Louisville. Pam Takayoshi was the chair of that superb conference and also the person who offered me the opportunity to edit this collection and for that I am grateful. I also appreciate the help and support of other members of the Watson Conference Planning Committee, Carol Mattingly, Brian Huot, Dennis Hall, and Terese Guinsatao Monberg, who came up with the theme for the conference that has served so well for the book.

In the Fall of 2002, I taught a graduate seminar on the theme of *Composing Identities* and the students in that course, through their generous and thoughtful conversation, helped me reflect and expand my thinking on these issues. Those students were Kara Alexander, John Branscum, Rick Carpenter, Kelli Grady, Jo Ann Griffin, Mickey Hess, Tammy Lubash, Dana Nichols, Iswari Pandey, Anne-Marie Pedersen,

Beth Powell, Rene Prys, Carolyn Skinner, Stacy Taylor, Darci Thoune, and Aaron Toscano.

I also want to thank Pat Sullivan, Mary Hallet, Amy Zenger, and Janet Bean, who have all helped me in in my thinking about these issues and this book.

My family as always deserves my thanks. Griffith and Rhys are always growing as my sons and as writers in ways that continue to challenge and delight me. Finally, I am grateful to Mary, who sees all my identities and loves me nonetheless.

PART I

Institutions and Struggles for Identity

2

SOCIAL CLASS AS DISCOURSE
The Construction of Subjectivities in English

James T. Zebroski

*What saved my butt was reading. I loved it. ...If I was propelled from
behind by fear of my Dad, I was pulled ahead by the written word.*
                                                        —Garger 1995

*If this were a story about gender identity, then I would be transgen-
dered. But since this is a story about class, and this is America, I cannot be transclassed.... Acceptance of one's own class identity, like the
acceptance of one's sexual identity, is—despite what those who decry
the use of labels insist—freeing. Rather than limiting one to what one
label (lesbian, working class) states, it expands the realm of the personal
experience.*
                                                        —Brownworth 1997

During the last week of June in 1970, I stepped onto a college campus
for the first time in my life. I was 18 and I had come to Ohio State that
week for freshman orientation. I had come to Columbus from Warren,
about 160 miles to the northeast, on a Greyhound bus. I had never seen
the Ohio State campus before except in the photographs included in
the brochures and catalogues that the university sent when I expressed
interest in applying. I had decided to go to Ohio State because a year
earlier I had read somewhere, probably in the local newspapers, that
OSU at that time was second only to Harvard in the amount of financial aid that it gave out. Once accepted in December I received a form
called the Parents Confidential Financial Statement, a bureaucratic
document required if one wanted to apply for financial aid which I knew
was my only hope for actually going to OSU. This Parents Confidential
Statement created one of the first conflicts that I can recall between
the working-class discourses that I was desperate to escape and the
middle-class discourses I would do *nearly anything* to join but was not yet
a part of. *Nearly anything* included having a big fight with my Dad about
this form. My father was anxious that I stay at home and work—ideally

in a factory as nearly all my friends did who were not on their way to Vietnam. Jobs in factories in 1970 were plentiful and paid extremely well. The sort of work one did in factories was not only understood and valued by my father but also by nearly everyone else I knew in my town. I was supposed to work in the factory, save that money by living at home, and go either to the local branch of Kent State which was in Warren or to Youngstown State which was about twenty minutes away. We had perfectly good universities in the area; there was no good reason to spend a lot of money to go away.

But I had decided I was leaving Warren and the factories and my father's control no matter what I had to do to do that. I had already registered for the draft in May as a conscientious objector; if that were my fate, at least I'd get out of Warren. I was seriously considering the priesthood back then as another escape route, but had serious doubts about celibacy. My determination to leave Warren was not at all untypical of my generation. Unlike our current generation of undergrads, there was precedent and cultural encouragement of sorts back in 1970 for people from my generation to break ties with family. There was a generation gap and it was easier to ally yourself with people your own age. Still, the desperation to leave Warren was about more than that and my father could smell it and he didn't like it.

The Parents Confidential Statement asked the parent of the student applying for financial aid to provide intimate details about the family's income, savings, property, expenses, and deductions. My father was aghast. He saw this as a serious invasion of his privacy—which it was. Only the Internal Revenue Service and maybe God knew about my father's financial business; not even my mother was privy. So here comes this young punk—my father's term for an eighteen-year-old male who think he knows it all—telling him to write all this deeply personal information down to send it off to complete strangers.

There was resistance. There was yelling. There was hollering. My father, after postponing it as long as he could, grudgingly agreed to provide this information, but instructed the young punk to first fill in all the nonconfidential info. So the young punk did that. I thought I'd use all my developing vocabulary skills to gussy up the language a bit, to make it a bit classier. Instead of simply writing "worker" or "factory worker" or even my father's usual "employee of Packard Electric" in the blank for occupation, I wrote *laborer*. A good word, I thought. A little fancy. A bit British. A word that covered up the reality that Dad worked in a factory.

A word that I never had used before in my life. My father read this and went ballistic.

My father was as angry as I had seen him and I didn't know why so he gave me a little lecture about how in his world—in what I am calling his discourse—laborer meant a manual worker. Someone who did whatever was left, someone who was several levels below a factory worker in prestige not to mention pay. A ditch digger was laborer. Father was not happy that I apparently had such a low estimate of his work and of him. Actually, I didn't have a clue about exactly what he did and even less of a clue about the discourse of laborers. I was just trying to enter a new discourse—a bit prematurely.

We got through it obviously. Three years later father told mother that that was actually pretty smart of me to get all of this financial aid, to get a free ride to a college like Ohio State. My mother passed the word on to me. That is how language worked in my family.

One last word about that June trip to freshman orientation at Ohio State. As soon as I actually got to campus and saw it, I was shocked. It was beautiful. I simply had not envisioned a college campus, especially one with 50,000 students, as park. Trees and huge open spaces and benches and squirrels. Where I came from schools including colleges looked more like prisons than parks. The second thing I began to see that hadn't been in my conception of university were all the buildings with fancy red tile roofs. I mean the place looked like pictures I had seen of Southern California. The only buildings that even had tile roofs in Warren were the county courthouse and Greek Orthodox church. The third thing that stands out in my memory was the fact that the campus was completely closed and barricaded after the anti-Vietnam, post–Kent State riots of the spring. Buildings still had broken windows from the riots. The taxi driver asked if I had an ID and when I told him I did not, he said they wouldn't let me on campus. The security person in the booth at the entrance to the Oval checked, and they let me in.

Now what I want to do in the rest of this essay is to focus on the discourse of social class behind this incident, but also behind our discussions of class and identity in composition and rhetoric. The next section delineates six differing, conflicting discourses that position us and in large measure shape the way we think, talk, and act on social class. After describing these conflicting discourses which work to constitute social class in composition and rhetoric, I will consider some of the implications of such a discursive view of social class.

THE DISCOURSES OF SOCIAL CLASS

By discourse, I mean the power of language practices to constitute their object. I am obviously following the lead here of Michel Foucault in his *The Archaeology of Knowledge* (1972), but also acknowledge the work of Jim Berlin, Lester Faigley, Susan Miller, and to a lesser extent Patricia Bizzell and David Bartholomae. The shortest and most precise description of the discourse of discourse, of the varied ways the term discourse is used, can be found in David Jolliffe's (2001) entry on 'Discourse' in the *Routledge Encyclopedia of Postmodernism* (101–3). In that entry, Jolliffe notes that discourse means (1) a passage of language, (2) a passage of language that reflects a group's practices, and (3) the power of language to influence and constrain in a group. This talk works within this third view. Discourse is a regulated practice that accounts for a number of statements. Norman Fairclough, cited in Jolliffe, states that "[d]iscourse is a practice not just of representing the world, but of signifying the world, constituting and constructing the world in meaning" (102). So discourses not only create by constructing, but also by excluding, by making invisible, by prohibiting, by silencing.

The discourses of social class then create the forms within which social class can appear and they create the range of possible identities which can emerge from the discourse.

In reflecting on my earlier class narrative, I can say that in 1970 a discourse of class shaped my idea of university, making some notions unlikely. Parks and tile roofs and financial aid were not in my discourse. Their absence made these things difficult for me to imagine. The idea that I might go the next step and apply to many colleges and barter for the best financial aid package was also absent from my discourse, nearly unthinkable. Even though one of my closest friends was going to Harvard, the very idea that I might apply there was alien even to my border discourse. That discourse made invisible a whole network of subsidies to the middle class in higher education. Even in graduate school, I had to learn too late to be of help about fellowships. The clash of social class discourses that occurred with the Parents Confidential Statement shows that the working-class discourse in which I was raised was not singular or sealed shut, but it also showed me that translating across these discourses was extremely difficult. For one thing, if you take up that role of translator across discourses you in some important ways become invisible to your family and your old friends—my mother does not have a clue what I do at work or at conferences like this and doesn't really want to know—but you also risk becoming invisible in important ways to the your professors and new middle- and upper-class friends. As I will detail at the end of this chapter, this is one reason why witness narratives are so crucial. They break the silence created by the discourses.

Now the discourse of social class is not singular. There are many class discourses. When we talk about social class, I hear at least six differing and often contradictory discourses. Once you enter any one of these discourses, your lines of argument, your key words, your values, not to mention your subject position and identities, are relatively established, at least at the start. One of the reasons it is so difficult to talk about social class in America is because these discourses of social class are relatively discrete and we often are simply in different universes of discourse in class discussions.

THE DISCOURSE OF POSITION

Social class in this discourse is a position in a hierarchy determined by some external and often easily quantifiable factor like income, education, and occupation.

The Parents Confidential Statement is the perfect example of this as was my father's lesson on laborers. Yet I also think this construction of social class was part of what my father was resisting. For him being working class was NOT about income or education or occupation alone. It was about social relations. The discourse of position is the ruling discourse on social class in America and so we should not be surprised that if we enter this discourse that it is extremely difficult to make class distinctions. In this discourse, we all mostly turn out to be middle class. This is then the discourse of the popular media. And when we euphemistically talk about "first generation college" students we too are in this discourse. Almost all scholars of social class in America address this discourse because it is so powerful, even when they do not locate themselves in it. Michael Zweig (2000) for instance in his new book *The Working Class Majority: America's Best Kept Secret* begins from a social relation discourse of class, but attempts to use that discourse to analyze the US Department of Labor's exhaustive data on occupation stratification. Doing so allows him to argue that 62 percent of Americans are in the working class.

THE DISCOURSE OF SOCIAL RELATIONS

Social class in this discourse is about power relations between people and groups of people. Traditionally, it has focused on what groups have power in the production process in the economy. Adam Smith, Karl

Marx, and many others argue that profit is produced by the workers. But then how to explain the bulging middle? G. William Domhoff (1998) takes one approach by defining and examining what he, after C. Wright Mills, calls the "ruling" class in America. He says,

> On top of the gradually merging layers of blue- and white-collar workers who comprise the working class and makes up 85–90 percent of the population, there sits a very small social upper class which comprises at most 0.5 percent of the population and has a very different lifestyle and source of income from the rest of us. Many Americans are not even aware of the existence of this upper class. They are used to thinking of the highly paid and visible doctors, architects, television actors, corporate managers, writers, and governmental officials and experts who stand between the working class and the upper class as the highest level of the social pecking order. ... But the "rich" are not a handful of discontented eccentrics, jetsetters, and jaded scions who have been pushed aside by the rise of corporations and governmental bureaucracies. They are instead full fledged members of a thriving social class which is as alive and well as it has ever been. (3–4)

Also, Erik Olin Wright (1985) in his book *Classes* locates his argument in a social relations discourse, and discusses contradictory class positions and making an important place for a wide range of credentialed and uncredentialed supervisors and managers in his theory of class. The discourse of social relations sees the world in us/them terms, pitting the numerous little people against the few rulers. The social relations discourse of class was the one my father felt most comfortable in. It is the discourse that emphasizes "what we have in common" and therefore is most useful in uniting people and in organizing them.

THE DISCOURSE OF WORK AND THE WORKPLACE

A little secret. If you want to talk with someone about social class and he or she is reluctant to talk about social class, move the conversation to work and the workplace. This is especially true now because as Jim Berlin, David Harvey, Richard Ohmann, and others have shown us we are living through a great transformation of capitalism that began about 1971 and is still ongoing called flexible accumulation or a post-Fordist regime of capitalism. Almost everyone has a horror story to share about the new workplace.

The discourse of work and the workplace focuses on social interaction and social stratification at work. It focuses on the changes in everything from technology to character that are occurring at work.

The Joseph Harris–James Sledd debate within our own profession is one good example of this discourse. Downing, Hurlbert, and Mathieu's (2002) recent volume *Beyond English Inc.: Curricular Reform in a Global Economy* and Eileen Schell's (1997) *Gypsy Academics and Mother Teachers* are others.

Composition and rhetoric is classed not simply in its appropriation of post-Fordist methods, among them the hiring of contingent labor. It is classed in its teaching, its scholarship, and in its professional practice. I have much more to say about this, but for now, let me just note that this discussion can begin with the facts of our employment—how many classes do we teach and how many students do we have each term. Not coincidentally, heavy loads correlate with colleges that have large numbers of students from the working class. By the way, I teach a 4:4 load at Capital and I have 73 students this term. Such facts are part of the social structure in composition and rhetoric.

THE DISCOURSE OF CULTURAL HERITAGE

In this discourse, social class is the cultural heritage, the way of life— what we think, say, do—that is created, preserved, treasured, and passed down by folk in the working class. It is a discourse of value and of everyday life.

The cultural heritage discourse is the discourse that folks from the working class exercise the most control over, so it should not be surprising to see so many academics from the working class turn to this discourse. It makes a kind of sense to both researcher and researched. Julie Lindquist's (2002) new *A Place to Stand: Politics and Persuasion in a Working Class Bar* and Robert Bruno's (1999) *Steelworker Alley: How Class Works in Youngstown* are just two rigorous, respectful, and imaginative examples of the importance of cultural heritage discourse of class in academic work. Of course, *Coming to Class: Pedagogy and the Social Class of Teachers* (Shepard, McMillan, and Tate 1998) and *This Fine Place So Far From Home* (Dews and Law 1995) are by now classics of this discourse and its genre. Though these two books are classics of the discourse of cultural heritage, they also draw heavily on the discourse of witness, more about which later.

Most of working-class studies is currently engaged with this discourse. Among the people very interested in class as cultural heritage are creative writers. There has been a virtual renaissance over the last decade or so of creative writers from the working-class publishing poems, stories, novels, creative nonfiction on this heritage. Jim Daniels has certainly been a leader in this. Following the lead long ago of people like Tillie Olsen (1978) and her book *Silences,* new presses have emerged including Bottom Dog Press, which has printed a variety of volumes including *Getting By: Stories of Working Class Lives* (Shevin and Smith 1996). Kent State University Press publishes a good deal working-class cultural heritage materials including the photography of James Jeffrey Higgins (1999), *Images of the Rust Belt.* And the Center for Working Class Studies at Youngstown State, the first institute of its kind in the United States devoted to working-class studies, has an important function of preserving what is becoming a vanishing way of life in the Mahoning and Shenango valleys and beyond.

THE DISCOURSE OF INDIVIDUAL AFFILIATION

In my analysis, I wanted to leave room for the pervasive American resistance or ambivalence to social class. I also wanted to acknowledge that there are no social class police enforcing your identity. I think this is an important enough phenomenon to warrant its own discourse, the discourse of individual affiliation which includes the ability to disidentify and reidentify as an individual with a class. To the person who says I am not from the working class, I say fine. In this discourse, you can choose to identify (or dis- identify) with whatever class you want. After all, my disidentification with my working-class cultural heritage when I was 18 made it easier at that time for me to imagine leaving home and going away to a place like Ohio State. However, to accept the discourse of individual class affiliation does not necessarily mean one must accept a Horatio Alger rags to riches narrative. To be sure, that genre fits here, but so do lots of genres which resist that utopian view. Acceptance of the effects of this discourse does not mitigate the other discourses. In fact, quite the contrary. The discourse of individual affiliation fits nicely and reinforces positivistic measures of social class, that is, the discourse of position.

THE DISCOURSE OF WITNESS

The final discourse of social class is also difficult to see, to analyze, and to study. It is far from evident. The discourse of witness is unlike the other discourses in that it is not at all about persuasion. The other discourses are very rhetorical in that effects are created on those who have been persuaded to locate themselves within the discourse. The aim of the discourse of witness, however, is most clearly not to persuade or to inform or to change someone. Its effects on others are either subtle or nonexistent. The discourse of witness is a speech act performative—a witness is created by witnessing, nothing more. This discourse says something like "I witness to the working class." Now someone else may well shape that witness for persuasive purposes, but the witnessing itself is not done primarily or at all to change someone's mind. Witnessing sometimes is done for or to a higher power, perhaps what Mikhail Bakhtin called the hero of discourse—to God or Science or History.. But I am not convinced that this discourse of witness is always done for some higher power. I am obviously drawing on religious and legal analogies here, but both of them break down fairly quickly. The discourse of social class that witnesses says something like "I am here. We are here. We exist whether you like that or not, whether you acknowledge us or not, whether you even hear us or not. We are here especially if you silence us and make us invisible."

Surprised by the large number of gay and lesbian contributors to their book on social class, Dews and Law (1995) in *This Fine Place So Far From Home* theorize a resemblance between the stories in their book and coming out stories in the gay community. They say,

> While our gender and race identities, comparatively stable and usually marked by readily visible signs, always sends messages whether we intend them or not, our class identity is a good deal less stable and marked by signs more easily concealed. In order to claim working class identity in a context that presumes middle class homogeneity, we must *do* something. I, like the authors, ...had to choose to disclose myself, a politically charged gesture for which the university has few opportunities; it in fact actively discourages such disclosure. In terms of self disclosure, working class autobiography is like gay and lesbian identity politics which is also threatening to the "standards" and "discipline" of the essentially conservative institution. (6)

There is something like that, something like a social class coming out story, that runs all through these other discourses of social class. It is a bit like Queer Nation's chant—"We're Here. We're Queer. Get used to it." Sort of "We're Here. We're Working Class. Get Used to it." The discourse of witness breaks the class silence.

CLASS AS DISCOURSE IN LANGUAGE AND IDENTITY

So what does all of the work we have done on the concept of social class as a discourse do for us? I think the concept of social class as discourse helps us in the following ways.

First, approaching class as discourse brings us back to what we all know best—language and the ways that language constitutes culture and identity. While I do think it is important to acknowledge and to understand the economic, political, anthropological, and sociological aspects of social class in the United States, I think that what English teachers bring to this conversation is our strong expertise and experience with language. Properly speaking, social class can only be approached in English as discourse since that is what our professional object is. This does not at all mean that we need to reduce social class to discourse. There are clearly other aspects of social class that other disciplines can better address than we.

A corollary of this is that when we view social class as discourse we can connect up our scholarship with others in and out of the department who use discourse theory to analyze text. We can draw on Foucault to Fairclough and many others. So this approach plays to the strength of the humanities.

Second, such an approach deconstructs the binary that usually accompanies identity politics or identity studies—that we shall either celebrate heritage or critique that positioning. The approach to social class as discourse argues for neither a celebration of heritage nor a critique of ideology, but for a study of the social and individual *in* language acts. Jane Hindman (2001) and Richard Miller (1996) provide a methodology for doing precisely this in our classrooms. Let also add that when we understand social class as discourse, we avoid the entire difficulty of the totalized and totalizing subject which can be appropriated for oppressive purposes. I think the likelihood of this happening in a culture like ours where social class has always been the least acceptable discourse is so low as to be not a consideration. Nevertheless, for those who are so concerned, appropriating Foucault's concept of discourse, most experts would agree, has built in safeguards against this totalizing tendency. These safeguards deriving from Foucault's counter-totalizing redefinition of power as local and positive.

Third, a discursive construal of social class acknowledges the "workplace" discourse post-Fordism in the academy and especially in composition and rhetoric. Our jobs and our professions are classed. Given nearly irresistible post-Fordist economic pressures on academe, we need to consider that there may be good reason to locate composition within the humanities within English. Poovey (2001) presents a very strong argument for this saying,

> The only way we can evaluate the effects of the market's penetration
> into the university in terms other than the market's own is to assert some
> basis for evaluation that repudiates market logic and refuses market
> language...I want to call this normative alternative "the humanities." I
> do so not because disciplines in the humanities necessarily or inevitably
> perform critique, but because, as a sector of the university least amenable
> to commodification, the humanities may be the only site where such an
> alternative may survive. (11)

Fourth, viewing social class as discourse reemphasizes geneologies,
that is, the writing and revising of histories of English and of composition and rhetoric in terms of the working classes. Composition has been
largely constructed through discourses our students, especially those
from the working class, over the last forty years, far more than by the
great ideas and hero scholars that fill our official histories. We need to
write these counter histories. Dixon (1991) provides at least a start in his
book *A Schooling in 'English'*. We must publicly acknowledge the heavy
debt composition has to colleges of education, to their teachers and
students, who, of all departments on campus, most heavily represent
the working class.

Fifth, social class as discourse presents a rationale and opportunity
for "studying up" the social ladder. In 1988 at the MLA Right to Literacy
conference, I noted, "I like Shirley Brice Heath's (1983) *Ways With
Words*, but perhaps it is time to complement that volume with a parallel
in-depth study of how Wall Street financiers create community and use
literacy. We need to match our vast literature on the life of oppressed
communities with a critical study of life and literacy in oppressor communities." Given the huge corporate scandals of recent years involving
Enron, Worldcom., Tyco, and many others, this proposal seems even
more crucial and relevant now as in 1988. I am still waiting for such
critical scholarship. Let me add that these scandals ought to be cause
for the champions of professional writing in composition and rhetoric
to justify their approaches showing us how they do not simply reproduce
a corrupt post-Fordist society.

Sixth, starting with social class as discourse, we can understand the
dual need to teach the conventions of ruling discourse *and* critique those
conventions through new forms. A recent RTE study by Penrose suggests that first-generation college students leave university *not* because
they perform poorly in academic literacy or get low grades, but rather

because they are dissatisfied by a university that does not seem to see them as a legitimate part of the academic community. *We must teach* genres *which open up a space for student experience,* that acknowledges their legitimate contributions. Forms like creative nonfiction, ethnographic writing, and multigenre projects are not nice supplements or alternatives to academic discourse; they are central if students are going to find form for their experience and stay in university.

Let me conclude by asserting that I see nothing in the discourse theory that I am proposing in this essay that takes away or abolishes agency. Indeed, discourse theory acknowledges the complexities of real agency. We can know of our agency in part through acknowledging the agencies of others on us. This is one of the functions of witness discourse, not so much to have effects on others in any short-term easy to identify way, but to trace out the agencies of others in our lives on us. Every time we speak of the effects of other persons on us, we speak of the potential agency that we have in a collective with others.[1]

3

EXCELLENCE IS THE NAME OF THE (IDEOLOGICAL) GAME

Patricia Harkin

Imagine for a moment that you are not a practitioner of composition studies but instead a bricklayer. You have earnestly prepared for your profession. You enjoy building strong, useful structures. Eagerly you arrive at the worksite where you have been engaged to build a wall. You look around, puzzled.

There are no bricks. Instead, you encounter a perky woman in a Liz Claiborne suit carrying a sheaf of thick beige paper engraved in gray gothic letters: *The Brick Foundation.* She explains,

> What you need to do is fill out this application. In five, single-spaced pages, you are to establish your bricklaying competence, explain the project, describe the bricklaying method you plan to use, estimate the time it will take you to complete the job, and provide a budget for mortar, trowels, and protective kneepads. Next, you find three other bricklayers familiar with your work, and ask them to take time out from their own bricklaying to write a letter in support of yours.

Frustrated, you ask whether there's a way for you simply to start working without producing all the bureaucratic paper. Rather than answer, Suit Lady tells you more about The Brick Foundation and its philanthropies—America has been good to the Foundation, she explains, and they just want to give back. Resigning yourself to the notion that you'll have to compete to work, you ask about the criteria the Foundation uses to make its decision. "We just look for excellence," Suit Lady says.

COMPOSITIONISTS AS COMPETITORS FOR FUNDING

This parable has, I hope, suggested that competition for the wherewithal—the actual raw materials—to do one's work is an inefficient way of getting a job done. Nonetheless, as compositionists in the academy, we often find ourselves competing for external and even internal funds to do the work that has historically been entrusted to us, work that used to be sustained by university and department operating budgets, work that, when grant applications are unsuccessful, no longer gets done.

When capitalism appears to be inefficient at one thing, it is often being very efficient at something else. This essay is about that "something else" and its effect on our sense of identity as professors and practitioners of composition studies. We might be said to have composed an identity for ourselves as persons who raise questions about how to define writing so that we can teach it. That identity has both research and service components. In part as a consequence of our success in establishing ourselves as researchers, many of us now find ourselves in a position wherein we are required to compete for the opportunity to deliver the service. For instance, I heard recently of a writing center director who is seeking grant funding because the English Department that used to support the center through its operating budget has withdrawn that support.

In other cases, the grant culture is capable of changing the work that we do, prompting us to do work that's fundable rather than to look for funding for work that we see as necessary and/or interesting. As an instance, I would cite a recent meeting I attended as a member of a think tank for a national professional organization charged with devising projects for the entire association to investigate. Someone suggested, for example, that the organization investigate and take a position on the use of contingent labor to teach writing courses. "But there's no funding available" was the immediate response. True enough. But it is hardly surprising that multinational capital is disinclined to fund studies that are likely to be critical of outsourcing. Maybe, though, an organization that represents teachers of English should look into it for free.

I worry about what it has done to us—this tendency to identify ourselves primarily as competitors for corporate funding rather than as teachers, historians, scholars, or (even) as activists for social change. What is the job that this competition is accomplishing? Why do we do it? One answer comes of course from classical economic theory: competition improves the commodity and (therefore) allows the invisible hand to set a higher price for it. Although the culture seems long ago to have decided that education is a commodity, many scholars and researchers in composition studies still believe that the work through which they define themselves—that is, inquiring into writing in order to teach it—is not entirely comprehensible in that way.

Another answer is that we do it because we are called to, actually called into being as competitive seekers after corporate and governmental capital. When university managers encourage or require us to compete for the funds to do our work, they do so in the name of *excellence*. In *The University in Ruins*, Bill Readings (1996) asserts that the posthistorical university is in fact best understood as a techno-bureaucratic institution-alization of "excellence"—an empty signifier that emerged as an answer to the peculiarly postmodern question:

How can incommensurable entities be competitively measured?

How, for example, in the absence of transhistorical, transcultural conception like truth, nature, or reality to which to refer does a review committee adjudicate among three proposals for grant funding—one to develop a computer application, one to offer a formal reading of "Lycidas," and one to conduct an ethnographic study of Puerto Rican dance? No problem. "Excellence" serves as what Readings calls a "prin-ciple of translatability." The unstated assumption is that each proposal is evaluated in its own disciplinary terms, which are then converted into imaginary units of excellence—a kind of academic *euro*—that can then be measured to produce a winner.

In his analysis, Readings is somewhat dismissive. His claim is that because the word "excellence" is meaningless, because it has "no exter-nal referent or internal content" (23), and because, in other words, it doesn't call on us to *be* anything but "excellent," it is not ideological. The implication is that after a few laughs at lunch over the university's new-est and most ludicrous use of the word "excellence," the serious thinker will return to her library carrel or his computer to continue a serious individually fashioned and self-sustaining inquiry, leaving the corporate types in the administration building to the play of empty signifiers.

"EXCELLENCE" AND IDEOLOGY

Notwithstanding my admiration for Bill Readings's analysis, I disagree strenuously with his assertion that "excellence," lacking internal con-tent and external reference, is not ideological. My argument is that, in the context of the contemporary academy, the content of the word "excellence" is competition, and its referent is winning. "Excellence," in my view, waddles like an ideology and quacks like an ideology, and it is quite useful to critique it as one. To do so is to see that the emphasis on excellence is not (as Readings would have it) silly, but really rather dangerous.

I'll begin with the definition of ideology that Readings and I share. In "Ideology and the Ideological State Apparatuses," Louis Althusser defines ideology as "the imaginary relation of individuals to their real conditions of existence" (1971, 162). This relation occurs when and because the subject is called upon—interpellated or hailed—by the apparatuses of the nation state—church, educational institutions, and so forth—and, through that hailing, is called into being. An ideology calls a subject into being by teaching her the "techniques and knowledges" (e.g., spinning wool into yarn, teaching writing through the use of peer group workshops) that are necessary to reproduce her way of life. In addition, every worker also learns what Althusser calls "the attitude that should be observed by every agent in the division of labor, according to the job he is 'destined' for: rules of morality, civic and professional conscience . . . [or, more abstractly] a reproduction of submission to the ruling ideology for the workers, and a reproduction of the ability to manipulate the ruling ideology correctly for the agents of exploitation" (132). In a very famous formulation, Althusser explains how a culture accomplishes this teaching:

> Ideology "acts" or "functions" in such a way that it recruits subjects among the individuals (it recruits them all) or transforms individuals into subjects (it transforms them all) by that very precise operation which I have called interpellation or hailing, and which can be imagined along the lines of the most commonplace everyday police (or other) hailing, "hey, you there!"

That call comes, and that being is evoked—even if the calling is inconvenient, even if it makes it necessary for you to believe and do things that run counter to your interests.

One classic example is the church. If I am poor, and my church calls on me to accept that poverty in this life, without complaining or trying to change things, because I shall be rewarded with eternal life in the next, then Althusser would call my religious belief ideological. That belief forges for me an imaginary relation to the real: it is a narrative I tell myself in order to make my real poverty intelligible and bearable. The church (acting for a God in whom I believe) calls, "hey, you, poor person! Yours is the Kingdom of Heaven." And I respond by accepting my poverty through all kinds of provocation. As a narrative, this notion that I shall someday, in some other life, be happier may have the corollary effect of making me less likely to participate in a strike or to declare a revolution against the persons to whom I sell my labor, the persons who keep me poor. In that sense the ideology supports a capitalist status quo.

By analogy, a university personnel committee calls upon us to compete internally and externally for grants, and we know ourselves to be members of the university insofar as we answer that call. "Funded researchers" get jobs and keep them, and so we strive to become funded researchers. In answering the call, we find rewards of sorts—raises, tenure, promotion, invitations to dinner at the Dean's. But if the analogy with the church is to hold, and I think it does, something also is lost in this imaginary relation we forge to the real conditions of life in the academy. What is lost, I think, is a different sense of identity—a way of knowing ourselves as researchers into questions that we ourselves raise as a consequence of actual problems we encounter in the classroom, library, or culture.

The terms of our inquiries change when we follow the money. As we construct our inquiries to follow the money, we also construct our "selves." All there is of you, according to Althusser, is what ideological state apparatuses call forth. There is no essential you beyond the reach of interpellation.

In the tradition Readings and Althusser describe, the university (as an ideological state apparatus) call upon a man (I of course use the gendered term self-consciously) to act as a subject of universal reason who strives to embody the best that has been thought and said in his nation state. One becomes the subject of universal reason through disinterested inquiry. But the notion of disinterested inquiry is sustained by—and perhaps only comprehensible in a context of—a notion of universal, transhistorical truth. If you believe in disinterested inquiry, you can also rather easily believe in competition. You can even believe that competition might get you closer to the truth.

In postmodernity, though, we've lost the notion of transhistorical truth. It has been replaced by disciplinary piety, an almost religious eagerness to demonstrate that we conduct our inquiries within the parameters of our discipline's regulated way of raising and answering questions, that we use its lexicon correctly, that we trust its experimental and analytic procedures, and that we reveal our results to other researchers through its representation techniques. One instance of such disciplinary piety might be the instruction to place an asterisk next to "refereed journals" on one's annual faculty activities report, as though the value of one's work is a function, not of its ability to describe and solve problems, but of certain *kinds* of competitive readings.

When this disciplinarity is located in a system that requires "competition" for limited funds—whether those funds come from external grants or from internal operating budgets—situations arise in which ethnographers are forced to compete with—to be measured against—formalist literary critics and cognitive linguists. The "judges" are then forced to invent "excellence" as (in Readings's good words) a "principle of translatability" that allows for the measurement of the incommensurable.

GRANTS, AGENCIES, AND POWER

The university calls on us to be measured—not in Aristotle's sense of finding a golden mean—but in corporate capitalism's sense of competing in terms of size. But by whose authority does this call come? For Althusser, of course, the conception of the nation state inheres in the relation between interpellator and the interpellated subject. That is, the educational system of which he wrote in 1969 operated as an arm of the nation state when it called upon its subjects to know the best that had been thought and said in (for example) France or Great Britain. But Readings suggests (and I agree) that in global capitalism that has emerged in the nearly fifty years since Althusser wrote, the nation state has become virtually irrelevant.

(Such an assertion may seem counter-intuitive at a time when, as I write this, several nation states are engaged in armed conflict. According to the terms of this analysis, however, it is arguable that corporate capitalism has used the names of the nation states who constitute the Coalition of the Willing in order to authorize its war for oil.)

If the nation state can no longer serve as the author of interpellation, it would nonetheless be unwise to throw the Althusserian baby out with the nation-state bathwater. Even though the nation-state may no longer be essential to interpellation, some governing power that can authorize an institution like the university system probably is. Multinational corporations, I think, are such a power. "Granting agencies" that serve as the philanthropic branch of such multinational corporations can, then, have the kinds and extent of control over the day-to-day behavior of ordinary people that were exercised by the nation state in older forms of capitalism. Like the nation state, they assign subject positions (like "funded researcher") on the basis of an idealized order, a structure of interrelations (like the hierarchy of research, teaching, service) that reflect the design of the institution and name its social function. Universities, for example, are designed as conglomerates of departments that embody disciplines. Two hundred years ago, teachers and researchers sought to produce subjects of universal reason. Today, they produce competitors—for grant monies, for rankings by national publications, for test scores, for larger and greater endowments, for internationally known faculty members, for graduate students. The multinational corporation has replaced the nation state; disciplinary piety has replaced transhistorical truth. But competition remains, and "excellence" emerges as the mark of the winner. Just as it fostered "truth" two centuries ago, the university now generates "excellence."

And we are called into being as competitors in its name. I would argue, then, that in this context it is the hailing itself—rather than the "content" of the belief system—that is the important part of Althusser's formulation. Today's narratives of excellence operate similar to the more traditional kinds of interpellation that Althusser describes. In today's stories, a university is "excellent," or, more precisely, *has* "excellence" (because part of the problem is the nominalization, and the reification) if somebody measures it—or a part of it—say its basketball team or its Department of Polymer Chemistry—as somehow *measurably* the best. *It is that measurement that produces the excellence.*

The "ideology" I find in the floating signifier "excellence," then, is the belief that we become subjects—not as Americans or Catholics or subjects of universal reason—but as competitively measured entities. Recently, the Center for Excellence in Teaching and Learning at a major university staged an internal competition for fifty thousand dollars in grant monies. Eighteen departments competed for this award on a form whose first question was: "how do you measure excellence in teaching?" The two "winning" departments got twenty-five thousand dollars each; the others got nothing. In this situation, the university decides to spend fifty thousand dollars on teaching, but then it decides to *superimpose* the notion of competition over that of spending money on teaching. And in that context, the notion of competing for twenty-five thousand dollars is evidently more appealing than the idea of sharing fifty. If I believe for a moment that the English department lost because it doesn't have as much excellence as the department of mechanical engineering—or that it won because it has more—then I've bought into that ideology. I have become a member of either an excellent department or a nonexcellent one.

But even as I answer the call, I really know that you can't compare the work of the department of mechanical engineering to the work of the department of English. Still, I compete. "You should strive to be excellent," they tell us. And we do, even though we know that excellence is an empty signifier.

This circumstance is important precisely because it is contradictory. Indeed it is that contradiction that marks it as ideological, this time in Fredric Jameson's sense of the term. In his *The Political Unconscious: Narrative as a Socially Symbolic Act* (1981), Jameson invokes the ethnography of Levi Strauss (among many other theoretical documents) to analyze the narratives that constitute what Althusser calls our imaginary relation to the real. In Jameson's account, these narratives, which he calls "the central instance of human consciousness" (13), emerge from an attempt somehow to bridge a double bind presented by the mode of production. Jameson then borrows a representation technique he calls the "semiotic rectangle" from the French narratologist, A. J. Greimas, as a "methodological starting point, as a set of categories to be explored [in order to] constitute the empty slots and logical possibilities . . . against which the content of a given social text is to be . . .sorted out" (46). A Greimasian analysis of the grant culture might look like this:

Prescription: compete to win Seek grants in order to measure yourself and your inquiry against others and defeat them.	Taboo: don't compete Pursue inquiry for its own sake; Different inquiries are incommensurable. The human subject is transcendently beyond measurement.
Nonprescriptions: compete and lose Even unsuccessful grant applications are good. They make you and your university more visible and will therefore be rewarded when you record them on your annual report of faculty activities.	Nontaboo: win without competing If you make yourself and the university visible through something other than the *usual* competitive pathways, that's OK, too. You can win by refusing to follow the rules, if you do so in a spectacular way.

The value of the Greimasian rectangle, in Jameson's formulation, is not that it *solves* a problem. Rather, one might say that it deploys four bad answers onto a grid in order to offer a heuristic picture of the ideological terms of the particular problem at hand. The rectangle makes the double bind visible, in other words, and prompts us to go on to the next step, which is to ask, "why *this* double bind, in *these* terms, *now?*" The answer to that question will illuminate the mode of production that gives rise to the double bind. The current mode of production, which Jameson calls postmodernism, is characterized by a multiplicity of contradictory interpellations (see his "Postmodernism, or the Cultural Logic of Late Capitalism," 1991, ix-xv). On the one hand, for example, we are told that we must compete to survive; on the other, we also know that (absent universal truth) competition between incommensurable entities is impossible.

THE COST OF GOING ALONG

We are called into being as contemporary academics in part through this double bind. We believe in competition among the incommensurable even though it doesn't make sense. *Credo quia absurdum est.* Excellence, as a principle of translatability among incommensurable scales of value, is ideological, then, because it's an *imaginary* conception that solves a *real* problem—the impasse between "competition" as a necessary component of capitalism and the undecidability of the postmodern. The University of Excellence calls on us to believe that even among incommensurable entities, even when meaningful measurement is impossible, competition—being measured—is good.

To go on, to get along, we have to make that double bind tolerable, or even invisible. We need, to return to Althusser, an *imaginary* relation to the *real* double bind, a way of hiding from ourselves, or hiding ourselves from the *contradictions* that have their source in history. To understand the historical source of these contradictions, it is necessary to remember that, two hundred years ago, people believed in truth. To support that belief they established a disciplinary system that taught people how to look for it. Now, even though we no longer believe in transhistorical truth, we retain the search engines designed to find it, engines that now carry us directly into the contradiction.

Those engines are competitive. They are still around because competitive measurement is crucial to capitalism. Please recall Treasury Secretary's Paul O'Neill's remarks about Enron: "Companies come and go. It's part of the genius of capitalism" (*New York Times*). The empty signifier excellence becomes necessary only in a culture in which somebody wins *because* somebody loses. What's won and lost is capital—of both the actual and symbolic varieties. Our lives as academics offer many examples of the genius of capitalism. I think especially of the kinds of calls that come in times, like now, of straitened budgets, demanding that departments compete—and offer measurements—in order to survive. In their essay "Excavating the Ruins of Undergraduate English," for example, Bruce Horner and his colleagues describe Drake University's requiring its English department to justify itself in terms of its value to the university (2002, 78–79).

Within the postmodern university, though, competitive measurement can only be accomplished by applying an empty signifier to the incommensurable. Measurement precedes essence (to borrow Existentialism's formulation) but the essence that measurement gives us is a chimera. Nonetheless, we believe in that chimera—at least enough to desire to be called excellent.

But how do we hide? How do we construct a narrative that allows us to live with the double bind? Instead of recognizing the system as absurd—and I use that term in its full existential sense—we hide its absurdity, and our own powerlessness in its face, by calling it a *game that we have chosen to play.*

Game is a phenomenological space in which meaningless measurements count. For example, merely carrying a football for a hundred yards is relatively meaningless. But carrying a football for a hundred yards between two goalposts while ten people are trying to help you and eleven others are trying to stop you is a touchdown—six game points. What makes this run a touchdown is the system of arbitrary rules that differs from "earnest"—from real life—precisely because those rules limit interference from actuality. The referees, for example, can be relied upon to prevent the guys on the bench from jumping up and tripping the runner. Rules make it possible to keep score. Scores make winners.

It's a game. It is true that our lives are governed by competitions in which a floating signifier is used as a standard of measurement, but never mind, it's just a game. Old folks tell young folks, tenured professors tell probationary ones, to learn to play the game. You get higher scores on computerized teaching evaluations by adjusting the questions rather than changing your classroom behavior. But those bubble sheets don't really measure anything, and besides, it's just a game. A department chair urges a candidate for tenure to rewrite her account of a Marxist thinker, not as an explication of his thought, but rather as a critique of "post-Marxism" because that's where the game is. A speaker urges a group of graduate students to teach argument—it's the only game in town. A member of the audience objects that there's more to the game than argument. The speaker, looking pained, responds that that objection is part of the game. You say my position is absolutist; I say yours is amorphous. That's the game. Your chairperson tells you that the only grants that count in the ranking of English departments are Guggenheim's, NEH's, and ACLS's. If you happen to be a department member who doesn't do the kinds of inquiries those grants support, you're cut from the roster before the season begins. It's just a game. Soon the "just" drops out. The game's the thing and winning is all-important.

From theoretical accounts of game, it is possible to see how the notion of game has come to be our bridge over the double bind. In *Homo Ludens: A Study of the Play Element in Culture,* Johann Huizinga (1950) describes the cultural function of medieval drama as a kind of *play* that helped believers to deal with the incomprehensibility of religious "mysteries." In so doing, Huizinga importantly discriminates "play" from "game" and establishes a continuum from play to earnest. Play is random. Game is play with rules. Children play in relative rulelessness. Adults engage in games whose comforting rules set up an alternate world from the terrifying randomness of everyday life. If the rulelessness of the everyday gets you down, you can play chess. There, a kind of certainty about winning or losing (with relatively low stakes) is relaxing. That certainty frees you to return to the world of earnest, where things are more serious and less certain. For Huizinga, both play and game prepare you for earnest. Like a puppy whose play with a toy allows him to practice breaking the neck of some imaginary prey, we learn through play to deploy the techniques that allow us to survive real life.

GAMES AND GRANTSMANSHIP

Although Huizinga's distinction between game and play is useful, it does not take us far enough. For an application to the specific circumstances of the postmodern, it will be useful to look at Jean-François Lyotard's use of Wittgenstein's theory of language games to examine the problem of justice. In his conversation with Jean-Loup Thébaud that Wlad Godzich translates as *Just Gaming*, Lyotard comes closer to the circumstances that I'm trying to understand when he describes the "social web [as] made up of a multitude of encounters between interlocutors caught up in different pragmatics" (1985, 73). There can, of course, be no transhistorical conception of "justice" to which to refer and adjudicate them. In the absence of universal standards, Lyotard says, game may be all there is—but that circumstance does not *necessarily* authorize relativism. Justice is not anything that is conventionally called "just," says Lyotard. If it were, Hitler's conventionally approved genocide (and by extension other more recent genocides) would be "just." One still wants to have a reference—an abstraction, even if that reference is not absolute, even if it seems to be altogether arbitrary. Lyotard offers a Kantian notion "the future of further inquiry [in which] there is a free field left open to the reflective judgment's capability" (76). In the context I develop here, I extrapolate from Lyotard to assert that we can create a local and contingent earnest, explain it, and work within it to accomplish something that seems—locally and contingently—useful. Such an "earnest" might be a project in community literacy, or a materialist analysis of an aspect of university life. In any case, for Lyotard, what would make such a thing worth doing is one's *informed and contingently ethical desire to do it* rather than its "fundability."

In other words, the problem is not grants *themselves*, but rather "grantsmanship"—the name I'll give to the (ideological) belief that a compositionists should aspire to be a "funded researcher" rather than as a person who seeks to theorize writing so that she can teach it. The difference is not in the activity itself but in the understanding—one's naming of the work that one does. It certainly is not possible in late capitalism for the university to eschew grants completely—nor does it seem prudent or possible to attempt to avoid competition. What can and should be avoided, however, is the notion that competition in terms of the empty signifier "excellence" is the only game in town and therefore the one that we have to play, uncritically, according to terms set by others for their own—very earnest—ends.

What I'm suggesting is that agency (even within late capitalism) still emerges from the perception of a double bind *as* a double bind. Agency comes when you see that the ways in which you are called into being contradict one another and run counter to your apparent interests.

How does agency come from perception? Perception can foster *articulation*. I use that term in Stuart Hall's sense, as "both a way of understanding how ideological elements come, under certain conditions, to cohere together within a discourse, and a way of asking how they do or do not become articulated, at specific conjunctures, to certain political subjects" (1996, 142). In "The Theory and Method of Articulation in Cultural Studies," Jennifer Daryl Slack writes that "[e]pistemologically, articulation is a way of thinking the structures of what we know as a play of correspondences, non-correspondences, and contradictions, as fragments in the constitution of what we take to be unities" (1996, 112). My epistemological effort here has been to make an ideological double bind visible as contradictory: we are enjoined to allow ourselves to be measured in a context in which we know measurement to be impossible.

"Politically," Slack writes, "articulation is a way of foregrounding the structure and play of power that entail in relations of dominance and subordination" (112). Politically, in this essay, I have sought to rearticulate competition and measurement as surveillance and control in order to reveal, for example, who profits and what is lost when grant writers focus on "what's fundable" rather than on inquiries that interest them.

"Strategically," Slack writes, "articulation provides a mechanism for shaping intervention within a particular social formation, conjuncture, or context" (112). Now, I shall attempt to suggest an intervention.

I would urge practitioners of composition studies to rearticulate game as earnest, to figure out what would count as earnest for us as individuals, and act on that judgment rather than submitting thoughtlessly to institutional measurements. For example,

Don't use the word excellence—not even in a grant application. If someone else uses the word, ask for a definition.

Don't ever answer any question on any form that asks how you measure excellence. Instead, if you actually do measure something, say what and why, even if your answer doesn't fit in the box.

Ask how measurements are arrived at—especially rankings. For example, if your chairperson announces that your department is ranked in the top twenty five percent of English departments, ask who did the ranking and what the criteria were.

Resist simplistic equations of excellence with time to degree, or with the prestige of the degree or press or journal.

Resist equations of excellence with professionalism. Model "earnest" for your graduate students (by, for example, explaining what would make a stronger argument) instead of teaching them to publish prematurely.

Don't supply measurements that will (or even can) be used for purposes of which you don't approve. Think carefully as you respond to questionnaires rather than scribble numbers so you can get on with the process of finding more money.

Resist zero-sum internal competitions, especially for funds that used to be (or that you think should be) part of the operating budget. Call attention to the ways in which the grant culture encourages us to compete among ourselves rather than cooperate—and try to change that.

Avoid competing for symbolic capital instead of the real thing. If the only prize in a competition is a certificate of excellence, don't compete.

Be mindful of the ways in which universities use external grant money, with all the strings attached, to do the jobs historically entrusted to it, rather than using their operating budgets. Strive to be alert to the expenditure of the actual capital it takes to sustain the grant culture in the academy.

When they call you to write a grant to build a wall, ask not only whom you're walling in and walling out, but also who's paying, who profits from the construction, and whether you really need the wall in the first place.

4

THE FEMINIST WPA PROJECT
Fear and Possibility in the Feminist "Home"

Shannon Carter

*Postmodern discourses are all "deconstructive" in that they seek to
distance us from and make us skeptical about beliefs concerning truth,
knowledge, power, the self, and language that are often taken for granted within and serve as legitimation for contemporary western culture.*
—Flax *Title*

*When the dominant group is homogeneous, its shared assumptions
stand little chance of identification, and when this group benefits
from maintaining these assumptions, there is even less chance that the
assumptions will be critically interrogated.*
—Alcoff and Potter *Title*

Narrating the rhetorical spaces in which I came to compose and continue to recompose one Feminist WPA Project involves a certain amount of
what Shirley K. Rose (1998) has called "indiscretion" and every indiscretion involves risk. This is a story of the fear and possibility at once limiting and inspiring the rhetorical and philosophical choices I made while
composing and, ultimately, *re*composing the Project in response to the
fluctuating nexus of power that similarly governs any social space—risk
further compounded by the tenure-track (rather than tenured) status of
my position, the traditionally and materially marginalized status of the
projects under my direction (the basic writing program and the writing
center), and the fact that the locus of this project is a challenge to the
status quo—the very systems at once authorizing my position and funding the learning spaces under my "direction" while limiting my choices
and shaping the possible and the valuable within those programs I have
been "empowered" to change.

Ultimately, this Feminist WPA Project embraced the epistemic privilege feminist epistemologists like Sandra Harding (1996) and bell hooks
(1996) argue marginality affords in an attempt to rework the system of
literacy education in ways that validate nonmainstream literacies and

worldviews rather than continuing to duplicate the dominant social order. The agents of change in this Project are (1) tutors working one-on-one with students in a variety of disciplines, at a variety of levels, with a variety of backgrounds, (2) peer-group leaders working with our basic writing students in small groups (less than seven), and (3) the non-mainstream students working with these tutors. Yet while my own story, including the acutely contextualized nature of the project itself and the difficulties I experienced, is quite personally and locally driven, the challenges I will explore are not unique. That is, any project attempting to subvert the dominant social order will be risky and will require rapid and constant shifts among multiple subject positions.

In *Rhetorical Spaces: Essays on Gendered Locations,* feminist epistemologist Lorraine Code (1995) illustrates the limits and fluidity of power with the useful metaphorical construct "rhetorical spaces." According to Code,

> Rhetorical spaces are fictive but not fanciful or fixed locations, whose (tacit, rarely spoken) territorial imperatives structure and limit the kinds of utterances that can be voiced within them with a reasonable expectations of uptake and "choral support," an expectation of being heard, understood, taken seriously. (x)

In every construction of public, professional, and personal identity, I must abide by the "territorial imperatives" shaping the exchange—not simply the verbal exchange itself but the actual subject positions I construct and the shape-shifting these spaces must continually endure.

As the director (not yet tenured) of a writing center and a basic writing program (always already marginalized), I must consistently weigh the feminist responsibility to challenge inequities with the risks inherent in this challenge. This balance is very, very complicated, for reasons I hope this chapter will illustrate. Through this Feminist WPA Project, I hoped to embrace the revolutionary potential of the learning spaces under my direction by working collaboratively with tutors to recompose the writing center and the basic writing program as spaces where students from nonmainstream groups could safely challenge the ways in which mainstream literacy education may unfairly exclude their very rich social histories in order to find space within the master narrative of the academy for the, in bell hooks' words, "oppositional world view" (hooks 2000) presented by marginalized narratives. In this Project, tutors, as research practitioners, would (1) chart the disruptions in literacy education, especially with respect to nonmaintream students and

(2) ultimately reshape literacy education in ways that open up space for nonmainstream ways of knowing.

While I continue to stand by the feminist utopian vision informing this Feminist WPA Project, I was to encounter several fault lines in the execution of this idealistically charged plan, and the flaws exposed in this narration should reveal even more fault lines in their expression. That is, risk informed my choices and my options in the performance of this Feminist WPA Project, but risk has also informed the narration of this performance. The risk shaped the earlier version of this essay that I sent to the editor, a version flattened and disembodied by fear—of not being "taken seriously," of misrepresenting my project, my colleagues, my students, and myself. Though this fear is always justified when one undertakes a new project, the shape-shifting and misrepresentations fear inspires become even more clear when we put these stories in print because print is static and linear and time must be "represented" rather than experienced, and the multitude of subject positions forced by the rhetorical spaces of the institution must also be frozen in time, separated from the rhetorical spaces informing these multiple subjectivities and, in the end, misrepresented.

In this chapter, I negotiate the power structures of print as I compose myself on the page, narrating the ways in which I compose my various selves within the academy and among multiple audiences (tutors, students, colleagues within and beyond the department, upper administration, the community) with varying degrees of power, all the time pressing against the norms the feminist me tells me must always be suspect for they always oppress (sometimes knowingly, often unknowingly) those who are not members of the culture of power the academy represents (and often dictates). The rhetorical spaces of print force me to misrepresent my Feminist WPA Project, including successes and failures, and the multiple subjectivities I have been forced to inhabit and compose and discard and recompose throughout the life of this project. These shifting and sliding subjectivities are necessarily frozen and somewhat muted as the performance of this project is narrated, forcing me to privilege some readings of these events over others just as we must when narrating any social space within the confines of the page.

DEFINING INSTITUTIONAL SPACES

Two years in the newly formed, tenure-track position of writing center and basic writing director at a rural, state university in a department with a Ph.D. program and a very active faculty (actively student-centered and actively productive in ways valued by the academy with numerous publications of books and articles) have offered this new academic many opportunities to negotiate risky rhetorical spaces. As I narrate the acutely situated story of my attempts to implement a WPA Project informed by feminist theories, I hope to make clear the ways in which the fear informing the spaces was rarely a response to openly adversarial relationships within the institution—I nearly always felt complete support in the design and execution of this Project, though I should admit that I only discussed the specific and radical ways in which I was attempting to recompose the writing center's identity with people whose conceptual systems clearly matched my own. The members of my department have been regularly, openly, and privately supportive; a few even helped me read the power landscape of the university early on when my inexperience and (sometimes) naiveté made these "territorial imperatives" illegible to me. The director of first-year composition has been an incredible and continuous confidant and mentor, and, unlike the experiences of many other writing center directors, the head of the department and other administrators and faculty in this department and beyond have never made me feel my budget was in danger or that the writing center was at all unappreciated. Yet, as Louise Wetherbee Phelps (1995) explains in "Becoming a Warrior: Lessons for a Feminist Workplace," we must "acknowledge the inherent asymmetry of power within any large social organization with any degree of hegemony" (324).

So while the tacit expectations and limits of my position and the programs I direct were never articulated in any explicit way, I did understand the power structures that shape the ways in which the possibilities of the writing center and the basic writing program can be, in Code's words, "heard, understood, taken seriously." In the painful rhetoric of the oppressed, in other words, I knew my *place* from the very beginning.

In "Keeping Close to Home," bell hooks (2000) helps her readers understand the importance of the "oppositional world view" those from marginalized groups can provide, if only the appropriate framework "for such naming" were available. As hooks explains, this oppositional world view

> must be articulated and named if it is to provide a sustained blueprint for change. Unfortunately, there has existed no consistent framework for such naming. Consequently both the experience of this difference and documentation of it (when it occurs) gradually lose presence and meaning. (221)

From the seemingly empowered position as director of the writing center and the basic writing program, I have worked hard to compose and recompose a "consistent framework for [this] naming," a space in which an "oppositional world view" can "provide a sustained blueprint for change" in the writing center and the basic writing program, areas traditionally marginalized and traditionally identified as the learning space struggling writers should call "home."

In 1989, Texas State Legislature quite forcefully defined learning spaces like these as the institutional "home" for nonmainstream writers in Texas public universities by requiring students unable to pass skills-based, standardized tests like the Texas Assessment of Academic Skills Program (TASP) to enroll in "remedial" coursework for which they would receive no college credit. These writing centers and basic writing programs were thus charged—no longer simply by institutional mandate but by Texas law—with changing these nonmainstream writers in ways that mimic institutional standards, further strengthening the power of institutional norms by forcing these students (by law) to conform to these norms or leave the campus entirely.

The first goal of this Project was to *compose the writing center as a center for research,* which means composing the tutor as research practitioner and the center itself as a learning space uniquely situated to observe the disruptions in literacy education, including why such disruptions may occur and what we can do about them when they do. In fact, such research may help us understand the ways we can reshape literacy education in response to the lessons we learn from these disruptions, especially moments where these disruptions may reveal injustices in the dominant social order.

Composing the writing center as a space where writers can come to understand the various forces shaping the "tacit expectations" of academic literacy was a second goal of this Project. That is, this Project required us to reshape the writing center as a space where writers can learn to read and understand the tacit expectations of the rhetorical spaces shaping the particular literacy project they are attempting to compose, including the instructor, disciplinary, and institutional expectations limiting and shaping the epistemological and rhetorical possibilities within that space. Most important, the writing center should be composed as a place where all writers can come to understand that academic literacy expectations are not natural but rather cultural and thus arbitrary.

In all cases, the feminist "home" informing the project is a deep-seated belief, informed by critics like Bruce Horner (1996), Min-Zhan Lu

(1994), and Victor Villanueva, Jr. (1997), in the tendency of mainstream literacy education to force nonmainstream writers to change—linguistically, politically, socially, culturally, personally. That is, arguments that linguistic choices cannot be separated from social, personal, political, and cultural choices and that standardized academic discourse is a cultural construct rather than the natural or "pure" state of language reveal the ways in which forcing students to conform to institutional norms in their literacy practices is a far less innocent political move than merely helping them be successful. As Nancy Maloney Grimm has argued in *Good Intentions: Writing Center Work for Postmodern Times* (1999), writing centers that do not recognize and work against this political truth are complicit in perpetuating unjust social practices, forcing our nonmainstream students to make one of two equally distasteful choices: either accept and assimilate into this dominant culture (erasing any difference) or leave the academy entirely. In these learning spaces, there is no room for the "oppositional world view" that hooks contends our nonmainstream writers can offer.

The writing center should be rewritten, then, in ways that challenge the tendency of literacy educators to erase difference and treat nonmainstream ways of knowing and communicating as suspect, thus forcing educators to understand that such tendencies to erase difference as one would erase a stray or unintentional mark while composing are implicit in teaching students to avoid error (that which is nonstandardized) and embrace standardized English, what bell hooks describes as "white supremacist, capitalistic patriarchy" (2000, 226), because such methods ask these students to adopt academic discourse with no regrets about the inevitable loss of their nonacademic, non-White ways of knowing and being.

As hooks explains,

> Within universities, there are few educational and social spaces where students who wish to affirm positive ties to ethnicity—to blackness, to working-class backgrounds—can receive affirmation and support. Ideologically, the message is clear—assimilation is the way to gain acceptance and approval from those in power. (226)

The message is especially clear to those from the margins—often those working in the writing center and the basic writing program: assimilate or leave. Learn to perform in ways the academy values or leave the academy. But because the force and inherent inequity within this academy is especially clear in marginalized learning spaces like writing centers and basic writing programs, we are, it would seem, in an especially powerful position to compose these educational spaces as places "where students who wish to affirm positive ties to ethnicity [. . .] can receive affirmation and support."

A POSITION FOR CRITIQUE

As Nancy Grimm (1999), Marilyn Cooper (2001), and Anis Bawarshi and Stephanie Pelkowski (2003) have argued, the writing center as a politically and, often times, *physically* marginalized learning space is in an excellent position to critique the institutional norms that, in fact, mute diversity by forcing writers who have not yet mastered the discourse of the academy to reconstruct their subject positions in ways that more readily mimic the dominant social order. Writing center scholars like Stephen North (1984) and Jeff Brooks (1991) have shaped the identity of the writing center as a place where, as North puts it in what has been considered the Writing Center Manifesto, "writers, not necessarily their texts, are changed" (1984, 438). As writing center workers and advocates have composed our writing centers in promotional materials, in conversations with students and faculty at our various institutions, and in the pages of our journals, we have continued to shape them as places where students can learn to write in ways the academy can value. It is only recently that scholars like Elizabeth Boquet (*Noise from the Writing Center*, 2002), Nancy Maloney Grimm (1999), and Marilyn Cooper (2001) have begun to challenge this construction of the writing center identity, calling upon us to instead shape our work and our centers in ways that work against the institutional norms that we now see as unfair to our marginalized students.

The nondirective methods perpetuated by what has become, for many, "writing center orthodoxy" encourages tutors to empower the writer by letting her do all the talking and all the work and forbids tutors to critique the assignment or the faculty member who assigned the project. According to critics, such methods actually reify institutional norms by failing to challenge these norms, thus treating academic ways of knowing as "natural" and anything deviating from that standard as "unnatural" or "immature." Grimm challenges our "good intentions" by forcing us to understand "literacy practices are *cultural* rather than natural" (1999, 33), something we can only begin to know when "teachers and tutors who are white and middle class [. . .] recognize that we, too, are raced, gendered, and classed subjects rather than just 'normal' people" (73). As I have explained, I hoped to recompose our writer center as a site for intellectual inquiry because, according to Marilyn Cooper, "writing centers are in a good potion to serve as a site of critique of the institutional structure of writing instruction in college" (2001, 336).

At this point, a further misrepresentation of the Feminist WPA Project is necessary for storying purposes: I must break the various identities I negotiated into those for tutor consumption, student consumption, and "public" consumption (the version of the writing center I presented to administrators and other faculty who may not share my epistemological framework). In doing so, I hope the various slips and dangers of the Project itself will become more obvious and the ways in which I have since rewritten this project will seem more innovative than reactionary.

The Writing Center at Texas A&M University-Commerce is pretty typical: writing center workers (peer tutors and graduate assistants working on degrees in, for the most part, History and English) work with writers at all levels in all disciplines across the campus, and while the percentage of basic writers working in our center is less than 30 percent, our center is deeply affiliated with the basic writing program because each of our basic writers is required to work with small groups and peer tutors twice a week, sharing concerns, paper topics, and evidence for and drafts of papers they are preparing for English 100 (one of our basic writing courses) or other writing-intensive courses not part of the basic writing program. I construct the identity of our basic writing program for tutor consumption in the pages of teaching notes that narrate the daily activities for the novice teachers who staff these basic writing labs. In keeping with the feminist principles of my WPA identity, however, I left ample room for critique of this composed identity. Whenever possible, the tutors, teachers, and I shared decisions that affected programs under my care, working to reach consensus with programmatic changes. Though these programs were already quite strong when I came in to manage them, the collaborative and consensus building techniques I had come to value and associate with a feminist managerial style allowed us to rework the writing center and the basic writing program in ways that better supported the diverse backgrounds of our students and the variety of literacy projects they were assigned. But in many ways, these feminine managerial styles actually left space for these tutors to reinforce the dominant social order instead.

The much more aggressive WPA Project Louise Wetherbee Phelps (1995) executes and then examines in "Becoming a Warrior: Lessons of the Feminist Workplace" was deeply informed by her feminist core value set as well, and as such she too felt compelled to employ feminine managerial techniques like shared authority, "cooperation, dialogue, nonhierarchical structures, and caring" (293). As she explains, creating "a safe utopian space"

> required both practically and morally that teachers of the program be treated as primary agents of change in themselves not as simply executing a director's will or serving as hapless instruments of ideology and institutional compulsion. (310)

I felt similarly compelled to share the power where I could, treating my tutors, whenever possible, as "agents of change in themselves," thus conflating the writing center identity I had constructed through this Project for student consumption with the one constructed for tutor consumption.

As a new, idealistic administrator filled with romantic plans of social change brought about by shared authority, cooperation, and caring, I could not predict disruptions in this feminist utopian project, disruptions I now understand were inevitable. Early on, I was certain that if given the chance, tutors and marginalized students alike would embrace the epistemic privileges informing marginalized learning spaces like the writing center and the basic writing program as an "educational and social space where students who wish to the affirm ties to ethnicity [. . .] can receive affirmation and support" (hooks 2000, 226). I felt it was my duty to shape the learning spaces under my direction in ways that invited change, and the only way I could do this as a responsible feminist was to share the authority with these tutors, collaboratively determining and reaching the Project goals, and thus reconstructing the identity of the writing center and, in turn, recomposing the academy in ways that transform these social spaces into territories less hostile to our nonmainstream students, perhaps even incorporating their marginalized narratives into this dominant social order.

Most problematic about the naiveté with which I approached and shaped this Feminist WPA Project was the ways in which I read the power of my particular position and the assumption that challenging the academy would be a project the traditionally successful undergraduate and graduate tutors working in the writing center would readily embrace. In fact, in some cases the tutors involved in this project felt not empowered by this attempt to redistribute power but angry, anxious, resistant, and frightened by it. In her own feminist plan to collaboratively reshape the writing program at her university along with the help of the teachers working in the program, Phelps (1995) encountered similar resistance (only on a grander scale) and only then began to understand "that an increase in authority, voice, and autonomy is not an unqualified good in and of itself" (311). As my own feminist utopian vision began to crack and peel Phelps' remark to an instructor friend began to resonate within the walls of my own writing center more and more loudly: "I've just begun to understand what an incredible risk I took—assuming that any group of teachers who just happened to be here could become capable of collectively inventing a new writing program. And that they would want to" (313). Until tutors began to resist my project, I was unaware of the hold the institutional norms would have on them, all of them students who have found success within the dominant social order and very few of whom felt that standardized academic discourse had forced them to change in any ways that made "keeping close to home" uncomfortable or even impossible. For these reasons, I was unaware of the extent to which pure collaborative managerial techniques, like nondirective tutoring strategies, may help my tutors reify institutional norms in their work with the nonmainstream students. Until I made the goals of this Project quite clear to them, I simply could not assume that they would work against any institutional norms that my feminist "home" had taught me unfairly constructed our nonmainstream students. If I believed the dominant social order had the power to dictate values and worldviews, I had to believe that this social order would be no less likely to shape the values and world views of my tutors. For the same reasons writing center orthodoxy may reify institutional norms by failing to challenge them, feminist managerial techniques may yield program goals that simply mimic the injustices of mainstream literacy I hoped the writing center would challenge.

So part of the trouble I encountered in this Project came from not only the inadequacy of some feminist managerial styles that are too "soft" to challenge the dominant social order in any real way—a disconnect I will explore in some detail later—but also the important ways that a marginalized social space like the writing center cannot openly challenge the institution upon which it, in fact, depends. To be sure, the public identity I hoped to shape for faculty and administrative consumption was most certainly not the one I described above. The writing center for public consumption is absolutely not the one that seeks to challenge institutional or societal norms. Once again, like a good Southern woman, I knew my place, and my writing center constructed on the political and, in fact, material margins of the academy/literacy education knows her programmatic place as well. In fact, I regularly negotiate rather risky rhetorical spaces in the promotional material and activities I create, distribute, and perform, and ask my tutors to perform.

OF ETHICS AND IDEOLOGY

For these reasons, in progressively complex rhetorical moves, I carefully manipulate those rhetorical spaces that could threaten the existence of my writing center or my tenure, assuring the consumers of the writing center's public identity that we are here to serve their students and only rarely (and then very carefully) educating them about the limits and possibilities of writing center work—in terms that are once invitational, and, I must admit, passive aggressive. In promotional materials like the letter I send to faculty across campus inviting them to attend an annual open house, I use rhetoric like "As you know . . ." (when I know many do not know), and I invite them to attend any one of our weekly tutor training meetings to talk to us about the specific literacy demands of their courses or their disciplines (sadly, most decide to use this time to help us understand the style guide appropriate for their discipline). As Patricia Dunn (2000) argues in her study of the matrix of power inform-ing writing center work via instructor's marginal comments on student papers, "When writing centers are run or staffed by those without ten-ure and criticized by those who have it, it is risky for directors to pro-test philosophical differences publicly" (30). At some level the writing center identity must be constructed in ways the institution will accept because we are absolutely dependent upon our institutional context, even for our very physical "home": the walls, the roof, the furniture, the power—in fact the monies that pay us to hire our workers and the monies we pay these workers once we do. As Muriel Harris explains in "Presenting WC Scholarship" "a writing center is a particular *place* [. . .] with an ever-present need to contextualize."

I must promise faculty that the writing center will, as North (1984) promised, "change the writer" or even promise some that the writing center will change the text, but I certainly should not promise to do what I can to change the institutional construct of literacy education. A writing center that is necessarily a part of the institution (materially, politically) cannot exist with such an adversarial identity. Again, I know my place. So disruptions will always exist between the public identity I construct for my programs and the true ideological construct of these spaces, and I do not feel that these disruptions endanger the integrity of the WPA Project itself.

More troublesome, however, are the disruptions that occur in my attempt to conflate the composed identity for tutors and the one for student consumption. As I explain, it seemed unethical to impose my social vision on my tutors in the same way I felt it unethical for our tutors and teachers to impose their worldview on their students, especially their nonmainstream students for whom this change would mean moving away from home so completely that, like Richard Rodriguez (1983), they simply could not return home. But because of the seductive force (and the power) of the master narrative and because so many of my tutors, though working in a marginalized learning space with many marginalized students, were not, in most rhetorical spaces, marginalized themselves, they were probably less likely to criticize that master narrative. Once again, they were excellent students for the most part (and always had been); therefore, they did not automatically challenge the institutional norms because, admittedly and quite understandably, they valued the dominant social order and hoped to teach these students what they felt they needed to know in order to find success within that dominant social order as well. Tutors are no more unsituated free agents than any one else, and they can not/will not automatically challenge the institutional constructs that often mute diversity any more than modern travelers from the West would challenge metaphorical constructs perpetuated by western maps that North is up and East is right. Without understanding the ways in which the value set informing American literacy education are cultural rather than natural, most tutors will continue to reify institutional norms by reading student diversity as deficit and helping marginalized students learn to overcome their nonmainstream ways of knowing in order to assimilate as completely and quickly as possible. Such instructional choices are rarely made with any malice. In fact, these novice teachers may reify institutional norms with the best of intentions—they want their student writers to succeed and it is likely the student writers want the same, by most any means necessary. The tutor may not understand the ways in which they may be forcing these students to abandon "home" for the academy. As qualitative studies like Anne DiPardo's *A Kind of Passport* (1993) have revealed, the dominant social order can be very seductive, especially for the professionally ambitious and traditionally successful students we hire to work in our writing centers. Indeed, our tutors with marginalized identity markers may be just as likely to "fail to acknowledge the culturally specific and arbitrary nature of academic expectation" as our tutors with more mainstream social histories, upholding the dominant culture without critiquing it in the face of diversity, albeit with what Nancy Grimm (1999) calls "Good Intentions." Thus, the Feminist WPA Project could only succeed with more directive and, perhaps, more masculine managerial techniques that helped tutors read student need in more culturally sensitive ways.

My own tutors cared about their students very much. Many of the tutors involved with the basic writing "labs" spent countless hours in my office fretting about students with poor attendance, resistant students, and students with wonderful ideas who simply "could not write." The levels of authority I felt compelled to share within the confines of the Project allowed tutors the space to rework their labs in ways they felt more appropriately addressed the needs of the students. In the rhetoric of the Project, the tutors were the "research practitioners," "organic intellectuals" in the unique position to explore the theory possible when applied to the real world, observing where theory breaks down and where it works. I trusted the research practitioners, and I felt certain the tutors in the writing center and those working from the teaching notes in their basic writing groups would be in a better position to observe the efficacy of the tutoring strategies I advocated, reporting successes and reworking failures. But these were novice teachers, and, as novice teachers, they may have difficulty reading what didn't "work." Worse yet, the determinations of efficacy may be made in terms dictated by the master narrative. In fact, in the race to help these students succeed in the academy, many of my tutors went in search of worksheets that would help these students construct a thesis or a paragraph "appropriately"—after all, wasn't that why they were here? Is it right to deny these students what they need to be successful in the academy, they may ask, often instinctively reading literacy education in the ways the dominant social order reads literacy—as a neutral and natural skill-set rather than a highly ideologically and culturally charged one.

Some of my tutors resisted the construction of the writing center as a place that would help students explore the differences between their lives and the representations of the dominant culture, often unable (or unwilling) to help these students develop strategies for negotiating these spaces in ways that simultaneously validate home and yield success in the culture of power because, in employing purely collaborative managerial techniques informed by the fear of imposing my own social vision upon them, I had left them in the dark and I had failed to recognize the powerful ways the master narrative would likely construct their own understanding of literacy education just as it had most everyone else's understanding—certainly those who had not been invited to challenge this master narrative. Given this, I can only imagine the kind of resistance my nonfeminist, noncomposition specialist graduate assistants and tutors must have felt when I came in and began asking them to help me rework these programs, programs I "direct" and programs for which I am best trained and for which I am, ultimately, responsible. As I've already explained, many excellent changes were implemented because this shared authority empowered so many tutors to help rework the program—multiple changes that supported the feminist utopian vision informing the Feminist WPA Project, albeit unknowingly. However, the desire for the "director" to offer "direction" was clear very early on. Many times, I would offer tutors several possibilities, hoping they would read the situation and implement the best solution. But while this seemed to be the best, most feminist approach, for the first few months (and with every new tutor that followed) I felt some degree of anxiety emanating from the tutor. Several even said, "Just tell me what you want me to do, and I'll do it." I could not. I felt doing so would invalidate my Feminist WPA Project.

So though we were able to rework the programs in some excellent ways, the expectation that someone needs to be "in charge" continued to dominate my interactions with a handful of these tutors and teachers. Specifically, these folks may have felt that if the designated "boss" has entrusted many important decisions to her staff, then perhaps the boss is unnecessary and perhaps an equally effective job is to be had without her. I am only aware of one staff member who felt this way, but one is enough to reveal a fault line in the system.

ISSUES OF POWER AND CHANGE

Early in this chapter, I suggested that rhetorical spaces may be a useful way to read the power landscape of any project challenging the dominant social order, especially those projects offering such challenges from the margins of the dominant social order, at once a part of and marginalized by the power landscape dictating norms and the dominant core value set. In "Feminist Writing Program Administration: Resisting the Bureaucrat Within," Amy Goodburn and Carrie Shively Leverenz (1998) warn us that "it is crucial that feminist administrators who wish to challenge the existing power relations understand the norms that nurture and support these relations" (276–77). This chapter is an attempt to understand these norms, and I hope new versions of this Feminist WPA Project will more adequately address them.

Too often, the WPA, and, especially, the female, feminist WPA, is not "heard," "understood," or "taken seriously" (Code 1995, x) by her audience. The feminist agenda is often not valued or understood because it takes on the status quo in spaces where the status quo is unproblematically valued. The female WPA's message is often not heard because she is a member of an undervalued group (a woman teaching composition, a largely misunderstood and thus marginalized subject area). The female, feminist WPA is dismissed in many rhetorical spaces in the academy unless she can shape effective arguments within the boundaries and "territorial imperatives" of the rhetorical spaces in question.

When we are able to move past the ideal, we are in a better position to successfully negotiate the rhetorical spaces involved in this new Feminist WPA Project. My work with tutors and teachers involved in the programs I direct must acknowledge the power landscapes and territorial imperatives shaping each and every rhetorical space and this work may, therefore, require more masculine managerial techniques like coercion and control. I am not arguing that we must completely abandon the more feminine managerial techniques like collaboration and consensus, but we must understand the ways in which dissensus and control are not failures in the project itself but rather opportunities to better understand the "territorial imperatives" structuring these interactions. At times, working against the status quo will require more forceful methods, but it is only in doing so that these programs can provide "the consistent framework" for the "naming" of the "oppositional world view" bell hooks tells us our students from marginalized groups can provide, if only given the chance.

5

WHEN 'MS. MENTOR' MISSES THE MARK

Literacy and Lesbian Identity in the Academy

Tara Pauliny

PROFESSIONAL DILEMMAS AND PERILOUS ADVICE

In a recent installment of her advice column in *The Chronicle of Higher Education*, Ms. Mentor (a.k.a. Emily Toth) counsels academic women struggling to negotiate their various identities (as minority women, mothers, untenured professors) with their sometimes disappointing and often misleading jobs.[1] Underlying the advice she offers is a stalwart feminist position: she "insists that women seize control of their work lives" and that academic women "self-promote," "speak about inequalities" and "be tough women, not docile girls" (Mentor 2005). Ms. Mentor's advice here is sound in its recognition of gender difference, racial inequalities, and in its uncompromising feminist stance. Where Ms. Mentor's guidance rings hollow, however, is in its forwarding of a heterosexist perspective. Both within this column and elsewhere,[2] Ms. Mentor's advice often elides sexuality's variance and neglects to note the precarious contexts encountered by graduate students and professors whose sexualities are nondominant. Just one year before the above-cited column, for instance, Ms. Mentor writes that "Matt," a graduate student who practices S/M, "must be *infinitely discreet* if he *insists* on practicing his sadomasochism." She "feels," in fact, "that his sex life is not her business, if he is doing *whatever he is doing* with consenting adults. But [. . .] he should not be *flaunting* it in college towns and scaring the horses" (Mentor 2004, emphasis added).[3] Not unlike homophobic discourse that relegates nonheterosexual forms of sexuality to the "privacy" of the bedroom where it can be discounted and ignored, Ms. Mentor's advice contains a (not so) subtle critique of S/M. Her use of the term "insists," and her caution against the assumably garish and inappropriate "flaunting" of "Matt's" sexual preferences, reinforces heterosexuality's cultural prominence, and promotes a context in which nondominant sexual practices and identities necessitate, at the very least, a closed door, but better yet, a retreat to the closet.

If the goal of advice columns like Ms. Mentor's is to help academic professionals successfully navigate the precarious terrain of their careers, that assistance should not only recognize the various contexts created by disparate identities, but it should also extend the egalitarian and political agenda offered by her feminism to queer academic dilemmas. Rather than articulating an "idealized" position in which professors are implicitly coded as either heterosexual or asexual, professional advice should recognize and address sexual difference. As a profession shaped in part by the diversity of our members, we need to investigate what it means to become literate within various professional contexts and with various sexual identities; we need understand what it takes to be "tough" and what tools we need in order to advocate for ourselves.

As a queer[4] addendum to an overwhelmingly heterocentric body of advice literature, my essay offers an alternative to Ms. Mentors' view of professional life. I locate sexuality as a key component of academic identities and professional literacy acquisition, and argue that the juxtaposition of "professional" and "queer" alters the shape of academic life. Furthermore, it is the performance of nondominant sexualities, I contend, that not only highlights the profession's inherent heterocentrism, but also offers bodies upon which to project such normative expectations and anxieties. "Coming out" therefore—whether partially or fully—and negotiating life as a queer professional, necessitates the recognition of institutional heterosexism and the need for tools designed specifically to address such difficulties.

A COMPOSITE IDENTITY: ONE PART TEACHER, ONE PART QUEER

During the years of my Ph.D. work, I lived part of my life as an out lesbian: I made my queer identity known to my family, friends, professors, and fellow graduate students, but not to the undergraduate composition and literature students I taught. My decision not to come out to my students was predicated on a number of reasons: I had only recently come to identify as a lesbian, and as such, I had some trepidation about how my students would react to hearing that I was gay. I was afraid they would no longer like me, and that my sexuality would overtake all their other thoughts and feelings about me as a person and as their instructor. More importantly, I worried about the pedagogical implications of coming out in the classroom: Did I have the right to come out?; If I did come out, were my motivations personal or professional?; and, Did coming out have a legitimate place in the classroom?

As I wrestled with these questions, and was outspoken about my lesbianism in other areas of my life, my queerness remained unspoken while I performed my role of teacher. This partition of identities was enabled, in part, because the classes I typically taught, Second-level Composition and Introduction to Fiction, were small—none ever enrolled more than 24 students—and although I often got to know students well during the term, I had little to no contact with them once they finished my course. Also, at an institution that enrolled over 50,000 people, there was little opportunity for me to work with students more than once, or to have contact with them outside the boundaries of our class. This short-lived connection among students and myself allowed for an intense, yet fleeting relationship to bloom. And since I had the freedom to choose my course themes and texts, we routinely debated the sex/gender binary, investigated the overlaps of public policy and social mores, and examined the pathological history of sexuality, although we rarely, if ever, came in contact with one another outside the confines of our classroom or my office.[5] The space we created was thus liminal. As a teacher, I urged students to see the personal implications of the gender binary, to connect the messages within literature to their own lives, and to understand writing as a persuasive and individual process: our work, I urged, was more than theoretical—it mattered to real people. It mattered, in fact, to us. Ironically, however, it was just this kind of individual connection with the course material that drove me to separate one of the most intimate and significant parts of myself from my teaching persona. Because I designed my courses around the themes of gender, sexuality, and identity, a decision that often provoked students' moral sensibilities and required them to engage with their personal beliefs, I didn't want them to have to wrestle with these same questions in regard to their instructor. My identity, I argued to myself, would only get in the way of their learning; it would derail their investigations and take too much precedence in the course.

With this decision, I mirrored Ms. Mentor's professional ideal: my feminist focus remained strong both in and outside the classroom, but I conceded that issues of gender and sexuality could most productively be taught when the instructor's sexual identity remained "ambiguous." Like the graduate student, "Matt," whom she advises to keep his S/M practice separate from his teaching life, I kept my sexuality confined to extracurricular spaces. If students couldn't easily read me as gay, straight, or otherwise queer, I posited, they likewise couldn't dismiss my courses' subject matter for their connection to my perceived "personal" politics. By choosing not to come out in the classroom, I believed that I was creating a classroom environment in which my identity did not overtly compel students to censor themselves or to try to appear "pro-gay" for the sake of pleasing the instructor. I had found a solution, or so I thought, to the complicated question of whether or not to out myself as a preprofessional teacher.

What I have since realized, however, is that my sexual "ambiguity" was most likely not read as such by my students. Given that I never named myself as a lesbian or clearly marked myself as other than heterosexual, it is fair to assume that I was read as straight. And since heterosexuality is culturally compulsory, as Adrienne Rich famously explains, and dominant culture forwards the notion that "women are inevitably [. . .] drawn to men [, . . .] that primary love between the sexes is 'normal,' that women need men as social protectors," and that heterosexuality is presumed as a 'sexual preference' of 'most women,'" it is probable that I was read in much this same way (Rich 1980, 642). So rather than enacting an open-ended identity in the classroom, I now believe that I passed—whether intentionally or not—as a heterosexual instructor.

My ability to shift in this way—from out lesbian to passing heterosex-ual instructor—was made possible by a particular set of circumstances and ideological ideals. For one, the urban environment in which my large graduate program was housed reflected a certain political geog-raphy, which, when combined with my preprofessional status, afforded me the privilege of a dual life: I could be a "straight" instructor in part because there were other places—literal and figurative—where I could comfortably perform my queerness. Then, at night and on the weekends I could spend time in queer bars and clubs, and in my graduate classes I could not only be open about my lesbianism, but I could also theorize the connections between sexuality and rhetoric: my particular specialty. Likewise, as a young, white, woman who looked vaguely alternative, I easily blended into the general college population. I could walk across campus, attend queer rallies, and frequent gay-owned businesses almost never seeing students I had once had in class. The easy availability and anonymity of queer spaces, combined with my preprofessional role, and perceived heterosexual normativity, allowed me to successfully negoti-ate the intersections of my distinctly different personal and academic cultures and helped me keep my sexuality and my teaching persona somewhat separate. I could perform two versions of myself because I had the space to do so; I could move between these identities because my status as a graduate student allowed such movement, and because heteronormativity facilitated this easy transition. I passed, then, because I performed an "identity in such a way that it seem[ed] to match a norm," and because my attempt at ambiguity was read within a context dominated by heterosexuality (Brueggemann and Moddelmog 2002, 313).

HETERONORMATIVITY AND ACADEMIC ADVICE TEXTS, OR, A QUEER ACADEMIC ABSENCE

As I was in the process of transitioning from graduate student to assistant professor, I began to rethink my decision to be closeted in the classroom, and went searching for advice about such matters. My review of the discipline's advice literature, however, was met more with absence and silence than reasoned recommendations. Unfortunately, of all the advice manuals currently available, none focus solely on the challenges faced by queer academics. Instead, what exists are numerous articles and books designed to advise academic job seekers and new professionals in general.[6]

On the whole, academic advice collections take a decidedly pragmatic or thematic approach. Their content and organization is often either shaped by the logistics of the hiring process, or arranged to reflect an overarching disciplinary focus. Instructional texts such as *Job Search in Academe* (1999), *Getting An Academic Job* (1997), and *Faculty in New Jobs* (1999) all follow a chronological schedule and fall somewhere within the timeline that includes preparing for the job market, interviewing, planning for the first-year on the job, and becoming acclimated to your new position. While these approaches do not preclude conversations about professional quandaries related to identity, or concerns that arise from various contexts and personal politics, they do take a fairly generic approach to the prospect of job acquisition and professional development. In the "Rehearsing and Ad-libbing" section of their book, *Job Search in Academe*, for instance, Dawn M. Forno and Cheryl Reed use first-person accounts to help prepare job seekers for inappropriate or odd questions from members of hiring committees. Quoting Ellen M. Gil-Gomez, they note how a candidate may be faced with "informative illegal questions" ostensibly meant to "uncover [. . .] sexual behavior and/or racial identity such as: questions about [. . .] birth control practices, [. . .] family planning, [and . . .] whether [the candidate] care[s] about the [culture she studies] or just [the] books [she reads]" (Forno and Reed 1999, 100).

Similarly, in "The Awards Ceremony," when the same text advises successful job candidates on the process of accepting positions and negotiating offers, concerns related to sexuality are dealt with cursorily. While answering questions about employee benefits and how to counter a job offer, the editors offer only the briefest advice about partner benefits, and do not suggest that such benefits might be used as one of many bargaining points (Forno and Reed 1999, 114–24). As a result, although identity and difference are afforded a minor space in this text, they do not play a fundamental role. Dealt with anecdotally, rather than substantially, these concerns become one of many idiosyncrasies included in the price of admission to the profession. Conspicuously, specific strategies for managing such situations, or a critical analysis of the institutional and ideological explanations of such "oddities" are noticeably absent. Rather, by way of advice, Forno and Reed suggest that, on the issue of benefits, "you will want to talk to the Human Resources Management director," and in regard to improper questions:

> You can never prepare for every sort of question that may get thrown at you. Sometimes, illegal or esteem-threatening questions are simply the result of interviewers who have received inadequate (or no) training in proper interview procedures. Other times, tricky questions give you real insight into the atmosphere you'd face if you accepted an offer from that particular institution. Our advice to you [. . .] is to come prepared to articulate who you are and what you want to do. (Forno and Reed 1999, 101)

What Forno and Reed neglect to mention, however, is precisely how "who we are" and how we identify offer particular challenges to the presentation of ourselves and our abilities—as well as to how those abilities and identities are read.

Unfortunately, Forno and Reed's volume is not alone in its limited approach; even texts that focus specifically on gender in the academy tend to do so in a decidedly heterocentric fashion. Sexuality—especially nondominant sexuality—is rarely considered within the numerous books and essays that examine closely the influence gender had, and continues to have, on women's abilities to attain academic jobs, to keep those appointments, and to be awarded tenure. Like feminism itself, these early gender-centered texts also neglect to consider fully lesbian or queer sexualities as they report on women's professional status, roles, and opportunities.

Even when lesbian sexuality (and I use lesbian here specifically since only one text I examined considered any identities outside the hetero/homo binary) is addressed within advice manuals, it is done so briefly and without paying critical attention to the heterosexist culture of the academy. Early volumes within this genre include such texts as *Academic Women Working Towards Equality*, (Simeone 1987), which details women's second-class status in the profession during the 1980s and, *Women of Academe: Outsiders in the Sacred Grove*, edited by Aisenberg and Harrington (1988), which scrutinizes women's place—at the time—and alienation within the academy. While both works are overtly and uncompromisingly feminist in their approaches and methodologies, neither interrogate heterosexism the way they do sexism. In Simeone's study, for example, although lesbians are mentioned within the discussion of how marital status affects male academics' view of women, the conversation takes place within one lone sentence. "Single women," Simeone writes, "whether lesbian or heterosexual, may be seen by men as more serious professional competition, but they may be threatening and confusing because they have seemingly rejected their most important gender-linked roles" (Simeone 1987, 139). Such an omission of analysis is surprising, given that earlier in the text Simeone acknowledges and laments lesbian invisibility within the academy (Simeone 1987, 70, 94–95). However, despite her recognition that lesbians' "achievements and contributions are sometimes ignored," and that lesbians are "further pushed aside by heterosexist intellectual constructs which see women primarily in terms of their relationship to males," lesbian's silence is nevertheless perpetuated when single women and lesbians are simplistically folded together (Simeone 1997, 70). Naming these two groups of women as equally distasteful and "abnormal" to their male colleagues, she does little to ameliorate or oppose such a characterization.

In a similar fashion, Aisenberg and Harrington's text, *Women in Academe*, also fails to challenge heteronormativity. Here, their lack of critical attention to the plight of lesbians in the academy rests, they claim, not in their hands, but in the fact that none of the women they interviewed for their study actually named themselves as lesbians. "We know that our interviewees [. . .] included lesbians," they write, "but none identified herself as such. Thus we have stories from these women that correspond in many aspects to those of heterosexual women, but we cannot draw explicit parallels or distinctions because the lesbian women themselves did not do so" (Aisenberg and Harrington 1988, xii). Lesbian invisibility, then, begets invisibility. Its absence disallows a critique of the very structures that maintain its oppression, and heterosexism escapes analysis because it perpetuates a system that works to silence its detractors.

While this approach to advice texts is certainly disheartening, it has not remained the norm. Thankfully, just as feminism amended its perspective with time, so too did books centering on women in the academy. In the 1990s, for example, when racial and sexual difference made significant inroads into feminism as a whole, this inclusion also entered feminist academic advice texts. These newer professional guides for women greeted their expanding audience of female scholars with texts that are reader-friendly and politically motivated. One of the earliest of kind, Paula J. Caplan's *Lifting a Ton of Feather: A Woman's Guide to Surviving in the Academic World* (1993) is also the one most sensitive to lesbian concerns. Rather than the additive approach adopted by some of the texts that follow hers, Caplan integrates sexuality—homosexual and heterosexual—directly into her various discussions of the profession. This consideration of sexuality begins early in her text when, in her discussion of the academic climate, she writes that there is "greater harassment and exclusion of women from nondominant groups and of feminists," that there is an "expectation that women will fit feminine and racial stereotypes," and that "general maleness, racism, and heterosexism [exist within the academic] environment" (Caplan 1993, 29–30). As the text continues, her focus on the treatment of nondominant groups remains clear when she advises graduate students to "consider organizing a group of students to request that seminars be held for professors about the effects of the chilly climate on the learning and achievement of women and on members of racialized groups, students who are not able-bodied, older students, and gay and lesbian students" (Caplan 1993, 117). And finally, at the end of her book, Caplan includes an exhaustive list of factors to consider when choosing a job and evaluating a university. This list, which spans more than eleven pages, consistently includes issues related to sexual identity. Two, among the numerous examples I could have chosen, illustrate Caplan's concern about institutions' "record of hiring and promoting women and people of both sexes from nondominant groups at all levels of the academic ladder," and whether or not universities have a "policy that discrimination on the basis of sex, race, age, disability [. . .] and sexual orientation is prohibited" (Caplan 1993, 162–63).

Caplan's approach, however, is not typical. In fact, a number of gender-focused advice books followed hers, and none treat sexuality as centrally as she does. Instead, most take an additive approach, devoting a single chapter to the concerns and situations of interest to lesbian academics. *Feminist Academics: Creative Agents for Change*, edited by Louise Morley and Val Walsh (1995) for instance, limits most of the text's attention to lesbianism within the academy to Debbie Epstein's chapter, "In Our (New) Right Minds: The Hidden Curriculum in the Academy." Other texts, such as *Career Strategies for Women in Academe: Arming Athena,* Collins et al. (1998), and *Troubling Women: Feminism, Leadership and Educational Change,* Blackmore (1999), rather than devoting a single chapter to lesbian matters, pay little or no attention to sexuality. Collins' text, for example, offers advice for handling subtle sex discrimination, navigating the precarious terrain of Affirmative Action, and taking advantage of the possibilities offered by administrative roles, but rarely mentions how lesbian sexuality might complicate these concerns. Lesbians are explicitly mentioned, in fact, only when "intellectual intimidation" is discussed. Likewise, Blackmore's volume, which reflects on how the restructuring of the academy has produced new dilemmas and potentials for women within the profession, only mentions lesbians when explaining some of the reasons why women in educational leadership positions are reticent to name themselves as feminists. "Many rejected the term 'feminism,'" she writes, "because of its depiction in popular discourses as being 'rabid', 'ball busters', 'man haters', and 'a lesbo', thus equating feminism with abnormality" (Blackmore 1999, 189).

Unfortunately, many advice texts are similar to those cited here. So although there are a few guides, like Paula Caplan's, which work hard to both note and analyze how the academy is homophobic and heterosexist, there are many more that deal with sexuality only in passing or with heterosexist remarks. Disturbingly, one of the most popular of these texts—Emily Toth's *Ms. Mentor's Impeccable Advice for Women in Academia*—is also one of the most egregious when it comes to handling issues related to nondominant sexuality.

Not unlike the column that commences this essay, Toth's text as a whole forwards a "don't ask, don't tell" philosophy in regard to queer sexuality. Repeatedly, she advises junior faculty members and graduate students to wait until they are tenured to come out, or even more alarmingly, wonders why such an individual would desire to come out at all. When asked by a new faculty member, for example, if she should come out as a lesbian, Ms. Mentor responds by asking "another question first: Why?" She then continues to make blanket and essentializing statements such as follows: "If you are teaching queer theory, everyone will assume you're a lesbian anyway"; "If you teach about lesbian and gay rights, or if you advise the local homophile [*sic*] group, or if you hang out in lesbian/gay bars, or if you speak out against homophobia—or even if you're unmarried with short hair—many people will assume you're a lesbian." And besides, she writes, "So what?" "Your sexuality is your own business" (Mentor 1997, 67–68).

Mirroring the advice she offered "Matt," the S/M practitioner, Ms. Mentor once again forwards a heterocentric perspective in which naming yourself as "married" or in a heterosexual relationship is considered standard, while doing the same in regard to queer relationships is "flaunting" your sexuality and making inappropriate reference to "private" matters. Such discourse reifies heterosexuality as the norm, equates homosexuality with deviance, and ultimately supports the heterosexist assumptions and practices of the academy—the consequences of which are not merely damaging to academic institutions, but also to individual readers as well.

Taken in its entirety, this cursory review of advice texts illustrates that, although there are currently myriad instructional texts available, few of them adequately acknowledge—never mind address—the particular difficulties faced by graduate students and professionals who do not identify as heterosexual or conform to regulatory gender and/or sexuality roles.[7] With this deficit in mind, I offer an account of my own: a story of how the transition from graduate student to assistant professor was complicated by my queer sexuality and my varying decisions to out myself. For although the MLA's *Guide to the Job Search* assumes that "by the time you leave graduate school and accept a job, you should have made the transition from thinking like a student to thinking like a professional" (and, on the same page, advises women to "wear a skirt and jacket" to interviews), my movement from graduate student to tenure-track professor has been neither seamless nor simple (Showalter et al. 1996, 35).

RENEGOTIATING THE TRIAL SEPARATION: THE RECONCILIATION OF MY QUEER IDENTITY AND TEACHING PERSONA

If my decision in graduate school to be closeted was motivated, in part, by internalized homophobia, it was also prompted by my desire to embrace and enact a theoretical understanding of ambiguity. I was attempting (however unsuccessfully), to perform a queer identity—to resist normalization, binary categorization, and essentializing. And because I premised my understanding of queer sexuality on "the idea that sexual identities as well as gender itself are historically contingent, socially constructed categories which can and have been assembled at different times," I aimed to reflect these concepts in my performance of self (Rudy 2000, 198). When I graduated, however, and made the decision to be an out lesbian in my new job as a tenure-track professor and Writing Center director at a Midwestern four-year comprehensive university, I came to understand how difficult (although certainly not impossible) it is to subtly thwart cultural conventions. Importantly, I also realized that transitioning from a graduate instructor who passes, to a completely out professional, reflected more than a distinction in rank and choice. Being out, I soon discovered, was a professionally risky endeavor.

When I revealed my sexuality on a day-to-day basis, I came to see that I also altered the ways my professional and personal identities intersected. I quickly learned, for instance, that if I wanted to be an out lesbian in the town of 60,000 where I live and work—which I did and still do—my sexuality and professional persona had to come into dialogue. In this new landscape, the spaces that at one time were safe havens for my sexual identity were now fraught with unmapped professional expectations. The knowledge of the academic panopticon—that, as a professor in a small town, I cannot escape my professional identity even in off-campus spaces—separated me both from the queer sites in which I was previously comfortable, and from the pedagogical safety of a passing teaching persona.

When I started working as an Assistant Professor in the Fall of 2002, one of the first service positions I agreed to hold was the faculty advisor for the Rainbow Alliance for H.O.P.E. (HOPE), our school's LBGTQ student organization. I was excited to take on this role since I saw it as a way to quickly connect to the campus' fledgling queer community, and because I was eager to lend my support to such an organization. As a result, I attended the group's first meeting of the semester, introduced myself as a new faculty member who identified as a lesbian, and agreed to be their advisor. Reflecting the "gung-ho" attitude adopted by many new assistant professors, I attended the group's Monday night meetings, met frequently with their executive board, and was present at many of their events. Departing from my earlier attempts at ambiguity, I now worked diligently to claim and proclaim my queerness. In my new, authorized role of assistant professor, I wanted to produce progressive pedagogical consequences; I hoped that by performing a lesbian identity, I would "call into question traditional expectations of the kinds of knowledge that can be shared with students," and that I would "redraw the lines between the intellectual and the personal, the sanctioned and the taboo, the academic and the experimental" (Brueggemann and Moddelmog 2002, 312).

As the semester continued, however, I began to notice that, while my newly acquired status as an out faculty member may indeed have begun to have these particular effects, it also came with some unexpected consequences. I quickly realized, for instance, that I could no longer move easily from my role as visible authority in the classroom to unremarkable layperson outside of the classroom. At this institution, whose campus stretches a mere few blocks, I was always recognizable as an instructor. No longer was I mistaken for an undergraduate student or even graduate student. I was consistently surprised, in fact, when students I never remembered meeting, or faculty and administrators I had not yet come to recognize, remembered my name and said hello as we passed one another in the library, student union, or academic buildings. While this kind of connection was welcoming, it was also unsettling. The comfortable anonymity of passing—to which I had become accustomed—was now gone; no longer could I move deftly out of my academic (read: heterosexual) persona into my queer one.

One particular incident that occurred in the middle of the Fall semester secured this change in my mind. To celebrate National Coming Out week, the HOPE group routinely planned activities to honor LGBTQ people and history. One of the most popular of these events was a drag show performed in the school's union. When I first heard of the show, I was impressed that such an event had already become a regular affair on campus, and I was pleased that so many students supported such a performance. I was also excited that I had the opportunity to be part of a community that showcased drag performances, since attending drag shows had been one of my favorite activities as a graduate student. My research, in fact, is based in part on the rhetoric of drag king performance, and I rarely missed local drag shows while completing my Ph.D. Drag, I thought, could function as a bridge between my graduate student life and my professional life; it could continue to be a queer space of comfortability as it also became a place where I interacted socially with those students I now advised.

On the night of the actual show, however, I learned that my new institutional context and identity performance reshaped my relationship to this queer space. When the performances began, I adopted my characteristically enthusiastic demeanor: I danced and cheered, clapped my hands, and got my singles ready for tipping. As I was enjoying myself I looked around and began to notice that some of the audience members were watching me almost as closely as they were watching the show. Feeling self-conscious, I soon realized that, within this context, I was not just another audience member, and that I certainly wasn't unrecogniz-able. So, when one of the female HOPE members appeared on stage dressed in the finest masculine hip-hop garb, I knew I was in trouble. Although I was proud of her and showed my support by standing and clapping, I stopped there. I did not approach her, make eye contact, or slip a tip into her waistband. This decision, it turned out, was seren-dipitous, because at the end of the show, the emcee, the president of HOPE, invited all the group members on stage—including me—and without warning, handed me the microphone and asked me to close the show. In this moment I realized that while I had gotten what I wanted: to be completely out, I had also given up my freedom to be just another queer attendee.

With this event, it became clear to me that my professional and per-sonal selves had now fully collided; by living as an out faculty member whose identity was integrated into her various academic roles, I lost the ability to separate these parts of myself. What I gained with this identifi-cation, however, was the potential for students to read their fears, hopes, and anxieties about homosexuality onto me. Since I now named my body as "other"/"lesbian," it became a text upon which students' reflect-ed and responded. And because, as Brenda Brueggemann and Debra Moddelmog contend in their essay, "Coming-Out Pedagogy: Risking Identity in Language and Literature Classroom," that the act of coming out, of "disclosing a historically abject identity [. . . gives] the teacher a body, and not only a performing body, but one that functions (or does not function) in physical, erotic, passionate, and sexual ways," my body became a site of just these kinds of interpretations (Brueggemann and Moddelmog 2002, 312). The HOPE students I worked with, for exam-ple, came to read me as much more than a faculty advisor meant to assist them in writing budgets and planning events. Rather, they assigned various responsibilities and roles to me: they wanted me to be a sympa-thetic confident, a vocal faculty supporter of queer issues on campus, an idealized version of a queer professional, and a nonconfrontational peer. And this disruption of spaces in which I could be comfortable did not end here. Once I came out, the classroom also became fraught with homophobic tension and heterosexist anxieties.

As an out lesbian instructor I was faced with reactions from stu-dents, the likes of which I had never before experienced. Although as a graduate student I had taught texts that dealt explicitly with gender and sexuality and those written by lesbians and gay men, I never once had a student complain—either in person or on course evaluations—about this decision. Even when students disagreed with homosexuality on religious grounds, they did not generalize this discomfort by criticizing me or the course's design. Once I chose to stop passing, however, all this changed. When I began to identify myself as a lesbian—sometimes by naming myself as such, sometimes by mentioning my female partner, and sometimes by making other casual comments that pointed to my sexuality—my students' responses to the topics of identity shifted. They were now more defensive, less apt to talk about these issues, and when they disliked a text for its homosexual content, they attributed this displeasure to the course as a whole.

To illustrate this response, let me offer an example. In my Second-Level Writing course, I focus the theme and readings around the medicalization of the female body, and I routinely teach Audre Lorde's *The Cancer Journals*. One of the main subjects of Lorde's text, of course, is her lesbianism and how it impacts her treatment by medical professionals. When we worked with this text in class (and this reaction has surfaced almost every time I teach this book), the students were reluctant to even name sexuality as one of the themes, never mind engage with it critically. Furthermore, my course evaluations for this course habitually contained comments that singled out Lorde's text and used it to condemn the entire class. Students wrote that Lorde's book contained "inappropriate lesbian content" that did not belong in a writing class, they claimed that the course would have been fine it if wasn't for all the "lesbian stuff we had to read," and they complained that the course was "all about lesbians." In addition to these persistent remarks, a few semesters after I began teaching this particular course, a colleague of mine overheard three of my students discussing me and claiming that "they knew I was a lesbian" and that they were going to make "their disapproval of my lifestyle" clear to me.

Of all the thoughts I have about these responses, I continually return to the fact that it was my outing of myself, and my decision to reject the privileges of passing, that precipitated these circumstances. And when I think about the ways I might engage these new challenges, I realize that the advice offered to me by Ms. Mentor and others like her, simply falls short. Because Ms. Mentor forwards an idealized position in which the professional and the personal are kept neatly separate, she leaves no space for a queer academic to perform as such. For if being out means being visibly queer at all times—in the classroom, the library, campus events—then the "personal" issues of gender expression, sexual identity, and sexual politics are also visible. Rather than facilitating the integration of the personal and the professional, Ms. Mentor's advice encourages silent acquiescence to heterosexist norms and leaves queer academics with few options.

NORMATIVE IMPLICATIONS AND THE DISCIPLINING OF THE QUEER

> *When a lesbian professor comes out in the classroom, she not only makes body, gender, sexuality, desire, and emotion legitimate subjects of discussion, but she questions the foundation of the institutional structures that has depended for its very existence on the systematic removal of these 'others' from its dualistic epistemology. Her body and sexuality make themselves present in the space that has denied them.*
> —Rebecca Mark ("Teaching from the Open Closet")

> *Like every discursive system, the culture of professionalism attempts to make itself omnipresent and thus transparent, invisible. It maintains power through a delicate balance of approbation and punishment, through explicit rules and implicit etiquette.*
> —Chinn ("Queering the Profession,
> or Just Professionalizing Queers?")

If, as Rebecca Mark's comments suggest, coming out in the classroom signals both a resistance to public/private boundaries and a defiance of heterocentric norms, then the exclusion of these acts—which is rife in advice literature—works not only to maintain the silence surrounding sexual difference within the academy, but also reifies and sustains regulatory professional norms. This rampant silence—and repeated acts of silencing—obscure the academy's dependence on and reproduction of heteronormativity and exposes its fetishization of liberal humanism.[8] Importantly, when the majority of current advice texts reiterate these conceptualizations, they perform a disciplining function: they encourage readers to conform to reductive and restrictive codes of behavior, they reproduce heterocentric regulations, and they persuade readers to assimilate these norms into their professional identities.

Subjects who reside within the academy are thus compelled to digest conventional heterosexual standards as they are simultaneously seduced into the humanistic ideal of the self-determined individual. Embedded within a university system that is predicated on "the assumption that [...] a set of attributes that can be acquired by various Others [that ...] will enable them to realize a stereotyped dream of success," academic subjects are often subtly (and sometimes overtly), encouraged to engage in the "process of acquiring such attributes [even though it] involves jettisoning undesirable traits and associations that [such Others have] brought with [them]" (Gibson et al. 2000, 70). So, when queer faculty and graduate students are advised to keep their "private" lives separate from their professional selves, when the legitimacy of coming out in the classroom is questioned for its (in)valid connection to pedagogy, and when discussions of sexuality are relegated to clinical, depersonalized discourse, subjects are confined to narrow professional identities that erase sexual difference and promote connections to regulatory cultural norms. Effectively, subjects are expected to accept "that power in the academy is consistently associated with a predictable and unchanging set of personal characteristics, and [. . .] that [their] self-representation must reflect only those 'power' characteristics and no other" (Gibson et al. 2000, 70). To be a successful member of the profession is thus to replicate a form of polite individualism in which subjects are "free" to advance as long as their work is rigorous and plentiful, and their professional performances mirror heterosexual kinships.

Connecting this perspective to the structure of the traditional nuclear family, Robyn Wiegman argues that professors' "marriage" to the academy "reiterates the structural dynamics of the patriarchal family," and elucidates the academy's reliance on heterosexual modeling which, in turn, demands the replication of heterosexual contexts, behaviors, and identities (1997, 3). Under this rubric, women become the wives and mothers of the profession, and their primary foci become textual (re)production and professional self-sacrifice. The "academy," continues Wiegman, "has required [women in the profession] to be its bride; it wants [them] to believe in [their] own suitability as a regular member of the family" (1997, 15). A successful female academic must then, be constantly engaged in the process of sustaining her "suitability"; she must submit to her place in the academic family and, as Ms. Mentor reminds us, be careful not to express any "lifestyle variations" she may have (as quoted in Gold 1998).

In the case of the queer female academics, whose "lifestyles" certainly stray off this "straight and narrow" path, familial/maternal expectations most definitely abound. If a queer woman is out on her campus, the demands on her time and energy reach far beyond the borders of her office hours and required service responsibilities. As my own experience illustrates, the queer academic is always visible and routinely called to duty. Whether she is asked to be the faculty advisor for the school's LGBTQ student group, to be the representative of "diversity" on committees, or to be the resource for all things nonheterosexual, her status is clear: she is expected to be the altruistic caretaker of queer-related students, issues, and sometimes new faculty hires. Furthermore, as a queer instructor, she is likely to become, as Michèle Aina Barale notes, "the perfect symbol for a variety of meanings. [Queer teachers] may represent all the possibilities of rebellious sexuality [. . .]; we can become sites for the expression of both [students'] liberalism and their bigotry, their fascination and their horror [. . . ,] and god knows that we play out parental roles that we can't begin to fathom" (1994, 19). Queer female faculty members often become, then, "alternate" mothers, once again reinstating the heterosexual model. Queer female faculty are expected to play the part of the dutiful spouse who takes primary responsibility for the care of "difficult" children, and assume the role of the devoted mother who tirelessly tends to her family's wounds and needs.

These queer academic subjects, however, while appreciated for their (often unpaid or underpaid) labor, are also expected to be silent commodities: "valued for [their] diversity," they are simultaneously "relegated to shadows." Within the official discourse of the academy, they can "only speak *about* but cannot speak *as* lesbians, except insofar as [they] are prepared, in such speaking, to make of themselves lesbian objects, objects of study, of interrogation, of confession, of consumption" (Mary Bryson and Suzanne De Castell 1997, 286). Within a university system whose foundation is built upon a paradigm of liberal humanism, academic subjects are presumed to have unified identities that can be easily assimilated into academic culture; they are expected to conform to an ideology in which difference is valued as long as it does not upset underlying assumptions.

Unfortunately, most advice literature (intentionally or not) disseminates, and ultimately helps to support, these principles. By recommending that their readers keep their nonnormative sexualities a secret, that they conform to expected codes of "politeness," and that they save any dissent until they have realized the "American dream" of tenure, these texts elide the intensely political culture of the academy and work in collusion with the disciplinary drive of the institution (Wiegman 1997, 4). The normalizing function of advice texts therefore assists the academy in "neutraliz[ing] the political aspects of identity performance" (Gibson et al. 2000, 70) and aids in the continuation of its "intentional silencing and exclusion of the female body and sexuality for which [it] was founded" (Mark 1994, 253).

Significantly, this cooperative relationship between advice texts and institutional norms is not only ideologically problematic—but also dangerous. Such a collusion privileges acquiesce over critique and works to safeguard the status quo. And, in a time when homophobia and heterosexism are endemic to institutions of higher learning, this problematic coupling should not be overlooked. To do so is to ignore material realities faced by academic subjects everyday—realities like those compiled by a recent campus climate study in which

> nineteen percent [. . . of those surveyed] reported that, within the last year they feared for their physical safety because of their sexual orientation/ gender identity [. . .] 51 percent concealed their sexual identity/gender identity to avoid intimidation [and . . . t]hirty-four percent [. . .] avoided disclosing their sexual identity/gender identity [. . .] due to a fear of nega- tive consequences, harassment, or intimidation. (Rankin 2003, 34)

Faced with such evidence, it is clear that issues of sexuality on campus are much more than theoretical; equity is not the only thing at stake here—safety is also at risk, and that, I maintain, is considerably more important than "not scaring the horses."

PART II

Identity in the Composition Classroom

6

SHE TOILED FOR A LIVING
Writing Lives and Identities of Older Female Students

Mary Hallet

I don't doubt for a moment that she loves her life.
And I want her to rise up from the crust and the slop
     and fly down to the river.
This probably won't happen.
But maybe it will.
If the World were only pain and logic, who would want it?
              —Mary Oliver, "Singapore"

I don't know what Martha Ballard looked like. Still don't know, after
all the years I've been working with her diaries. She became for me a
voice, but that took a long time. Before she was a voice she was a mark
on the page.
       —Laurel Thatcher Ulrich, *The Midwife's Tale* (the film)

DOWN AND DIRTY

"In general," the college administrator pronounced, tugging at his tie, "older students do not know how to write academic essays and need lots of help. They are also less sophisticated when it comes to college life."

I was 40 years old, a nontraditional undergraduate enrolled in a women's liberal arts college on the East Coast, about ready to graduate, and thinking about my future. My college experience at this school had been a good one, largely because the institution had invested much time and money in the building and strengthening of its nationally known nontraditional students program. For the most part, faculty and college administrators seemed to take a holistic approach to older female students, not only in terms of what these students brought to the classroom, but also in terms of their experiences and lives outside of the academy.

Because of what I perceived as their more enlightened stance toward older female students, I was always stunned to hear the occasional negative comment such as that made by this particular administrator.

I had been appointed as a nontraditional student representative to the college's admissions committee, and had learned through the course of my tenure on that committee that tensions rose when hard decisions had to be made about the "desired" population of the institution and who should be admitted. These tensions were exacerbated when financial considerations prevailed. In this case, the decision had been made to eliminate the college's blind admissions policy, an approach to admitting new students based only on their qualifications rather than on their ability to pay tuition. Up until this point, students admitted who could not pay were awarded financial aid packages. This is, in fact, how I myself had been able to attend this particular school. But now this policy was coming undone.

It's not that I did not believe older female students new to the academic environment struggled with writing (I certainly had when I when I first arrived), nor that I did not think that older students, often first-generation college students, approached college from a sometimes uninformed perspective. It's just that the administrator's proclamation simply did not ring true for me. I knew, for example, that every spring nontraditional students, who comprised a small percentage of the campus population, were often awarded at least half of the college's academic writing prizes and that they traditionally occupied a good many of the summa cum laude slots on the graduation program. Because of these paradoxes, I began to see how, no matter what facts pointed toward real academic achievement on the part of nontraditional students, some academics still perceived the older female student as alien to the academy, and a threat to academic space and standards.

About this same time the Career Resource Center at the college sent out a pamphlet to prospective employers to counteract age discrimination in hiring. On the cover of the pamphlet was the picture of a professionally dressed white woman between 40 and 50. She carried a briefcase and smiled confidently at the camera. Bold letters at the top of the pamphlet announced: "The Benefits of Hiring Older Workers." Inside a list of reasons proclaimed why hiring older workers might be a good idea: we were not only more mature, experienced, and dependable, but we tended to call in sick less than younger workers. We could be counted on to be productive citizens. Like vintage machinery, if well cared for, we could go on indefinitely.

This pamphlet mildly offended me, and many of my peers as well. We couldn't quite pinpoint exactly what it was that irked us about this pamphlet; surely it was produced with good intentions—to combat age discrimination in hiring. Nevertheless, it touched a nerve with us, and I believe it did so on several levels. First, we could not conceive of a similar publication about our younger peers who were also about to graduate, a pamphlet that announced, "Hiring Younger Workers," and that listed the productive attributes of young people in the same way: dependable, seldom get sick, get along well with others, likely to have many productive years ahead of them. The pamphlet made us feel a little bit like sturdy work horses with good teeth and lungs. But it was the word "workers" that irritated me even more. It seemed to me that my younger peers identified themselves, and were identified by the college, as being women with careers—not as workers.

In retrospect, I see that my association with the word "worker" was complicated, and not one for which the college could have been entirely responsible. I had been raised by a widowed mother, a strong woman with a high school education who took care of four of us as best she could on her legal secretary's salary and my deceased father's Social Security death benefits, but still had to sometimes hit up her reluctant brother, a warehouse manager, for occasional handouts. Before returning to college after a hiatus of twenty years, I had been a data entry operator for the Colorado Department of Revenue, and later for oil-related businesses in Denver before the oil industry itself went suddenly, violently, belly-up. I had also been a membership specialist (translated data entry operator) for a large national organization. In most of these jobs my female co-workers and I were relegated to the kind of open cubicles the comic strip *Dilbert* makes fun of: small stall-like spaces with walls just high enough to separate us from one another and from the college-educated staff who had their own offices with doors and windows; but low enough so that we could always be seen and our activity and production monitored.

When I finally got my B.A., I spent the summer before going on for my Masters degree working for a temporary agency. I was 41 years old; my younger co-workers, male and female alike, called me the "temp-girl," and I worked in a large bank's mortgage department answering the unwanted calls from economically disadvantaged people who were responding to the bank's federally mandated program designed to give such people a shot at home ownership. The young mortgage officers at the bank hated these calls and had hired me to run interference. If these people, who were desperate to own a home, expected a quick call back, they had another thing coming. I was ashamed of the role I played at this bank, and ashamed to be back in a low-hierarchy clerical position.

I realize now that much of my response to the college's brochure had to do with a sense of shame that I, like many low middle-income or working-class people, carry with them as they see themselves climbing the ladder to professionalism and middle-class success. It has taken me years to overcome that shame and to value my identity as a first-generation college student with a less-than-privileged economic background, and I find now that I can stand up with backbone and a great deal of pride to professors such as the one in my department who recently claimed that, because I had not, as he had, come from an academic home or professional family background, I had to negotiate a "larger learning curve" in the academy.

This struggle to come into my own as an academic—one who not only came through the academy's back door as a first-generation college student, but who did so at a "late" age—has encouraged me to reconsider my writing pedagogies, especially when teaching nontraditional students. Because I sometimes teach an autobiographical writing course for evening students at my university, I often teach to a classroom of older female students. As I teach these students, I have a heightened awareness of the multiple ways they construct identities in the classroom, ways that are often antithetical to traditional views of academic space and purposes. I have come to recognize the complicated and often vexed identities of these students—both as they are realized in autobiographical writing and as they are often distorted through un-theorized pedagogies and unquestioning acquiescence to naturalized notions of academic standards and intellectual space. In the rest of this chapter, I suggest ways of considering the positions of older female students in the academy, and approaches to their writing that will allow for the fleshing out—rather than the *flattening* out—of their contingent, layered, and fluid identities.

WORKING WOMEN ALL

The textured, mutable, and interlocking identities of older female undergraduates can best be explored within a framework of varying and often contradictory perspectives: the generalized and the particular, the academic and the personal, the intellectual and the embodied. In this essay, I explore the tensions that arise from these diverse perspectives, particularly those that inform (and also vex) learning, writing, and teaching. In doing so, I show how the identities of older female students are often imagined according to, or constructed by, their reproductive and "laboring" histories, as well as by their supposed proximity to dirt, materiality, and embodiment. I will also show how the often unconscious association of nontraditional female undergraduates with maternity and physicality simultaneously positions these women as "always already" outside the academy while attempting to limit them to "pure" academic spaces. Finally, I will suggest ways that we can use these tensions to help such students compose life stories that position them as historical and political subjects both within the academy and their communities at large.

I begin this essay with two quotations, both of which I refer to here to launch my discussion of older women students in the academy, cultural and academic perceptions of such students, and how these women construct and perform through autobiographical writing what John Ernest calls "multiply contingent identity" (28). The first quotation is from Mary Oliver's "Singapore" (1992), a poem in which the speaker narrates her encounter with a cleaning woman in a restroom in that country's airport. Entering the restroom, the speaker sees the woman in one of the stalls, stooped over a toilet bowl, cleaning ashtrays. With this image, and indeed with the poem itself (the only one of its kind in a collection of poems largely characterized by their references to nature), Oliver calls to question common assumptions about poetry—especially *her* poetry—that a "poem should always have birds in it," and that a "person wants to stand in a happy place, in a poem" (72).

Although the reader of Oliver's poems may indeed wish "happy" and stable places, in this poem she encounters an artificial space, a human-made site inhabited not by the flora and fauna of Oliver's other poems, but by a woman laboring on the ground over a toilet bowl. Both the space and the woman are imaged in relation to human excrement, to the residual grime of ashtrays, and to the "natural" dirtiness of the human body. For all its references to embodiment, however, the space of the poem itself is strangely—and paradoxically—both ephemeral *and* finite. The site cannot be described as a liminal space, as such a term would suggest a potential boundary crossing, and would thus lend to the space a transforming quality it does not have; neither the poem's speaker nor the cleaning woman will necessarily transition from one side of this space to another. Earlier in the poem, in fact, upon witnessing the woman at work, "disgust argue[s] in [the speaker's] stomach," as she signals her freedom and eagerness to leave the space by groping "in [her] pocket, for [her] ticket." Meanwhile, the cleaning woman stays put. Left behind in the latrine, suspended amid the "crust and the slop," kneeling before the toilet bowl scrubbing "airport ashtrays, as big as hubcaps," she remains anchored in the repetitious dailiness of her duties (72).

Certainly, in its wish for possibilities beyond "pain and logic," Oliver's poem gestures toward hope. Nevertheless, the poem's speaker locates this hope not in the woman's life outside the poem's frame—that is, within family, community, and culture—but rather as emanating from the woman's acknowledgment and affirmation of the speaker herself: "I mean the / way she folded and refolded the blue cloth, / the way her smile was only for my sake" (73). While I do not want to reduce the poem to political and socioeconomic binaries, there seems to be some sense at least in which the woman's light and life is activated by, and thus indebted to, the speaker and the metaphorical images that construct both space and identity in the poem. The woman, the poem's title indicates she may not be a White Westerner, and whose constructed setting is a nowhere space inaccessible to nature or community, remains alien and out of place.

In the second quotation I use above, from the documentary *The Midwife's Tale* (1998), nature as metaphor for human experience gives way to a discursive and embodied human presence, a more viable presence than the one presented by Oliver. Here, with the historian's subject coming to voice ("she became for me a voice"), as well as the "markings" on the page made by the subject herself, we see a more dialogic relationship between experience and interpretation of experience, between analysis of a subject and the subject's construction of identity through her own written record. If we consider the quotation in the context of the documentary from which it comes, we note the pronounced interrelationship between observer and subject. Whereas Oliver's speaker's relationship with the working woman in the Singapore restroom is constructed solely through the speaker's voice and perspective, in *The Midwife's Tale*, relationships and identities between historian and subject, not to mention between subject and community, intermingle and shift. Moreover, since the historian derives her interpretation from her subject's diary itself, the subject's discursive voice, rather than simply the historian's observation, becomes central to the midwife's identity, as well as to the identity of the historian who studies that voice.

The historian who narrates *The Midwife's Tale* is Laurel Ulrich, who published a book by the same title in 1990. In the book, Ulrich historically contextualizes the diary of the midwife Martha Ballard, an eighteenth-century working woman from Hallowell, Maine. This diary, as with other similar documents written by women in colonial and postcolonial America, had been ignored for years by other (mainly male) historians, as it was deemed to concentrate too heavily, and only, on the work and trivial details of domestic life, rather than on larger historical events, such as battles and the signing of important national documents. But as Ulrich herself points out, "[i]t is in the very daili-ness, the exhaustive, repetitious dailiness, that the real power of Martha Ballard's book lies" (Ulrich 9).

In 1997, Ulrich collaborated with writer and producer, Laurie Kahn-Leavitt, to produce a film version of *The Midwife's Tale*, a dramatic recreation shown as part of the PBS series, *The American Experience*. In the film, representation and construction of the subject's identity are complicated by the triangulation of her experience through the layering of—and fluid connection between and among—the midwife's diary, the historian herself, and the actors who represent Ballard, her family, and her community. In several scenes, for example, viewers see Ulrich por-ing over the diary, trying to make sense of what Ulrich calls its "scratch-ings"; as Ulrich mouths the words of the diary out loud, the viewer also hears the voice of Kaiulani Lee, the actress who plays Ballard in the film, speaking the same words. As the voices and identities of Ulrich and Ballard meld together, the scene shifts from Ulrich to the actors repre-senting Ballard, her family, and her community. With this shift, Ballard becomes, vis-à-vis the actor who portrays her, not just a fully embodied object of study, but also a participating subject in her own story.

Thus, while we can only imagine the life circumstances and network of relationships of the working-class woman in Oliver's text, Ulrich's story and the circumstances of the midwife's labor are literally fleshed out for us, and even given an almost three-dimensional character through the tightly interwoven triad of text, historian, and actor; the words and images of each of these subjects intersect, interrupt, and interact fluidly, sometimes overlapping, sometimes separating. As with Oliver's poem, work and labor are at the heart of Ulrich's narration. In Ulrich's text, though, images of labor are complicated by Ballard's multiple roles and her intense capacity for work: as colonial housekeeper, as midwife and healer, and as an almost dogged recorder of her own life and history. The connotations of "labor," moreover, become even more complicated when the viewer considers Ballard's association with birthing mothers and the labor of childbirth.

Ballard's role in birthing and healing lend to her work and life a similar relationship with human "dirt," or the "crust and the slop" of the cleaning woman in Oliver's poem. Ballard's association with the stuff of the body—indeed, embodiment itself—is highlighted in detail throughout the film: Ballard attends countless women giving birth; assists men, children, and women, victims of eighteenth-century epidemics, coughing up blood; empties slop jars; trails her skirts through the mud of unpaved streets as she is called to sit with a dying woman; is shown down on her knees, incessantly cleaning up her own family's "crust and slop." Yet her "working class" life opens up far beyond the four walls of the cleaning woman's latrine as depicted solely through the eyes of Oliver's speaker. Not only do the horizons of Ballard's life expand to include family, community, and Ballard's profession as healer, they also push beyond temporal confines to include historian and actor as participants in Ballard's life and story. While Oliver's poem constructs working-class life only through the fleeting gaze of the artist herself, Ulrich's text and the documentary arising from it reveal the multiple dimensions of a working woman's life as seen through a variety of eyes and as lived in relationship to various communities, both in the past and in the present.

Of course, Oliver's poem is what it is; the conventions of poetry, and especially of the short poem form in which Oliver normally writes, do not allow for the kind of expanded discussion and perspectives that characterize the historian's book and the documentary connected to it. I like Oliver's poem, the questions it raises about poetry in general, and Oliver's own poetry in particular, as well as its courageous foray into new territory, its brave consideration of a single working-class life. I use it here in relation to Ulrich's work largely metaphorically, as a way to discuss issues of identity construction among and by older female students in the university where I teach, students who, for the most part, have held working to lower middle-class kinds of jobs, and who have complex lives and relationships outside of our classrooms.

As I juxtapose Oliver's poem with Ulrich's historical interpretation of the midwife's life, I use Oliver's poem to highlight what I see as a common tendency among academics to objectify working-class older women who return to school by viewing them only through our own lenses and positioning them in a limited and enclosed intellectual space. Simultaneously, I use the documentary *The Midwife's Tale* to offer alternative, concurrent, and multiple approaches to perceiving and teaching such women. To this extent, I compare the speaker in Oliver's poem to teachers who define the identities of their older female students solely according to their *own* perceptions and experiences as academics. (Most of these teachers, unlike the older women in their classrooms, have taken a direct and linear path to their academic careers.) At the same time, I discuss Ulrich's documentary not only as a way of opening up our field of vision to the broader and highly contextualized lives of the women we teach, but also as a classroom tool that helps us do so.

SITES OF LABOR: MAKING ROOM FOR MOMMY

If the speaker in Oliver's poem stands in relation to the cleaning woman as some academics stand in relation to older female students in the academy, what useful parallels might we draw about the ways we define those students' identities? Oliver's speaker depicts the cleaning woman's identity mainly as constructed in response to the speaker's own gaze; in this sense, the teacher in the writing classroom, as well as the scholar who writes about such students, often teaches to, and defines, older female identities as constructed only in relation to her or his individual classroom and pedagogies. Because we often have the perception of a fixed academic space occupied equally by students of all ages, life circumstances, and backgrounds, and because our relationships with our students are most often limited to that perceived space, we often imbue the classroom site with a significance it may not necessarily have for older students, much as the speaker of Oliver's poem sees, leaves, and limits the cleaning woman to a single enclosed space and identity constructed solely in response to the speaker's gaze and by the poet's words.

This tendency to telescope the older female student's experience into a single site of identity and intellectual achievement, and to perceive that space as an ultimately significant site, erases from the subject's body—in some figurative sense at least—important identifying marks, particularly those having to do with the "dirt" of reproduction, mothering or reproductive (non)history, human relationships, and what is commonly described as women's work, or working-class labor. The result of such erasure is a streamlined intellectual identity confined and defined by a streamlined and decidedly terminal academic space. To expand our view of the older female student and to acknowledge an intellect "soiled" by human labor and relationships risk admitting into the academic spaces of the writing classroom that which is commonly perceived as alien and even threatening to the academy. I see as proof of this alienation the complaints of colleagues concerning students whose first priority is not their academics, but rather their work and their families. Somewhat ironically, such positioning of older women students according to their relationships, or according to their reproductive histories (whether or not they have had children), does not necessarily result in the recognition of complex identities; rather this kind of positioning attempts to streamline "laborious" identities so that they fit into a single one-size-fits-all academic space.

My focus earlier in this essay on images of "crust and slop," as well as on the proliferation of different kinds of dirt related to the body and associated with working-class lives and environments, lays the ground-work for my discussion here of so-called sterile academic and intel-lectual sites and the alien figures that some see as contaminating those sites. As one of my colleagues exclaimed recently on a university list-serv: "Some people are simply not university material!" The suggestion of "material" here hints at embodiment, as well as a textured toughness resistant to the kind of shaping it might take to fit that material into a desired form or space.

Beyond this notion of rigid (rigorous) shaping, however, are also negative images of the body—that is, identities as constructed through physical and somatic experience. Such bodies are often seen as not only contaminants in the university classroom, but also as antithetical to the intellectual mission of the university itself. Too often, the texts written by these bodies are judged as physical manifestations of the writers them-selves, especially when surface and compositional "flaws" are deemed reflective of not only the writer's (lack of) intellect, but also of her or his right to enter the university as a participating body.

Deborah Mutnick (1996) best illustrates this linkage of bodies to so-called flawed composition in her study of basic writers: "As in other types of oppression—sexism, for example—the basic writing student is often viewed as alien and inferior, the 'body' of his or her texts regarded contemptuously" (xxiv). Such an image of the body as out of control can be extended to nontraditional female students whose physical lives and concerns spill over both into and out of those academic spaces that some teachers and administrators wish to contain. It is no surprise, in fact, that suspicion of the working-class female body (indeed, of *all* bodies constituting other than the academic class) parallels what Kylie Message (1998) calls the streamlining of the abject female body in the 1950s, around the same time that the G.I. bill allowed working-class male students into American university classrooms. Examining Australian advertisements that replicate those of American magazines, Message notes that

> . . . the increasingly attractive postwar forces of modernism and consum-
> erism were inherently tied and marketed toward women and the home

. . . . Women were bound and sentenced by the filth of their maternal bodies and to regulate their family's dirt . . . . Represented as being passively bound to this association with filth, housewives were encouraged to participate in an economy of consumerism by imperatives to cleanliness . . . . [and] the body of the housewife was encouraged to conform with modernist designs of streamlining. (2–7)

By quoting Message, I am not suggesting that all older nontraditional students are mothers (I was not one), nor that their identities are necessarily constructed by motherhood. Rather, I am arguing that the older female body is often associated with its reproductive history. That this is true is evidenced in the constant pinpointing of older women according to their reproductive pasts. Whereas older men in public life are not necessarily defined as fathers or grandfathers, older women are often described in the media according to their reproductive histories. Recently, for example, while interviewing workers at a bomb-making plant, CBS's Bill Geist spoke with a number of men of various ages, including some over 50, without once referring to their roles as fathers or grandfathers. When he approached a woman of about 60, however, he introduced her as a grandmother. This focus on the maternal history of women and their roles as caretakers suggests that unconscious associations with embodiment and uncontained "filth" are more pronounced with women than with men. Here, then, we may recall the woman in Oliver's poem, a working-class woman contained and defined by her small space and the "crust and slop" that characterize that space.

This notion of an identifiable (and identifying) space for containment becomes a central issue for composition theorist Jonathon Mauk (2003), who notes that many students not containable within traditional academic spaces actually occupy *no* space at all:

Although the average college student is impossible to profile, a vast number of college students share a common trait: they are unsituated in academic space. Or put another way, academic space is not an integral part of their intellectual geography. They are first-generation college students; they are commuters; they are part-time community college students; they are "nontraditional" (above twenty-four years old), with jobs and families . . . And, collectively, their presence portends change for academic space. (369)

Mauk sees these students in a state of "nowhereness," and suggests that the assignments we give them "need to create a *material-discursive where*"

for these students (379). Likewise, John Ernest (1998)—a nontraditional student turned academic—extends "terms of identity [that] are both
positive and negative" (27) to his own sense of academic space. Noting
that "we define ourselves both according to who we are and according
to who we are not" (27), Ernest sees working-class and nontraditional
students as being both "in and out of the game," or both insiders and
outsiders within official academic sites. "According to the official academy," Ernest argues, "education is a high ideal, a shining city on the
intellectual and social hill, a lifetime pursuit, both the means and an end
itself" (33). By pinpointing a *nowhereness* (non)occupied by working-class
and nontraditional students, both Mauk and Ernest emphasize the need
for identities as constructed not only by place, but also by what Kristie
Fleckenstein (1991) describes as a coextensive "[w]ho and where (thus,
what)" (286). Ernest agrees with Fleckenstein when he asserts that "class
is both defined and experienced relationally" through "multiply contingent identity" (28), an identity that shifts and shapes itself according to
relationships and the spaces they occupy.

It is with this sense of sites and identities as intermingled, fluid, and
ultimately relational that I turn here again to Ulrich's *The Midwife's Tale*.
My intent is not to be prescriptive, nor to offer easy solutions that help
nontraditional female students construct identities. However, I believe
that texts like Ulrich's, and documentaries such as the one that springs
from Ulrich's text, are exemplary in the way they allow for the construction of the kind of multiple contingent identities Ernest describes. The
film highlights, first, the importance of primary "pure" autobiographical documents, in this case, the midwife's diary, a text that defines the
midwife almost solely in economic and bodily terms, with each entry
concerned with births, deaths, illnesses, and economic exchanges made
for professional services. Second, the film situates the diary in historical
terms and makes it (and the midwife) a valid subject for academic study.
Finally, the embodied details of the midwife's life, as well as of her community and family, are fleshed out—made whole—for the viewer. These
different modes of signifying the woman and her work speak to a sense
of relational identity not contained in a single site, but rather transcend-
ing—or at least concurrent with—different spaces and temporalities.

SHE TOILS FOR A LIVING: DOCUMENTING LABOR

In more practical terms, the documentary lends itself to the kinds of
writing assignments Mauk (2003) recommends, assignments that provide "a conceptual place (a topic) while also prompting students to

make meaning out of the people-places that constitute their daily lives" (381). To encourage this kind of meaning making, I use *The Midwife's Tale* along with other texts, memoirs and autobiographies that narrate the experiences of others, and that include the perspectives of those from different cultures, races, and ethnic backgrounds, and also the perspectives of both men and women. In recent classes, for example, students read James McBride's *The Color of Water* (1996), James Carroll's *An American Requiem* (1996), Elva Treviño Hart's *Barefoot Heart* (1999), and Adeline Yen Mah's *Falling Leaves* (1997). Using these texts in addition to the documentary ensures that most students will find a way to "relate" to the course and also to the stories of others. While reading these texts, they are able to recognize the significance of people and places in the construction of autobiographical identities.

While all of these texts are equally important to the class, however, I lay the groundwork for our discussions by beginning with *The Midwife's Tale.* By doing so, I encourage students to contextualize autobiographical experience in terms of labor and gender. I also reveal autobiographical documents, and the subjects who write them, as essential components of history. While they are watching the film, for example, I ask students to list all the different kinds of labor that characterize the midwife's story: the historian Ulrich at work over the midwife's diary, for example, or the midwife on her rounds and women laboring in birth. I also urge them to pay attention to gendered divisions of labor in the film. At the same time, I have students make note of the triangulated voices that tell the midwife's story—the midwife's words as written in her diary, the historian interpreting them, and the actors representing the midwife and her community. With these observations, students begin to see that autobiography, as well as the autobiographical subject and audience, are complicated and contiguous elements. For older female students in particular, the recognition of the complexities of rendering daily labor, and the contingent qualities of work, family, and community, help them see their own lives (which they often view as mundane) as threads in a larger cultural tapestry and as events on a continuum of historical moments.

Immediately after viewing the documentary, we open up analysis of the midwife's experience to other issues, and discuss Ballard's experience in relation to other women of her time, particularly women of color and from different economic backgrounds. At the end of this discussion, we form a kind of rubric together, one that helps each student begin to position herself or himself as an autobiographical subject. The rubric headings include: Labor, Class, Gender, Race, Family, and

Community. Once students have discussed these elements in relation to the documentary, they are prepared to begin looking at them in their own lives.

The next step toward writing their own autobiographies is a series of diary and journal keeping entries. For the first couple of weeks of class, I have students keep what I call a working diary, one that concentrates only on the so-called mundane details of daily labor and relationships. Much as Martha Ballard recorded only the sparse details of her daily life (weather conditions, babies delivered, one sentence summaries of often momentous family or community events), students also make daily entries listing only the bare facts of work, family, and community. When they have completed this diary, they exchange it with a partner, who then plays historian, working to interpret and flesh out her or his classmate's life. By doing this, students come to recognize the difference between merely relating chronological facts for oneself, and writing with an audience in mind. They also begin to recognize themselves as historical subjects.

More important, perhaps, students learn to view work and economic class as crucial components of life and the construction of life narratives. For older female students in particular—especially those who have worked in lower paying clerical or blue collar positions before returning to school, or those whose work has been centered in the home—this kind of recognition of daily labor and its importance not only to autobiography, but also to history, allows them to bridge the gap between the personal and the academic. Not only are they invited to incorporate daily details into their academic writing, they understand the personal and historical importance of such details.

Finally, as we progress to other texts, students begin keeping a journal, which is distinguished from the diary by its fleshing out of details and its more expansive reflective nature. As they compose this journal, I encourage students to build on, rather than drop, the "mundane" facts of their diary entries, so that they are less likely to gloss over those elements of work, class, race, and gender that underpin their life's stories, and are also less likely to sublimate those elements to the narration of such "life-altering" events as marriages, births, and deaths. In fact, they come to see such life events as largely dependent upon their personal positions as political, historical, and working subjects.

I do not claim here that all students in my autobiographical writing classes end up writing perfectly detailed autobiographies characterized by a fully developed political and historical awareness. Nevertheless,

I have had the pleasure of witnessing older female students find an expansiveness in their lives and writing that permits the opening up of academic space from a site of "nowhereness" to a territory of intersecting identities, temporalities, and historical positionings. Thus, what Ulrich calls the "exhaustive dailiness" of the diary becomes the means of constructing not individual and isolated identities, but rather dynamic identities rooted in relationships, histories, and the rich messiness of embodied experience.

7

LITERACY, IDENTITY AND THE "SUCCESSFUL" STUDENT WRITER

William Carpenter and Bianca Falbo

What would it mean for the field of composition to study the literacy habits of undergraduate students identified as talented, privileged, and academically successful? What new information can this group of writers tell us about the relationship between literacy development and education? How might our pedagogies and our theories benefit from examining the ways in which these students discuss their literacies?

In this chapter, we investigate these questions by examining the written literacy narratives of students working as undergraduate Writing Associates at Lafayette College, our home institution. We seek to contribute a different perspective to current research in literacy studies, which, as the programs from the most recent Watson Conference and CCCC demonstrate, has come to focus almost exclusively on nontraditional students. Instead, we focus on the literacy habits of students who are reasonably well prepared to do academic writing, but whose (mostly successful) experiences with writing have not encouraged them to reflect on the different identities they construct (and have constructed) through literacy and at various literacy sites. Our aim, then, in looking at writing by "successful" students, is not to gather "tips" on good writing, but rather to think broadly about the means and ends of academic writing.

Although we think our project offers a different perspective, we nonetheless see ourselves working in the tradition of scholars such as David Bartholomae (2001), Mariolina Salvatori (1988), and Min-Zhan Lu (1999), who have made powerful arguments about students' texts as complex cultural artifacts that invite and demand sustained critical interpretation.[1] Though our students differ, in particular, from the kinds of students Bartholomae and Lu write about, like them, and like Salvatori, we are similarly concerned with the ways in which our students negotiate academic discourse, and we try to situate that struggle with respect to the politics of speaking (or not) in the academy. In addition, there are a number of longitudinal studies that have been important precedents for ours, including Marilyn Sternglass' *Time to Know Them: A Longitudinal*

Study of Writing and Learning at the College Level (1997), and, more recently Lee Ann Carroll's *Rehearsing New Roles: How College Students Develop as Writers* (2002) and Nancy Sommers' project on undergraduate writing at Harvard (2003). Though the discussion in this chapter is not the result of a longitudinal study, it does mark for us the beginning of a long-term project about the ways in which participation in our College Writing Program changes the Writing Associates' perceptions of themselves as readers and writers. Our reading of the narratives, so far, has been based on three questions: How do new Writing Associates describe themselves as readers and writers? How do returning Writing Associates describe themselves as readers and writers? To what do new Writing Associates attribute the changes they see? Like Sternglass, Carol, and Sommers, then, we are looking at how writers develop over time, but for the purposes of the present discussion, we focus exclusively on students' reflections on their writing. We are not interested in the quality of writing in the narratives, but rather in how our students write about writing.

Briefly, then, here is some background about our institution and our program. Lafayette College is a private, highly selective, liberal arts college in Easton, Pennsylvania, with a student population of approximately 2,200. Lafayette has always been a competitive institution, but in recent years, the College has raised its admission standards, admitting students with higher GPAs and standardized test scores. Many of these students identify themselves and have been identified as highly literate, meaning that they have always been recognized for good critical thinking, reading and writing skills. Since 1985, the College Writing Program has recruited and trained 30 to 50 Writing Associates a year to work with professors teaching the College's first-year and sophomore seminars and other writing courses. Writing Associates come from all majors and generally have at least 3.0 GPAs. In addition, they have excellent communication skills, and they participate in a range of campus activities.

Writing Associates occupy a unique position on campus, as they are simultaneously students, peer readers, and professional representatives of the CWP. They function not as editors or proofreaders, but as informed and intelligent readers who help students formulate tough questions about their own writing. Writing Associates also provide faculty with invaluable feedback on assignment design, student progress, and strategies for the evaluation of written work. (Writing Associates do not grade student work.) The College Writing Program sponsors a summer workshop each year as well as weekly staff meetings in which Writing Associates discuss the theory and practice of writing. In preparation for the summer workshop, new and returning Writing Associates alike compose literacy narratives—histories of their experiences as readers and writers. The work of reflecting on their literacy histories helps prepare Writing Associates to see their peers as individual writers who likewise have literacy histories of their own.

Our chapter, a qualitative study of more than 130 literacy narratives written between 1999 and 2001, compares narratives by new and returning Writing Associates in order to show how participation in the College Writing Program shapes their identities as readers and writers. For most, working as a Writing Associate complicates what they previously assumed about the work of writing. New Writing Associates' narratives tend to be success stories about how they have always had a "natural" talent for writing, or how their perseverance in the face of a demanding teacher or assignment eventually paid off in the form of a good grade, an award, or a lesson about why writing is an important skill. Returning Writing Associates' narratives focus on students' revised assumptions about writing as a process over which they have varying degrees of control. Most returning Writing Associates attribute changes they see in their writing, or their thinking about writing, to interactions with their peers. As one returning Writing Associate wrote, "by examining others' writing, the Writing Associate also ends up examining his or her own written work. . . . I learned that writing is not an absolute process" (Menon 2001).

LITERACY NARRATIVES BY NEW WRITING ASSOCIATES

Thanks mainly to Kenneth Burke, we know that all ways of seeing are ways of not seeing, too. In organizing our realities into coherence we favor some interpretations over others. We construct narratives that identify certain relationships among events and leave other relationships, other possibilities, unrecognized. Our decisions in organizing and constructing our narratives materialize in the language forms we utter or write. Thus we create artifacts that communicate simultaneously what we see and what we do not. In so doing, we open ourselves to interpretive strategies of others who seek to comprehend the relationship between what is said and what is not, who search for the ways in which our narrative decisions uncover certain truths while burying others.

New Writing Associates are asked to write literacy narratives in which they "identify a handful of formative experiences" that have affected their senses of themselves as writers. The assignment asks specifically that the narratives be written "as a story, arranged in chronological order." So in sense, a key interpretive strategy is made for them by us:

that they arrange moments in their literacy development as a progression of sequenced events. To help the Writing Associates invent ideas, we include a list of broadly defined events—such as one's first attempt to spell a name or one's most difficult writing assignment in high school—recognizing, of course, that such suggestions might limit the scope of some writers as it broadens that of others. The assignment then asks the Writing Associates to reflect on the significance of these events in shaping their identities as readers and writers, a concept we leave broadly defined so as to encourage the Writing Associates to reach their own conclusions about the effects of their upbringing and schooling on their language use.

This is an interesting rhetorical situation for the new Writing Associates. Not yet fully oriented to the theoretical and practical frameworks surrounding their position, and perhaps still feeling the need to impress those who hired them, they must work within a genre that few have any experience with.[2] Given this unfamiliar rhetorical situation, as well as the assignment's implicit and explicit demands to create sequential relationships among events, it is little wonder that new Writing Associates often write within familiar narrative forms. For most, these forms mirror those of the heroic narrative, the telling of the hero's journey toward home or some other promised land. The hero is the earnest student confronted at various times by progressively difficult tasks, each of which teaches her something about herself and about academic writing.

For many of the new Writing Associates, academic literacy is achieved—or at least perceived to be achieved—through struggle, though it is a kind of struggle marked mainly by gaps in a string of academic successes. In other words, struggle occurs when the usually successful methods for responding to assignments no longer garner the same rewards or higher grades. These moments introduce obstacles for the Writing Associate—heroes to overcome, lest they perish in the marshes of academic mediocrity. They often write of the demanding language arts teacher who had to be appeased, of the difficult assignment that had to be unlocked, and of the physical and emotional terrains of the educational system that had to be navigated. In some scenes there is confusion and frustration, as the students confront unsettling moments of failure or diminished performance that force them to seek a hidden map for writing or to unravel the riddles of their teachers. In other scenes, the students rediscover success as they learn to refocus their energies and apply what they have learned from their struggles. The ease with which these narratives come into focus under the hero-lens speaks not only to expectations stated and implied in the assignment, but also to these young writers' perceptions and theories of the interdependent relationships among education, identity, and writing.

Adam Scheer, hired as a junior in 2000, writes a narrative indicative of those of his peers. In his section on the transition between high school and college, he tries to analyze the relationships among his high school's standards, his performance, and his own identity as a student and a writer.

> I was always very much turned off by the educational realities of my high school, for it seemed that grades and most of the other evaluation mechanisms had very little to do with the content of the student's work and even less to do with his/her overall academic prowess. My grades were good throughout high school, but not great. Although I was able to identify the shortcomings of my high school and understand that my grades there did not define my worth as a student, I was not able to truly internalize this. Going into my freshman year at Lafayette, I did not have a tremendous amount of confidence in my academic abilities. One paper later, I was a different student.

The passage encourages two conflicting readings: that Scheer's own "academic prowess" was not recognized by his teachers, resulting in decent grades but also a diminished self-esteem; or that Scheer's "good . . . but not great" grades reflect some level of grade inflation at the school, resulting in academic success but also a fragile self-confidence. Scheer explains that grades at his school did not represent effort or ability, but he does not explain whether the discrepancies are caused by over- or underappreciation of the students' work. And while he does give himself credit for recognizing his school's "shortcomings," he does not divulge what those shortcomings are, nor what he means when he admits that he could not "truly internalize" the idea that his "grades . . . did not define [his] worth as a student." That the entire passage rests on ambiguity signals Scheer's own uncertainty about how well his high school prepared him for college. The hero faces a test of his confidence—albeit a short one.

We read Scheer's description of his high school as a key dramatic component of his narrative, one that enables its heroic story arc. Its ambiguity aside, the majority of the passage offers reasons for Scheer's penultimate point: that as a first-year college student, he initially felt underprepared for academic work. The high school becomes a metaphorical limbo, a place that does not allow Scheer to claim an identity as a student or a writer. As the last sentence of the passage suggests, this state of existence does not last for long. "One paper" written after high school frees Scheer from his academic limbo, returning the hero to the path toward success, but also allowing the narrative to continue along a comfortable, familiar story arc. The sudden transition at the end of the passage is indicative of transitions found within the new Writing Associates' narratives. In Scheer's case, it enables him to present a difficultly as a narrative convenience, one that re-emphasizes his ability to overcome adversity. Scheer, like other new Writing Associates, associates his literacy development with his successes over adversities, rather than with the adversities themselves. This is a crucial point, for it implies that these students, at this stage, consider literacy as a problem-solving heuristic, and see themselves as quick-learning problem solvers. Note, for instance, how Scheer explains the revelatory experience of writing his first college-level paper.

> My first paper as a Lafayette student was for my FYS [First-Year Seminar] class and had to be only a few pages long. I wrote about the many archetypes concerning men that suggest they cannot achieve true intimacy with each other. I would have rather written about the prevalence of iron deficiencies in prematurely balding men or the role of the earthworm in the animal food chain. Regardless of the topic, I knew I was going to try my hardest to write a coherent, well-organized, thought-provoking and overall solid paper. After a short writing process, a few meetings with our Writing Associate, and the teacher finally grading the paper, I was convinced that I had found a good blueprint for my future writings and that I would continue my development as a writer. Over the rest of my FYS course and that entire year, my progression continued. Once again, however, that progression was to be hindered as I spent my sophomore year studying in Malaga, Spain.

The problem in this passage is a much more external one than that of the previous excerpt; Scheer faces an uninteresting, and perhaps uncomfortable, topic for his paper. He seems to have lost, rather quickly, the internal strife of a writer unsure of his abilities and has replaced it with a confidence borne of hard work and good planning. The hero-narrative form he has chosen encourages him to stress individual struggles with assignments at the expense of a holistic analysis of his writing abilities. Absent from this passage—from the entire narrative—is any discussion of how he comes to value and to achieve "a coherent, well-organized, thought-provoking and overall solid paper." Rather, he presents the steps he took to achieve this paper, his "good blueprint" for college writing. By presenting these characteristics as unquestioned goals, Scheer presents himself as one who can perform the most demanding of tasks, thus marking himself as a successful writer. The topic on which he writes so well is ultimately of little importance, as is the process he performed and the help he encountered. More important for Scheer, he acquires what he thinks are some of the general skills needed to succeed as a college writer. His last sentence, reminiscent of that in his previous passage, continues the story arc by presenting another challenge—writing in a second language—which will be overcome by perseverance and which will teach him additional skills. Like many of his new Writing Associate peers, Scheer discusses his literacy development as a succession of skill-acquiring episodes that enables him to overcome academic challenges.

Other new Writing Associates' narratives complicate the hero story arc more than Scheer's, but most present literacy development as a result of changes in academic standards. Kate Edelstein, for example, at first evokes miracle imagery to explain how she learned to write in high school. "[M]y grades flip-flopped around in the B-C range until one day, as if the clouds parted and I saw the light, I got it. I wish I could explain what I mean by this, but something just clicked." Edelstein cannot maintain the quasireligious rhetoric for very long, though, and by the next sentence she is explaining what she means.

> It was really not until my junior year in high school when my AP U.S. history teacher told me, "Kate, you need to reread your paper like you know nothing about the subject on which you are writing." That was it. What would a stranger say about my paper? What would they question about it? . . . . I began asking myself these questions and adjusting my papers accordingly. . . . With these questions came more praise from my teachers and better grades on my report card. By the end of high school I had really learned how to write an effective paper.

Edelstein's narrative tells of her learning to write reader-based prose instead of writer-based prose, an important development in any student's literacy education. We would not expect her to have that sort of vocabulary to describe what she undergoes. We are, however, interested in the extent to which the realization triggered by her teacher is interpreted by her to be the sole elixir needed to succeed as a high school writer. Unlike Scheer, Edelstein articulates some of the process that enabled her to think more carefully about her audience and to write more successfully for her teachers. But just like Scheer, she centers her narrative on a comfortable motif: that of the hero overcoming an obstacle by acquiring a particular skill.

Some new Writing Associates seek to subvert the heroic narrative formula, but their attempts often result in their positioning themselves as heroes nonetheless. In other words, the hero motif appears even as Writing Associates recount moments in which they do not overcome a specific problem. For example, Catriona Mhairi Duncanson, an international student hired in 1999, offers a stinging critique of her grade school and high school English courses. She depicts herself in her narrative not as the hero who can surpasses an obstacle on her way toward better writing, but rather as the rebellious hero who can recognize, endure, and subvert a rigid pedagogy.

> When I moved to America, seven years ago, I was introduced to the infamous district writing sample and the five-paragraph essay. The hardest part of a writing sample was sticking to the formula, and limiting my opinion to five paragraphs. . . . I fought with teachers over the length of essays. I did not finish my papers until I had finished what I wanted to say. When I was old enough to deserve an explanation, I was told that students need to start with a rigid model and they will learn to branch out from there.

Duncanson recognizes an adversarial relationship between herself and her teachers, one in which her individuality is at stake. She takes it as a point of pride that "sticking to the formula" gave her the most difficulty, not inventing ideas or structuring paragraphs. In Duncanson's narrative, she is an anti-hero of sorts, the Cool-Hand Luke of the English class. And like Luke, she learns to submit when victory becomes impossible. Later in the same passage, she explains that the "rigid model" expected in her English courses taught her only "to be abrupt." "I became submissive to my English teachers," she writes, "and I saved my more eloquent work for papers in history class because they were less regimented." We read her passage as an attempt to reclaim some authority in her past literacy moments and to establish herself in the present as a survivor—activities performed by other new Writing Associates throughout their narratives as well.

The hero narrative format so easily detected in these texts leads us to some preliminary conclusions about how these students identify themselves as writers. Clearly, most have been rewarded in the past for writing organized, sometimes lockstep papers, and that training may have affected the analytical lenses they apply in their narratives. New Writing Associates try to construct as coherent of narratives as possible, perhaps in attempts to systematize what are often unsystematic patterns of literacy development. These are not students comfortable with disorganization or meandering exploration. Indeed, they may have been penalized for such things in the past. They prefer familiar, though not rigid, structures, and they thrive in environments where they can work from "blueprints" for their assignments. They are eager to please authority figures, yet capable of recognizing the dangers such eagerness poses to their individuality. The new Writing Associates view their educations as series of shifting standards and expectations, signaled usually by changes in schools or teachers. Their narratives show us that these students claim identities as writers by demonstrating swift abilities to accommodate (or, in Duncanson's case, reject intentionally) these difficult transitions.

LITERACY NARRATIVES BY VETERAN WRITING ASSOCIATES

The literacy narrative assignment for returning Writing Associates asks them to describe their histories as writers of the last year in a "focused and detailed history of the recent past which could serve as an addendum—but also as a development of some of the questions posed and discoveries made previously." Like the assignment for new Writing Associates, this one for returning Writing Associates asks for a story. But, returning Writing Associates rarely produce "tidy" narratives. Rather, when we read their narratives, we see the following patterns: Returning Writing Associate's narratives are more conscious about writing as a recursive process—one, that is, with multiple, recurring, subprocesses, as opposed to one driven by abstract forces like "inspiration" or "creativity." Veteran Writing Associates also tend to be more critical of their own composing processes, though many also admit they struggle to follow the same advice they give their peers. Veteran Writing Associates, in general, are more conscious of the *difficulty* of writing well. In comparison to new Writing Associates' narratives, veteran narratives are not, by and large, plotted as progress narratives where hard work and perseverance pay off. For veterans, hard work and perseverance may lead to an improved understanding of how writing happens rather than an improvement in their writing per se.[3]

Consider, for example, the following passage from Andrew Colton's narrative, written after his first year in the Program, which describes his revised understanding of his writing process:

> It used to be commonplace in my world of academia to hand in a paper, cross my fingers and hope for the best a week or so later. The story is much different nowadays. The phrase "rough draft" is no longer an excuse for a crappy paper; it is an integral part of the paper. The draft is read and analyzed, not simply for those sneaky spelling errors or the inconspicuous absence of punctuation, but for Higher Order Concerns that make or break a paper.

We are struck, initially, by the phrase "my world of academia." The possessive pronoun "my" which modifies "world of academia" sets up a distinction between "academia," on one hand, and then Colton's *experience* of "academia" on the other. Although Colton is talking in general terms, rather than about speaking within a particular academic discourse, the way he appropriates for himself a habitable space from which to speak is similar to the process of identification Bartholomae describes in "Inventing the University," whereby students "have to appropriate (or be appropriated by) a specialized discourse, and they have to do so as though they were easily or comfortably one with their audience" (515). Like many of our students, Colton was taught, at some point, how to write papers in drafts. Either because he didn't understand the goal of a rough draft—or perhaps because he did—Colton's appropriation of the form results in his using it in a way other than his teacher intended: "as an excuse for a crappy paper." As Bartholomae explains, "writers who can successfully manipulate an audience (or, to use a less pointed language, writers who can accommodate their motives to their readers' expectations) are writers who can both imagine and write from a position of privilege" (515). The "position of privilege" for Colton is knowing how, in Bartholomae's words, to "bluff" (511) his way through a rough draft.

Writers like Colton are, of course, on the margins of Bartholomae's discussion, which focuses primarily on how basic writers struggle to negotiate a space from which to speak in the academy. And, currently, such writers are on the margins of research in Composition. But as Colton's narrative reminds us, Bartholomae's argument describes a problem faced not just by basic writers but by writers in general, albeit in different ways and to varying degrees.[4] Colton both does and does not have control over his writing. On one hand, even though he does not completely understand the required form (or, perhaps, does not accept its value or necessity) he can nonetheless produce it. This ability gives him a degree of control over his writing. But on the other hand, he also describes a loss of control: once the paper is written, he is left to "cross

[his] fingers and hope for the best a week or so later." Of course, such a sentence might have been written by any student about his or her writing process.[5] But we find this kind of "wait-and-see" approach especially prevalent among our students, most of whom are competent writers, but who have not had the opportunity to reflect on what makes their writing successful (or not).

It is tempting in light of Colton's narrative to conclude that training in the Writing Associate Program is responsible for his revised understanding of writing. The last sentence of the above passage, Colton "read[s] and analyz[es]" his rough draft not for sentence-level errors, but "Higher Order Concerns." Reading for "higher" as opposed to "lower" order concerns (i.e. "sneaky spelling errors or the inconspicuous absence of punctuation"), is a strategy Writing Associates learn early on and one they rely on for talking to their peers about works-in-progress. Like many veteran Writing Associate narratives, this one shows how Colton uses his Writing Associate training to help him read his own writing. Courtney de Thomas, for example, describes her disappointment at being told by her thesis advisor that an early draft of the project was "not Thesis appropriate writing": "The inexperienced writer who Linda Flower talks about in "Inventing the University" was me!"[6] She writes, "I was unable to compose 'reader-based prose' (446); I knew what I wanted to write, but I could not write as if I was writing for a psychological scholarly journal."

Though it is apparent in veteran Writing Associate narratives that training allows these students to reflect on their writing, veteran Writing Associates, Colton and de Thomas included, most often attribute changes in their writing to interactions with their peers. The above discussion from Colton's narrative, for example, is framed in this way:

> Undoubtedly, the most formative experience of the past year occurred during my time as a Writing Associate. First and foremost, it's obvious, but still vital, to point out the new perspective gained from serving as a peer editor. It used to be commonplace in my world of academia to hand in a paper, cross my fingers and hope for the best a week or so later. The story is much different nowadays. The phrase "rough draft" is no longer an excuse for a crappy paper; it is an integral part of the paper. The draft is read and analyzed, not simply for those sneaky spelling errors or the inconspicuous absence of punctuation, but for Higher Order Concerns that make or break a paper.

As he represents it here, Colton's "new perspective" on his writing comes "first and foremost" from working on writing of—and with—his fellow students. Though, of course, the training he receives in staff meetings is what helps him do this work, it is not what he mentions "first."

For some Writing Associates, the meta-awareness gained as a result of working with their peers causes not just a shift in identity, but, at least initially, an identity crisis. They discover, for better and worse, that they are not the writers they think they are. Jenelle Zelinsky, for example, describes her struggle focusing a paper she had to write after gathering "an overabundance of information":

> As a beginning Writing Associate I had trouble teaching writers to improve their problem areas because as a writer myself I never had a problem focusing. I just wrote my papers in one sitting scribbling furiously for hours, with the ideas simply falling into place in a logical order in my head. As a Writing Associate I was a hypocrite—I never outlined, never stated a clear thesis, never did much of what I found myself preaching to other writers. This had always worked fine for me. But, when my raw method of writing started to fail me I suddenly took my own advice and found it to work quite well.

Zelinsky's story sounds, perhaps, like the kind of success story told by new Writing Associates: She met a problem head on and persevered until she resolved it. And, we might wonder what she means when she writes that following her own advice "work[ed] quite well." In the paragraph that follows the passage above, however, she provides more insight into the process of changing her thinking about her writing, a process facilitated by interaction with a fellow Writing Associate:

> My conferences with my own Writing Associate were also different. I found myself thinking more like a Writing Associate, trying to act as that ideal student, rather than the quiet, listener that I had been the year before. My questions of her were more focused as I saw the errors in my own writing as I identified them in other's [*sic*] writing. I also accepted my resentment for her constructive criticism. Writing is very personal, and criticism often seems like an attack on feelings and thoughts rather than on words. Coming from a peer, it becomes extremely easy to dismiss because the Writing Associate is "no better" than yourself. But, I made sure to listen carefully, ignore these feelings of annoyance, and change my problem areas as she had pointed out.

It is uncertain whether the "errors" Zelinsky mentions fall into the category of "higher" or "lower" order concerns (e.g. does she mean "errors" in the thesis, organization, transitions, etc. or "errors" at the level of the sentence?) But the idea that the questions she asked her Writing Associate "were more focused" as a result of working with other writers suggests she has learned to see her writing differently. Perhaps more important, she has begun to re-imagine a different relationship to her writing. Recognizing that "writing is very personal," she understands why she resents advice, especially from a peer. As she explains in her narrative, this awareness helped her to be a better writer and a better Writing Associate: "Each gave me the understanding and the insight necessary to become better at the other." Again, though, we recognize that this is a "success" story of sorts. Ideally, that is, a Writing Associate's experience in the College Writing Program brings about the kind of changes Zelinsky describes. What interests us is the emphasis on a change of thinking about how writing happens, in particular, a recognition that producing "good" writing is intellectual work and not a matter of luck (crossing your fingers), inspiration, or natural ability. The change we think most significant, then, is Zelinsky's emerging awareness of the "personal" as well as the social dimension of her writing.

While some Writing Associates, like Zelinsky do, indeed, point to changes for the better in the writing, the majority report that, at least initially, their writing seems to get worse. Heather Bastian writes, for example, that she became "completely frantic" about the papers she wrote during her first year as a Writing Associate:

> Every sentence needed to be perfect. My cohesion needed to be perfect. My organization needed to be perfect. My thoughts needed to be perfect. This was the first time I felt pressure to write a perfect paper, and my anxiety level skyrocketed.

The way in which Bastian lists her concerns is interesting: sentences, cohesion, organization, thoughts. The order reflects (though perhaps not intentionally) a situation most writers have encountered at one moment or another when faced with the task of revising their own writing. Tinker with a sentence, and you may find (or cause) cohesion problems. Revise for cohesion, and you may also discover (or create) problems of organization. And so on. Tinker long enough, and, inevitably, you end up revising your thinking. In the concluding paragraph of this narrative, which she wrote at the beginning of her second year in the program, Bastian notes that she hopes to overcome these anxieties about her writing (which are also affecting her ability to work effectively with her peers). The implication, then, is that she has not yet overcome them.

In her narrative, Bastian describes herself as in the process of revising not just her writing, but her thinking about writing. Although she is anxious, she manages to learn from the situation "through a lot of thought and reflection about what went wrong." Like most veteran Writing Associates, Bastian's understanding of the changes she sees occurs through a process of "reflection," initiated by the ways in which her assumptions, themselves, are "reflected" through interactions with her peers as well as engaging with her own writing.

SOME WORKING CONCLUSIONS

The literacy habits of students like those who appear in this piece might often be taken for granted by educators, since so many resources are often (rightfully) targeted for students who have difficulty navigating the educational system. But we believe these students' experiences and reflections provide a valuable means of insight into the effects our theories and practices have on how all students employ writing in their academic, personal, and professional lives. Our readings of the narratives suggest that these students' identities as writers are formed first by extrinsic responses to their texts rather than by the content of their texts themselves. What teachers tell them about their writing, what grades they receive, how parents and peers respond, the effects their writing had—the Writing Associates discuss these responses in their early descriptions of their writing identities in far more detail than the characteristics of the texts. This speaks to a rather materialistic view of writing—and perhaps of identity, too. New Writing Associates' narratives often describe their literacy training as the amassing of what we might call academic currency: grades, comments, praise, criticisms, results. This currency, materialized in the documents and artifacts they create and receive, has enabled many of these students to prosper in the educational economy (while causing a few, such as Duncanson, to identify themselves as marginalized). In such a materialist view, the obstacles Writing Associates must overcome appear as dips in this economy, as moments when the currency is harder to come by. Transitions to new schools, dealings with new teachers or assignments, and exposures to new subjects make for unstable times, which lessen these students' performances in their classes, thus lessening whatever cultural/educational capital they attained. When the obstacles are cleared, the currency becomes stronger, and the associates' identities as successful students, as successful members of the economy, strengthen as well.

The economic metaphor speaks to how very literally these students have identified with their grades and assessments. As the new Writing Associates we discussed earlier demonstrate, success (or lack thereof) in school and, more specifically, in academic writing often serves as the foundation for writerly identities. Many times in the narratives they refer to their earlier selves in ways that denote an intricate connection to the comments heard about their writing: "B student," "creative writer," "inventive thinker," and so on. When we remember that students spend at least nine months in school each year, seven to eight hours a day, five days a week, we can understand how grades and scores, so prevalent in our nation's assessment-obsessed schools, can heavily influence how students identify themselves as writers. The more successful student writers, it seems, not only embrace these labels, but use them as motivation to figure out and respond to the changed expectations they experience during their time in school. Like some members of upper economic classes fearful of losing status, some of these students look for ways to assimilate into new environments without thinking about what such assimilation means in terms of individuality and self-knowledge.

Narratives by returning Writing Associates, however, tell us that the importance of external labels may lessen for some students as they begin to take more thoughtful positions toward their writing and their education and as they mature into their various social settings. The economy of education does not dissipate for returning Writing Associates; grades and rewards still provide a type of currency. We see that new associates describe writing and learning processes as means to such currency and, ultimately, their identities as student writers. Returning Writing Associates, though, often write of these processes as indicative of their identities. The processes may lead to good grades, but more important, they represent these writers' own interpretations of why and how they write as they do. The returning narratives show students complicating their identities as writers by focusing less on extrinsic responses to their writing and more on their own intrinsic responses to their questions and concerns within the composing process.

These findings lead us to consider some implications for the teaching of writing. First, we question the role of extrinsic rewards. As many of the new Writing Associates' narratives demonstrate, such rewards—grades, test scores, stickers, prizes—often become the ends of the writing process. They also play some role in how students identify themselves in regards to education and their peers. Clearly, it is time for the fields of Education and Composition to examine more closely the purposes of graded writing courses at all educational levels. Our study also encourages us to explore how extrinsic rewards (or lack thereof) affect students' writing and reflection processes. We wonder if such rewards hinder the literacy development of students identified as successful writers.

Finally, Writing Associate narratives speak to the important role that reflective practices play in students' improved awareness of themselves as individuals who think, read, write, and speak in the world. Veteran Writing Associates seem capable of applying to their own writing the same reflective strategies they encourage in their student conferences. We cannot say to what extent this ability is related to Program training, but we suspect there is a correlation because of how—in writing and in conferences—they appropriate and adapt critical methodologies and language they encounter in staff meetings. It seems as though the training they receive provides a critical vocabulary for reflecting on their writing, and, consequently, helps them see the range of identities they assume and construct as writing (and written) subjects. But such reflection, we strongly suspect, is also the product of regular interactions with peers (Writing Associates and other students alike), in which Writing Associates discuss the work of writing and its subsequent artifacts. These interactions provide opportunity to test the uses and discover the limits of their working critical vocabulary, and, thus, as Freire (1970) might say, to make that vocabulary part of themselves.

We know that reflective practices have become part of the mainstream in composition courses, but we wonder what role they have (or should have) in other college courses in which students must demonstrate mastery of the material in writing. Most of our students assume that writing plays an important role in critical thinking; but hardly any of them understand how that might be so. As a result, most see writing as merely a reflection of their thinking rather than a technology by means of which they discover what they think. Returning Writing Associate narratives make a strong case for why—and how—teachers should make reflection (what Freire would call "consciousness of consciousness") (60) part of any course in which writing is a vehicle for learning. Why?—because, as we have seen with our returning Writing Associates, all of whom are solid writers, students don't know something unless they understand *how* they know it. How?—writings assignment that let students explore and situate their emergent ways of knowing the material. As writing program administrators, too often we see assignments that ask students to summarize or paraphrase a reading assignment—as if those mechanisms or and purposes behind these kinds of reading strategies, widely practiced in the academy, are self-evident. Not surprisingly, many students struggle with such assignments. And the ones who can produce the appropriate responses often cannot describe how they did; thus the work has no relevance or lasting meaning. Based on what our Writing Associates tell us about how they develop as writers, it seems that a student's relationship to his or her own processes of knowing is crucial to learning, but is also hard won—it occurs in fits and starts, and the trajectory is not necessarily obvious. As teachers, we can facilitate a student's understanding of this process, but, perhaps, it is naïve to imagine we control it in any authentic way.

8

SPEAKING FROM THE BORDERLANDS
Exploring Narratives of Teacher Identity

Janet Alsup

What does it mean to be a secondary school teacher? Those who have been high school or middle school teachers know that secondary school teaching is demanding work. They have taught 130-plus adolescents per day, spent weekends and evenings grading papers and planning lessons, and have negotiated the competing demands of various stakeholders including administrators, community leaders, colleagues, and students. They also know that the profession is often perceived, both by "insiders" and "outsiders," as *more* than a job—as a way of life or a "calling." A teacher is seen as an individual who should go above and beyond the call of duty for the benefit of the young people with whom she works.

This definition of teaching as a "calling" has both positive and negative consequences for those in the profession. On the bright side, cultural conceptions of teachers as "heroes" should mean that they are revered and respected. (I remember a recent series of television ads that featured a voice over urging young people to "Be a hero. Teach" and coffee cups proclaiming, "Teachers make a difference" written next to a red apple.) However, the down side, and also the irony, is that only rarely are teachers the recipients of such reverence in American culture. Because the standards are so high, and the price often so great, few teachers are awarded "hero" status, and the rest are labeled mediocre at best, or simply inadequate.

There is a fundamental paradox in our cultural model of teacher, a paradox that affects teacher education: for a teacher to be a hero, our society says he or she must be selfless; however, research demonstrates that only the teacher who has developed a rich, well-rounded identity, or sense of self, is truly successful in the classroom. An effective teacher must be "self actualized" (to use the phrase coined by Abraham Maslow in 1962 and later used by bell hooks in 1994) to the extent that it is possible and reflective about all aspects of his or her self, namely the intellectual/cognitive, the emotional/spiritual and the physical/material. In short, the successful teacher must be self*less* and self*fish* at the same time.

Perhaps the first years of teaching are the most difficult. According to Dwight L. Rogers and Leslie M. Babinski (2002), much has been written about the problems of new teachers, and ample research has been conducted on the topic (Bulloughs 1987; Feiman-Nemser 1983; Grant and Zeichner 1981; Ryan 1970). Yet, they write, "despite all of the research and all of the books and articles written about the difficulties endured by beginning teachers, the first year of teaching continues to be an exceptionally difficult time for most of them" (2). All of our research and writing, while it may be published in respected journals and by academic presses, has not really helped the new teacher. According to the most current figures, only 50 percent of new teachers' careers last longer than five years (Gordon 1991; Huling-Austin et al. 1989). And, if that is not bad enough, according to Robert Bulloughs (1987), many of the teachers who remain in the profession end up structuring their classrooms in ways that are inconsistent with their pedagogical beliefs (Rogers and Babinski 2002, 3). They cannot find ways to teach as they were taught during their university education, so they revert to lifesaving measures that simply keep them afloat in the classroom.

To learn more about how to successfully mentor new teachers, I conducted a longitudinal, qualitative, interview-based research study from January 2001 to spring 2003. This study began with the following goals:

- to examine the philosophies of teaching English held by the participants and the modification of these beliefs over time;
- to describe classroom practices of the participants, their change over time, and how these changes are connected to the aforementioned beliefs;
- to explore issues of self-confidence about teaching and participants' level of comfort in the classroom and how these change over time;
- to describe changes in how the participants define their roles as English teachers over the time of the study; and
- to offer suggestions for mentoring pre-service and beginning teachers and for further research directions for understanding teacher development.

The study evolved and eventually came to focus on teacher professional identity development, a concept that encompasses all of the above questions. My goal was to recruit six to eight student participants; seven volunteered, and one dropped out of the project after the first year.

The six remaining participants were all white women, between the ages of 19 and 23. This gender and ethnicity is representative of the students in the English education program at the university where I teach (in my program, students are 74 percent female and 95 percent white). In addition to the interview data, I collected relevant artifacts such as lesson plans, philosophy statements and literacy autobiographies the pre-service teachers wrote for classes, teaching metaphors they created, and notes I took when I observed them teaching during their internship experiences. Therefore, there were ample sources of data to establish "triangulation," or the assurance that multiple sources were analyzed and compared before stating results (Denzin 1987). I used the "categorical content" approach to data analysis which is often called "content analysis." In this approach, categories of the studied topic are defined (codes), and examples from the text are placed into these categories/groups for analysis (Lieblich et al. 1998, 13).

As a result of my research, I argue that in order to be successful in the classroom, a secondary school teacher must develop a sense of professional identity that incorporates his or her personal subjectivities with the professional/cultural expectations of what it means to be a "teacher." This incorporation, this merging, this professional identity formation, happens through a new teacher's participation in various genres of discourse that facilitate a dialogic engagement with students, mentors, teacher educators, family, peers, and even internal dialogues with other personal subjectivities or ideologies. Such discourse, as it becomes more complex and sophisticated, can result in the physical and emotional embodiment of teacher identity as well as increased pedagogical effectiveness.

This is not to say that the eventual goal of the teacher is to iron out all ideological tension so that teaching is "smooth sailing"; such consensus among subjectivities is not likely or even desirable. However, the various identity strands making up the self should be able to coexist to the extent that a professional teaching life can be enacted efficiently and effectively—at least most of the time. When such discourse occurs that allows for the intersection and integration of various subjectivities and identity positions, I call it "borderland" discourse. The "borderland" is a term that I have taken from James Gee (1999), who uses the term in a study he did of urban middle and high school students from different ethnic groups who "came together" on the schoolyard. When they came together they used borderland discourse to communicate, discourse that was "a mixture of the various neighborhood peer discourses, and some emergent properties of its own" (22). It is at the borderlands of discourse, and by association at the borderlands of various identity positions that the pre-service teachers began to discover how to move from being student to being teacher and how to respect personal beliefs and passions while learning to embody a teacher identity. I believe that engagement in such borderland discourse is the first step toward developing a professional identity as a teacher and a productive personal pedagogy combining professional knowledge and skill with personal beliefs and orientations.

DEFINING THE BORDERLAND

I am not the first educational theorist or researcher to recognize the importance of teacher identity development. Richard P. Lipka and Thomas M. Brinkthaupt (1999) write that it is essential that teacher educators and mentors of new teachers help new teachers balance their "personal development . . . with their professional development" (2). They explore why paying attention to the personal, in addition to the professional, is important for a workable teacher identity to result. Jane Danielewicz (2001) proposes "a pedagogy for identity development" and describes "the qualities that must characterize our teaching in order for the students we encounter to become something other than students" (1). Parker Palmer (1998) identifies three paths to identity development, be it personal or professional: the intellectual, the emotional, and the spiritual. According to Palmer, an individual should address all three parts of this triadic identity. Palmer aptly calls teaching "a daily exercise in vulnerability," as the teacher attempts to find his or her "inner teacher" and teach from a place of "integrity" that incorporates these three aspects of the self (17). Deborah Britzman (1991) calls becoming a teacher a type of identity "transformation," and argues through the case studies she presents that in order to become a teacher we often ask students to give up or suppress aspects of their personal selves that do not conform to the cultural model or "script" of the secondary teacher (4). We suggest to them through a discourse of objectivity that they should not reveal their personal ideologies or make pedagogical decisions based on their racial, ethnic or gender subjectivities; on the contrary, and in order to be fair to all students, they should be intellectually neutral (and, of course, academically rigorous) as often as possible. However, this suppression of personal identity is only a sham, a facade, as personal subjectivities and ideologies do not disappear; they simply remain, and even fester, as sites of tension and discomfort.

Theorists and researchers (with the exception of Britzman) often oversimplify the identity development of pre-service teachers as a bringing together of two conflicting identity positions: the "personal" and the "professional." The idea is that once both aspects of the personality are attended to and nurtured, a holistic sense of professional self will result. My research attempts to complicate this binary understanding of professional identity. The six participants in this research study demonstrate that professional and personal identities are multiple and ever changing, rather than singular and consistently opposing. Therefore, a teacher's identity is a "weaving together" (Gee 1999) of various different subjectivities and situated identity positions as expressed through genres of discourse and influenced by multiple life experiences.

Borderland discourse explicitly facilitates (and rewards) the bringing of personal subjectivities or ideologies to the classroom and connecting them to a new teacher's developing professional self. Sometimes the new teachers were not able to experience or express borderland discourse and felt a great deal of tension and discomfort taking on the role of teacher. If the professional and personal identities and related subjectivities/ideologies seemed too distinct or even contradictory, the pre-service teachers could not close the gap, and some of them opted out of the profession. Three of the six teachers in this study decided not to be teachers after their college graduation because of extreme tension between their student and teacher subjectivities or between their perceptions of the idealized, culturally accepted professional identity and their personal beliefs or ideologies. The tension and discord were simply too powerful to negotiate.

One of our goals as teacher educators is the creation of opportunities for borderland discourse that will enable pre-service teachers to combine their personal and professional subjectivities and create a new, albeit recognized, discourse of professional identity. The discourse community of secondary educators might accept such borderland discourse because it contains some recognized characteristics; however, the discourse may also stretch understandings of professional identity within these traditional boundaries.

NARRATIVE: THE DOMINANT GENRE OF TEACHER IDENTITY DISCOURSE

Engaging in narrative discourse is one way the new teachers in this study facilitated their professional identity development. This power of narrative is reflected in the work of psychologists and psychiatrists who have long used the "case study" and life history narrative to understand people's problems. Many social scientists assert that personal narratives do not simply reflect identities they *are* people's identities (see Bruner 1991, 1996; Gergen 1994; Gergen and Gergen 1986; Hermans et al. 1993; McAdams 1993; Polkinghorne 1991). Jerome Bruner (1986), one of the preeminent scholars of narrative, writes that people lead "storied lives," and defines narratives as essential to the making of the self. Bruner goes so far as to say that if the human being was not able to create and tell stories that both differentiate and establish connection, he or she would lack a sense of real selfhood (2002, 86).

Narratives have been used in educational research and theory since the 1980s with great consistency, for purposes such as action research projects and sharing of pedagogical expertise. Recently, several educators and researchers such as Ivor F. Goodson (1992), Leslie Rebecca Bloom (1998), and Stanton Wortham (2001) have written that analyzing or interrogating narratives new teachers tell concerning their educational histories can be a way of helping them overcome long-held and overly simplistic belief structures about what a teacher should be and what a classroom should look like. In other words, such narrative interrogation can help them overcome the temptation to simply teach as they were taught no matter what current research and theory tell them. Such interrogation of narrative histories is especially important as many studies have shown that teachers tend to teach as they remember being taught, and that they are not influenced that much by their teacher education programs (Lortie 1975; Knowles and Holt-Reynolds 1991). This large body of research supporting the influence of narrative educational memories demonstrates the importance of the examination of such narratives during the education of a teacher.

In this study, engaging in narrative discourse facilitated as well as reflected the development of professional teacher identity of the six participants. There were a total of 357 stories told by the participants over the two years of interviews. During qualitative analysis, I thematically coded these narratives, and six major types of stories emerged: (1) narratives of tension, (2) narratives of experience, (3) narratives of the embodiment of teacher identity, (4) narratives about family and friends, (5) narratives about seeking voice, and (6) borderland narratives. In the rest of this chapter, I describe a few of the most instrumental of these narratives and provide examples from the discourse of three of the pre-service teachers—Carrie, Karen, and Lois. Specifically, I will discuss a narrative of tension, a narrative of embodiment, and a borderland narrative.

THE PERSONAL CONFRONTS THE PROFESSIONAL: A CLASH OF SUBJECTIVITIES

An important finding from my narrative analysis was that unresolved tension between discordant subjectivities and associated ideologies lessened the chance of the participants developing a satisfying professional identity. In the analysis of the narratives, three major kinds of tension were revealed: (1) personal beliefs versus professional expectations, (2) university ideologies or educational methods versus the practical ones experienced in secondary field placements, and (3) "student" versus "teacher" subjectivity as pre-service teachers moved from the role of university student to that of high school teacher. Tension that was experienced by the pre-service teachers concerned issues as diverse as classroom authority, professional confidence, opinions about pedagogical methods and curricular emphases, approaching classroom discipline, and negotiating family and career.

The three students who told the highest total number of narratives of tension decided not to take traditional teaching jobs after graduation and expressed confusion about their future professional lives. These students (Sandy, Carrie, and Karen) told 34, 27, and 16 of these narratives, respectively. Others who were able to negotiate these tensions because of awareness and acceptance of nonunitary or multiple subjectivities and/or because of engagement in borderland discourse were able to find, and begin to embody, a workable professional identity. Their tensions did not go away or become insignificant; instead, these successful pre-service teachers found a way to honor and integrate the various subjectivities and ideologies central to their lives. However, this process was difficult, and Sandy, Carrie, and Karen did not complete it by the end of the study.

There were 27 narratives told about the confrontation between personal and professional subjectivities. These narratives described ways that the pre-service teacher was struggling with maintaining a sense of self while taking on the professional identity of teacher. The two students who told the most of these narratives, Carrie (told 12 narratives about personal–professional tensions) and Karen (told 15 of these narratives), chose not to become secondary teachers immediately after graduation. Unfortunately, we often imply to new teachers that the successful teaching life is relatively uncomplicated. In fact, many choose it for that reason—they think that teaching will allow them to privilege other parts of their lives, such as family, over their careers. However, this "myth of normalcy" (Britzman 1998, 82) is not always reality. A teaching life can be fraught with ideological tension and conflict, as the educational establishment and related cultural scripts portray acceptable education within certain moral and political boundaries, boundaries that are not always comfortable for the new teacher.

For example, Carrie experienced a great deal of tension between personal and professional subjectivities, namely about curricular focus. Her interests lay in the areas of women's literature and feminist theory, and the classes she enjoyed the most as a university student tackled issues of gender, sexual orientation, and the cultural conceptions and inequities related to them. However, in Carrie's experiences in local secondary schools, she became convinced that such topics would not be accepted as a part of secondary school curricula. In the third interview with Carrie in September of 2002, she said,

> The thing is the more that I'm realizing over the past few years is that the environment that I loved so much and that I wanted to recreate is going to be very rarely recreated [in the secondary school]. . . since a big aspect [of mine] is wanting to get into my areas of interest that have developed more into the feminist and queer theory and wanting to approach those and being restricted [in high schools] with what books I can show to my classes, what topics I can talk about—even if I'm not doing an entire unit on homosexuality, you know, am I going to get yelled at or whatever for having it come up in the classroom? I'm like, why the hell am I going to even be there?

This statement is an expression of tension, a tension that Carrie could not resolve by the end of the study. Since Carrie defines herself as a lesbian, her tension is compounded by a belief that her "marked" body will not be accepted in the secondary classroom and that a life as teacher will mean a lifetime of hiding an important part of herself. This problem of embodiment is explored more fully in the next section through the stories of a second student, Karen.

DENYING THE MIND/BODY SPLIT: FACILITATING THE EMBODIMENT OF TEACHER IDENTITY

Developing teacher identity involves embodying the discourse of teacher. Brent Hocking et al. (2001) write that discourse itself is an attempt at embodiment because it attempts to close the gap between the outer, material world of sensory input and the internal, intellectual or emotional world. Freud's notion of the id and the ego addresses the falsity of the mind/body split. He writes that the ego is "first and foremost, a bodily ego; it is not merely a surface entity, but is itself the projection of a surface" (1961, 27). In other words, the idea or understanding of the "self" is always wrapped up with the material body, and the embodiment of emotional or intellectual concepts of self. French psychoanalyst Jacques Lacan also insists upon the connection of mind and body. His "mirror stage" asserts that the child first comes to think about "self" when he or she sees his or her reflected image and begins to be aware of self as divided: the internal, individually defined self, and the corporeal self as seen and interpreted by others. While the postmodern tendency is to make gender constructions, class inequities, and other identity positions almost completely a result of discourse, feminist scholars such as Judith Butler (1993), Teresa Ebert (1996), and Bronwyn Davies (2000) are among those who insist on the inherent relationship of the discursive to the corporeal.

When I write about teacher identity and the discourse used to facilitate it, I am describing discourse not only as a way to bridge the gap between internal states—such as subjectivities, situated identities, or ideologies—but also between these internal states and the physical enactment of "teacher." In short, the new teacher has to figure out how to place herself in the "body" of the teacher, a body that is often culturally defined as white, female, middle aged, politically conservative, and heterosexual.

The narratives students told in this category concerned issues of gender, body size, age, class, sexuality, race, and ethnicity. Much like the narratives of tension, if the narratives of embodiment of teacher identity expressed an overwhelming concern about the disconnections between the pre-service teacher's perception of self and the perceived cultural script or model of the teacher body, then the student often did not choose to become a secondary teacher upon graduation. The students who told the largest number of narratives expressing confusion or frustration about embodiment issues had the most difficult time integrating into the profession. Carrie told a total of 12 narratives of embodiment tensions, and Karen told a total of eight; again, both of these students decided not to take secondary teaching jobs upon graduation.

Karen had difficulty with the notion of diversity and multiculturalism, as it was discussed in her educational classes. Karen, a white working-class student from Indiana, felt that much of the discourse about diversity was nothing more than "politically correct" identity politics. She was deeply unsettled by a "Literature of Black America" class in which students engaged in a discussion of whether white teachers should be able to teach African American literature. She was angered and confused when her African American teacher suggested that perhaps this should not be allowed. She told me she thought her own cultural heritage was being disregarded, even though she did not seem to have a very strong idea of exactly what this heritage was. This tension between her working-class white upbringing and the "diverse" discourse of the university was consistently expressed in our conversations. Only toward the end of our time together, when Karen took a middle school coaching job at a school with primarily African American students, did she begin to work through these ideological tensions. In fact, she wrote me a long letter in which she tackled them. In December of 2002, she wrote, in part, "I have told you that I was called racist everyday. But the situation was that from the moment some of the parents came into our first practice or when they came into the parent meeting I held, they judged the fact that I was white."

Often the notions of multiculturalism as they are discussed in education courses center around the idea of a kind of "color blindness" or rhetoric of sameness. This false objectivity might make pre-service teachers such as Karen less likely to think about and interrogate their own subject positions. However, Karen's discourse reflects her struggle with her racial and ethnic identity. She was beginning to understand that she also has a race, and that her race might be an obstacle to communication in certain contexts; she was beginning to understand that race was not something that she only thought about in terms of the "other"—it was also something she had to apply to—and understand about—herself. In other words, she was starting to figure out how to live in her own skin (her white skin) and in her own body, as a teacher.

TOWARD A PERSONAL PEDAGOGY: AN ANALYSIS OF BORDERLAND NARRATIVES

Engagement in borderland discourse was important to the pre-service teachers' development of a professional identity and eventually, a personal pedagogy. The most immediately and obviously successful teacher education students in this study were those who were given the opportunity (and the necessary guidance) to begin to see complex connections among their educational memories, their university education, their practical school and teaching experiences, and their personal or core ideologies. The creation and expression of this borderland discourse can be seen as a political act, an act of enriching and broadening the discursive and material identity of the teacher that is often perceived as narrow and restrictive.

Lois engaged in a great deal of borderland discourse, discourse that communicated connections between student and teacher subjectivities, personal and professional ideologies, and/or university coursework and practical field experiences. She told me a total of 14 borderland narratives; in contrast, of the three students who chose not to become teachers at all, one told two borderland narratives, the second told none, and the third only one. Lois' mentor teacher often facilitated this discourse, although at other times, Lois took the initiative to build bridges (so to speak) between the various aspects of her self. Consequently, she had a very satisfying student teaching experience and went on to accept a secondary teaching job the following year. Here is a quote from an interview conducted with Lois in September of 2001 about her student teaching experience that exemplifies her borderland discourse:

> One of the first things she [her student teaching mentor] said was, "I don't want you to come in and model the classroom exactly the way I do." She said, "You know, if something I do works for you and that's the way you want to do it, then go for it. But I want you to come in here, and I want you to do things the way you want to do them." She said, "I will help, you know, and I will offer you advice, but I want you to come and I want you to find your own way." Not necessarily my own way, but find what works for me. If me being more strict with discipline is the way, if I wanted to move certain students then I would. I would move those students. But then, I would see how that worked for or against me.

Lois is in the process of developing a personal pedagogy, a pedagogy that incorporates her multiple subjectivities or identity strands. I believe she *is* finding her own way. By engaging in narrative discourse about this development her understanding of her own growth only increases, and with such enhanced meta-awareness or reflexivity, Lois' professional identity can only become richer, more complex, more effective, and more satisfying over time.

BRINGING THE BORDERLAND TO THE METHODS COURSE

The discourse the pre-service teachers used to describe their identities, subjectivities, and ideologies assisted them in learning to occupy multiple borderlands between identity positions (such as student, teacher, lover, mother, or feminist) and, eventually, understand these borderlands as sites of professional and personal power instead of spaces of tension and confusion. Eventually, spending time in this discursive borderland led to the beginnings of a personal pedagogy integrating individual beliefs and experiences with professional goals and expectations. It is at these borderlands that the pre-service teachers discovered how to move from being students to being teachers and how to honor personal beliefs and passions while also embodying a teacher identity that in our society, as Deborah Britzman (1991) writes, is so-often overshadowed by simplified and stereotypical cultural models and media scripts.

How can teacher educators create opportunities for borderland discourse for our students? Findings from this research can be applied to assignments appropriate for the English education class. I have used what I learned about narrative and teacher identity to re-think an assignment I have given many times in my methods classes. To take advantage of narrative's potential to shape and reshape teacher identity, I revised the "practice teaching" assignment to become the "pedagogical discussion."

This assignment asks the students in my class to take turns leading a discussion about teaching a literary text and the narrative histories that influenced their pedagogical decisions. The student leading the discussion describes her goals for teaching the chosen text, provides specific ideas for classroom activities and assignments, and gives suggestions for assessing student learning (as well as alignment with our state's 9–12 standards for the teaching of English language arts). Additionally, the pre-service teacher writes an essay reflecting on these goals, activities, and assessments and explaining why he or she made certain choices about teaching the selected text. In this critically reflective essay, the student is asked to include (1) discussion of research or theory that supports the pedagogical choices, (2) anecdotal or narrative evidence from past classroom experiences (either as a student or a teacher) demonstrating the appropriateness of these choices, and (3) discussion of his or her teaching philosophy and how it is consistent with the aforementioned pedagogical choices.

The reflective essay is shared with the student's peers who respond to both the pedagogical ideas and the reflective essay. To get the discussion started, the student poses questions to the class such as "What do you like about or agree with concerning my pedagogical choices?" "What suggestions or ideas might you add?" and "What narrative or anecdotal evidence do you have that is similar or different than mine?" The questions posed are determined by the student's interests and concerns; however, a key component of the assignment is that the pre-service teacher is asked to provide narrative, theoretical, and philosophical support for her pedagogical choices, and her peers participating in the discussion are asked to respond to these narratives with educational narratives of their own. Through the discussion, the student presenting has the opportunity to critically examine the educational history that influenced his or her beliefs and discover to what extent this history, as well as the theory and research cited, is a sound basis for her pedagogical decisions and educational philosophy (Alsup 2005).

By expressing, deconstructing and critically examining the narrative, experiential knowledge underlying their current beliefs about teaching, pre-service teachers may move past simple imitation of classroom practices and expand their vision of what constitutes effective pedagogy. They might honor their educational memories while also interrogating them through new intellectual lenses, thereby taking a first step toward understanding ideological tensions as potential sites of professional and personal discovery. Through such borderland discourse, pre-service teachers can become more effective secondary English teachers, as well as self-actualized human beings.

9

"WHO ARE THEY AND WHAT DO THEY HAVE TO DO WITH WHAT I WANT TO BE?"

The Writing of Multicultural Identity and College Success Stories for First-Year Writers

James R. Ottery

No matter what theoretical approach they offer, the rhetoric/readers of first-year writing courses have, for at least the last decade and a half, made an ostensible bow to diversity and multiculturalism. While not altogether abandoning the essays of Anglo-European American writers such as Virginia Woolf, George Orwell, and E. B. White, most of them now feature the writings of prominent American authors whose ancestors were not originally members of their homeland's dominant culture. Such writers include Frederick Douglass, Sojourner Truth, Zitkala-Sa, Helen Keller, James Baldwin, Malcolm X, Richard Rodriquez, Mike Rose, Maya Angelou, Sandra Cisneros, and bell hooks, to name only a few. The inclusion of a broad range of cultural perspectives is meant to reflect the fact that the population of university campuses now mirrors that of the nation, insofar as cultural diversity is the norm rather than the exception. First-year writing program directors and instructors now feel that students in general education courses should be able to relate to minority writers better than those from what was once regarded as the cultural mainstream. However, the question of whether students do remains open.

The truth, as it seems to me, is that many entering first-year students, especially those from backgrounds similar to those of the writers named above, are more likely to relate to more immediately available representatives of popular culture—whether "mainstream" or "minority"—than they are the authors of literary essays and creative nonfiction. Such students often find their cultural models in popular culture icons, such as Eminem, Tupac Shakur, and Shakira. Yet such icons say little to students about the experiences and subjects that have shaped and informed the authors represented in their first-year readers. Popular culture artists don't speak to students of the nightmare of intellectual deprivation that is all too often the unremitting experience of those marginalized by slavery (Frederick Douglass), the urban ghetto (Malcolm X and Mike Rose), or the more elusive, generalized ghetto of sex and race (Maya Angelou, Sandra Cisneros, James Baldwin, and Richard Rodriguez). They don't speak to students of the will, desire, and self-determination required to emerge fully embodied from intellectual impoverishment. Nor do they ponder retrospectively the separation between nightmare and illumination. Nor do they attest to the difference that crossing from one marginal position, the nightmare of intellectual oppression, to the other, the enlightened point of view, makes *within* the mind and heart of the one who makes the journey.

In short, the icons of popular culture, despite their much-touted "diversity," offer students a banquet of images or "eye candy" that often are so familiar that they require little more than a glance in order to be recognized. This instant of recognition, where the "eye" becomes a mirror of self-regard, a master of two dimensions of *imag*-inary understanding, belies a third and a fourth dimension of real knowledge. The story of struggle and self-determination marks the point of separation between intellectual deprivation and enlightenment and conveys the effect of the journey from the unschooled identifying state to the one that develops in higher learning. Having no clue that the third and fourth dimensions of knowledge exist, and glued, as so many are, to the latest popular image, our students may be excused for asking of the authors in their readers, "What do *they* and their stories have to do with me? How can reading them help me to fulfill my goals? What do they know about becoming a lawyer, a computer graphics designer, an engineer, a business manager, an artist, an entrepreneur, and so on?"

Still more first-year writers might wonder about the relevance of the story of another marginalized American, an Indian by the name of Samson Occom, were his writings to appear in their readers. Although once published in some few collections of American literature, Occom's writings, like the author himself, have long since been superseded by the more contemporary representatives of marginalized groups. Yet Occom's story might be called the Urtext of those now published in first-year readers. Moreover, it might provide our culturally and ethnically diverse students a prototype against which to measure their mainstream aspirations, their diverse versions of the American dream.

Occom's diary conveys an experience of marginalization that is not only outside the American cultural mainstream, it is also removed from the mainstream of marginalization. It begins, "I was born a Heathen and

Brought up in Heathenism at a place calld [*sic*] Mohegan." Without calling attention to the fact, this statement marks the significant difference between the early and late Samson Occom. It is a difference embodied in Occom's tacit acknowledgement that the lack-of-culture into which he was born—Heathenism—constitutes his real place of birth, its significance trumping that of the geographical birthplace, Mohegan. In short, the word "Heathenism" marks the limit between the two world-views represented via Occom's writing, the one unmarked by history and letters and the other illuminated (and shadowed) by both. Via Occom's story, the latter view turns back on and illuminates the former, showing the author and presumably his readers what the first Occom lacked. It was a negation, a gap or hole in perception, for which his Western education provided the cure. And it was this cure, the path from "Heathenism" to the ideals of a culturally and spiritually enlightened consciousness, that Occom wished to make available to other Indian Americans. The most effective way of doing this was to disseminate his story in writing.

Occom began his formal education at the age of 20 in 1743 under the tutelage of the Rev. Eleazar Wheelock at Lebanon, Connecticut (Ottery 1989). At the age by which today's college students have completed twelve years of primary and secondary education and perhaps their first year of college, the "heathen" Samson Occom began to learn to read and to write in English, Latin, Greek, and French. Four years later, Occom left Lebanon, according to one of his early biographers, "to take charge of a school in some part of New London" (Love 2000, 39). From headmaster he would go on to become a popular preacher and hymn writer, and an internationally successful fund-raiser. Largely because of funds raised by Samson Occom in England, Dartmouth College, which Occom thought was intended to be an Indian college, was founded (Ottery 1989).

In addition to founding, he thought, an American Indian institution of higher learning, Occom also helped to found an experimental Christian-Indian community in New York. Like Dartmouth, this community was modeled on Western institutional ideals, chiefly the democratic principle of home rule and New England town governance, concepts suggested by its name, Brothertown. Also like Dartmouth College, this experiment in Indian community-building and self-governance met with limited success, in large part because the white colonists discounted the Indians' claims of sovereignty in matters directly touching them, such as *where* and *how* they might live. As a result of the colonists' preemption of authority in matters of tribal autonomy, the Brothertowners were relocated several times. In the shuffling of Indian tribes from the East into the Midwest, including into the area that is now Wisconsin, the Brothertown community ended up on the Eastern shore of Lake Winnebago not far from Fond du Lac. Eventually losing that land as well, the members of the Brothertown community dispersed. Today the descendants of Samson Occom and other Brothertowners seek federal re-recognition of *our* tribal, sovereign status.

I am Brothertown Indian 20261 and the Brothertown's founder, Samson Occom, is my ancestral cousin.

STORIES OF GAIN AND LOSS IN IDENTITY TRANSFORMATION

I tell this story here, as I often tell it to students in my first-year classes, because it is part of my identity and I believe that it illustrates something of what is at stake when students choose to enter the discourse of higher learning, a discourse represented by the authors of the essays in their first-year readers. Paradoxically it may seem, the university discourse demands a sacrifice—a certain loss of origins, including a loss to some degree of the mother tongue. This primordial loss is the price for dreaming the American dream. At a first glance, Samson Occom's life exemplifies such a sacrifice for such a dream. For, having overcome his "Heathenism," as his biographers indicate, Samson Occom was a great success in his career, his "chosen" field of Indian education, preaching the gospel, and community building. As I have tried to make clear, this highly successful Indian, this "Heathen" brought up in "Heathenism," owed much of his success to his having become literate, to his having learned to read and write—in order to become articulate in English and other Western languages.

The primary reason that I tell Occom's story in my classes is that the significant role literacy plays in achieving success in an incorporated, text-based world is not a bad lesson for first-year writing students to learn. Yet there is another side to the story, just as there is to all stories of gain and loss in identity transformation. This story bears witness to how an individual's identity within the dominant, white, Western culture of the United States is *re*-formed by the learned language of that culture, by, not to mince words, the university discourse.

This discourse, which is also the discourse of capitalism,[1] demands from us all that we sacrifice the origins, the traditions, the tongues, the rituals, the tribal fabric into which, from birth, any child is woven. Yet these elements of self identification constitute themselves from a set of circumstances that construct a sense of our own meaning and our own worth that we might describe as a sense of self, a sense of being one. It is founded on and constituted of certain knowledge: of having been born in a certain place, at a certain time, to certain parents, into a certain familial and social structure. It is welded from the necessities of representing oneself for others and being represented by others within a family of speakers operating within a certain set of discourse conventions and daily uses of language. Such self-identification more or less guarantees any person a subjective position in language and thus to a *sovereign* sense, a secure yet fragile sense of what it is to be one self in a world of others.

Yet insofar as it imposes a weight of sameness on those it assimilates to its cause, the university discourse belies such a claim. It is a discourse that holds out the promise of a sovereign universe constituted of beings united by and committed to its preservation. In the discourse of a conferred and deferred status of sovereignty, the materiality of language has a *material* effect upon identity. This weight manifests itself in the question of what one is for others. It is manifest in how one represents oneself for others, both those within and those outside the boundary of one's primary discourse community. The reciprocal effects of the university discourse structure—one assimilates it in order to become assimilated into the world of those who function via its design—reshape identity. Yet what is its design, what is the *structural* effect of the university discourse structure? This design has to do with the reason that Samson Occom learned to read and write in English. Occom became not only literate and articulate in the white man's language, but he also became *articulated* to that cultural body that speaks its tongues—the language of commerce, of business, of medicine, of law, of trade—so as *finally* to experience salvation from the alienating effects of a marginalized and therefore incomprehensible mother tongue. This step was the prerequisite to his becoming successful in the New World, a world built on the foundation of the ancient civilizations of the Western world.

In becoming thus educated and cultured in order to be thought literate, Occom assumed the burdens of a culture and civilization not his own. Thus Occom's retroactive story of the success of his effort positively spins the negative effect of Occom's process of acculturation and assimilation. That is, it attests to Occom's willingness to relinquish the "burden" of "Heathenism," a burden that was presumably greater, thanks to the arrival and virulent spread of the white man on the North American continent, than the laborious process of mastering the university discourse. In submitting to such a process, Occom took upon himself the burden of the new discourse structure, choosing, as it were, to bear this new burden in order to yield the fruits that laboring under its yoke promised. This burden was the necessity of reshaping a new self-identity, a new way of being-in-the-world, a being composed within and by the terms of a new language.

W. DeLoss Love's 1899 biography of Occom, *Samson Occom and the Christian Indians of New England* (2000) illustrates this point. The window Love's biography opens onto the prevalent attitude of his time toward Indian identity transformation is invaluable. In Love's ineluctable purview, induction into the ways of Western civilization and Christianity in particular would not only improve the quality of American Indians' lives, it was for their good, the only good for which they had a right to hope. Awash in Christian supremacist idealism, Love depicts a grateful Occom, always fully conscious of and thankful for the opportunity granted to him to be educated by the Reverend Eleazar Wheelock and "even" treated as a guest in his home. For Love, it is simply an article of faith that the "refining influences" of the Wheelock home "were a great blessing" to Occom. Moreover, Love asserts, because he was allowed to associate with Wheelock's "other pupils," the Indian youth became acquainted with "the deficiencies of his *heathen* training and was quick to profit by the examples set before him" (my emphasis). And of course Love retroactively proves prophetic. In looking back at his lost origins from his newly acquired status as a man of education and culture, Occom implicitly judges them against the "refinements" of civilization and finds that, from the vantage offered by the new perspective, they seem lacking: "I was born a Heathen and Brought up in Heathenism at a place calld [*sic*] Mohegan."

While Occom was "lucky," enjoying and suffering, as perceived from a modern point of view, a gain and loss as a result of the weight of the discourse structure that shaped the course of his literacy and thus his life, American Indians in the aggregate were not so blessed. The indelible product of the university discourse structure is a judgmental gaze. This standard dimension of civilization crushed the American Indian population for hundreds of years before and after Occom's time. Indeed, I would argue that the university discourse—the discourse of Christianity, the market, and the law—was the primary cause of the destruction of the American Indian way of life, as the following observation from Rudi Ottery's (1989) *A Man Called Sampson* suggests,

> The Puritan colonists felt they could conquer Indians at will and gloried in the terror their conquest had inspired among the Indians. The Puritans

had convinced themselves that as God's chosen people, their will was in accordance with His. They regarded the Indians as inferiors who were outside the laws of moral obligation, so they could do what they wished with them. (30)[2]

Doing "what they wished with them" ranged from the massacre of women and children of the Pequod (Occom's mother's tribe) at Mystic River in 1637[3] to the less physical, but no less deadly application of *force* known as acculturation and assimilation.

The force of assimilation brings me back full circle to the connection, as I see it, between the fates of Occom and many of today's college students, especially those from the populations that bell hooks describes as "oppressed" (hooks 1998, 79). (Not that the force and effect on identity in college-level literacy acquisition doesn't affect all college students—it is only more visible in the groups described above.) The issue of literacy acquisition and acculturation has for at least the last three decades furnished the site of many of the battles, known collectively as the "culture wars," fought in American colleges and universities. In the 1970s, this war resulted in the CCCC declaration of a student's right to his or her own language. More recently the issue emerges via the concept of rhetorical sovereignty. Of special interest in this regard is Scott Lyons' (2000) work on the sovereignty of American Indians in American Indian rhetoric.[4]

The very existence of the battle over the right of a people to claim title to the language of the stories that embody its myths, traditions, and ancient ways of knowing indicates the burden that the language of acculturation represents for so-called "oppressed" racial and ethnic minorities.[5] It is certainly a determining factor in the discourse of those of us who teach writing and also write about our teaching. In teaching at an open admissions institution, for example, I observe first-hand everyday the weight of the burden that language imposed on students as they struggle to compose their identities via writing—*in the discourse* that might structure and thus *materialize* their dreams of college, career, and personal success.

THE CHANGES THAT HAPPEN IN COLLEGE

Because I daily witness this struggle, I have come to believe that one of my first duties is to help students in my first-year writing classes to realize that going to college *must* change who they are. I tell them that their desire to succeed in college *must* inform their identity and dictate their choices. I insist upon weekly, if not daily, reflections—in writing—on who they are at the moment, who they want to become, and what they must do in college and in life to bridge the gap between these two limit points. Reading about such abstract ideas as identity formation and the gains and losses that come with change and pondering in writing the effects of such change constitute the "practical" literacy "skills" that my writing classes impart. For that is how my students begin to discover what *they*—the stories of those authors in their reader—have to do with what my students want to become.

By now perhaps, you glimpse the paradox of the locus in which I, and all of us to some degree, find ourselves as we try to help our students become literate, both able to "read and write" and to be "educated and cultured." The university discourse impersonally carries and conveys the weight of personal and cultural prejudices.

In "Considerations for American Freireistas," Victor Villanueva, Jr. (1997) writes of this lapsus, the abyss between education and culture. It is Villanueva's position that the two prevalent trends among American Freireistas are (1) "to reduce politics to discussions of the different cultures and histories found in the classroom" and society and (2) "to convert the classroom into a political arena that aims at pointing out injustices and instigating change" (623). Villanueva argues "that to achieve a pedagogy that aims at more than mere reform we must begin by acknowledging the unlikelihood of dramatic revolutionary change in the most immediate future." Furthermore, he argues, "less dramatic but no less revolutionary change might come about by our becoming more aware of the workings of hegemony . . . [turning] to advantage the ways hegemony exploits traditions and the ways hegemony allows for change, ultimately making for changes that go way beyond those allowed by the current hegemony" (623–24).

Villanueva illustrates, at a cultural and political level, the loss–gain factor of identity change that students in my classes find themselves having to encounter. The essays I ask them to read constitute stories that embody this encounter. I often begin with Malcolm X's "Coming to an Awareness of Language" (Malcolm X and Haley 1995). Most students are aware of Malcolm's reputation as a black revolutionary, a fiery religious activist, and political leader. While those aspects of his identity are implicit in Malcolm's jailhouse education piece, less implicit is the method by which he became literate and the radical manner in which it redefined and reoriented him. For in developing literacy—the acquisition of both an education and the cultural awareness that accompanies it—the man who entered prison calling himself Detroit Red also acquired the ability to examine Red's boundaries—the personal, social, and historical reference points that had shaped his thought and behavior to that point in his life. Thus in the tradition of Samson Occom, but taking that tradition to a limit unimaginable in Occom's time, Detroit Red emerged from the last prison cell he was ever to occupy as the formidable thinker and speech-maker, Malcolm X.

The story of Malcolm X's identity transformation begins with Malcolm's retroactive summary of his strongest identity trait: "I've never been one for inaction. Everything I've ever felt strongly about, I've done something about" (9). This tendency to act on his convictions led him, as he explains, to writing letters to which he never got replies. In looking back at his former identity, Malcolm X sees what he could not see from behind its narrow bars. Lacking the vital sense of audience that might have garnered them readers, the letters were little more than illiterate rants declaring that "the white man is the devil," penned in "ragged handwriting" that didn't even go "in a straight line" (10–11). Moreover, their writer didn't even know how to address the envelopes that contained them. Frustrating it must have been. Yet this frustration constituted the first step the man of action was to take on his road to literacy. The other significant step occurred because of the sudden, searing envy Malcolm felt in the presence of another prisoner's glibly displayed "stock of knowledge," a raw desire to regain the position of envy and admiration in the gaze that Malcolm himself had held on the streets: "I had always been the most articulate hustler out there" (10).

The conjunction between these two events opened up within Malcolm the sense of a gaping hole in his being, similar perhaps to the one that his former "Heathenism" represented to Samson Occom. Lacking a Reverend Wheelock to guide him along the path to education in the white man's tongue—the language of law, business, commerce, and philosophy—Malcolm devised his own "homemade education." Having asked for a dictionary, tablet, and pencils, he began copying down the symbols and letters, the definitions and phrasing, which operate this tongue. By the time he had finished copying the entire dictionary, from one cover to the other, Malcolm had not only acquired an astonishing vocabulary, but also a knowledge of history, geography, and etymology. This knowledge he rigorously applied to and augmented with books from the Norfolk Prison Library. The end result was the freedom of the life of the mind, the freedom to roam in the infinite rooms of the prison house of language. The excerpt from the Autobiography that I use in my classes ends with Malcolm's ringing affirmation of this life, a cliché that speaks afresh to every student who, in reading it, takes it to heart: "Although still in prison, I had never felt so free" (11).

Once a class finishes reading this remarkable personal story regarding the transformational power of literacy, I ask the students to trace Malcolm X's identity transformation. We begin with its earliest incarnation in the child and adolescent Malcolm Little and trace its metamorphosis from the street hustler Detroit Red, to the civil rights leader Malcolm X. In tracking the major steps of the process, the students inevitably make two astonishing discoveries. First they see that, for the storyteller, Malcolm X himself, the evolution of this identity is made visible by writing. They also discover that the things that Malcolm X felt strongly about remained constant throughout the entire process, essentially fixed and unalterable. What does change is the manner in which this message is expressed. Structured by the rhetorical strategies and aims of the university discourse, strategies that Malcolm developed along with the ideas to which such strategies lend shape and substance, Detroit Red's "crazy" rant becomes a passionately stated, yet cogent and arguable thesis: "The white man is responsible for the black man's condition in this wilderness of North America" (11).

As my students read, discuss, and learn more about Malcolm's childhood and street life, they almost invariably begin to see the logic of the antisocial behavior exhibited by Detroit Red. As a child, the former Malcolm Little had watched while an angry white mob lynched an innocent black man; had learned that, while pregnant with him, his mother, along with her other children, was terrorized by white-robed Ku Klux Klansmen; had felt his hopes of becoming a doctor or lawyer dashed when a white teacher told him "you people don't do things like that." Moreover, as if forever to punctuate the rape of young Malcolm Little's self-identification, Malcolm X also learned that he was the by-product of an ancestral rape, the mother of his mother having been raped by a white man.[6] This knowledge, always already there within his consciousness, as my students are quick to realize, ultimately informed and drove Malcolm's process of transformation. It knotted together the separate periods of his life into one formidable and articulate representative, the relentless social critic, Malcolm X.

My students also begin to see, almost in spite of themselves, that loss of the mother tongue is necessary in order to function as an adult. For Detroit Red's loss *is* Malcolm X's gain. Without the one, there would not be the other. They see that ultimately the university discourse, the discourse of the oppressor, offers the only feasible way out of oppression by affording a path back through it and out again at another place, a locus of critique and self-understanding.

WRITING ABOUT IDENTITY TRANSFORMATION

I'll close by describing a typical final essay assignment in my writing classes and then discussing one student's written response to it. For this particular assignment, I asked the students to read excerpts from Richard Rodriguez's *Hunger of Memory* (1998) and from bell hooks' *Talking Back: Thinking Feminist, Thinking Black* (1989). They first outlined the essays in their reader-response journals. Then they wrote a personal experience essay prompted by passages from each text.

Rodriguez's book is famous for enraging many liberal educators with its stance against bilingual education in the public schools. Thus my first writing prompt challenges students to think about the implications of Rodriguez's position: "It is not possible for a child—*any child*—ever to use his family's language in school. Not to understand this is to misunderstand the public uses of schooling and to trivialize the nature of intimate life—a family's 'language'" (1998, 64). I ask them to write their reading responses to the following questions: "What do you think about Rodriguez's statement? What is your experience regarding 'private and public language'"?

The bell hooks excerpt is a response to Rodriguez. Hooks argues that Rodriguez suggests that "attempts to maintain ties with his Chicano background impeded his progress and that he had to sever ties with community and kin to succeed at Stanford" (1998, 83). My second prompt includes two passages from hooks' essay. In the first one, hooks writes,

> Often I tell students from poor and working-class backgrounds that if you believe what you have learned and are learning in schools and universities separates you from your past, this is precisely what will happen. It is important to stand firm in the conviction that nothing can truly separate us from our pasts when we nurture and enrich that connection. An important strategy for maintaining contact is ongoing acknowledgement of the primacy of one's past, of one's background, affirming the reality that such bonds are not severed automatically solely because one enters a new environment or moves toward a different class experience. (82)

In the second, she writes,

> Even in the face of powerful structures of domination, it remains possible for each of us, especially those of us who are members of oppressed and/

> or exploited groups . . . to define and determine alternative standards, to decide the nature and extent of compromise. (83)

The prompt then asks students to write a response that demonstrates their understanding (paraphrase/summary) of hooks' writing. Once they have done that, they are asked to interpret the statements based upon their own experience regarding people and events that might alienate them from their roots. Within the writing process, the Rodriguez reading response acts as essay prewriting, while the response to hooks moves student writing toward an essay draft. These writings are shared and peer evaluated as a way of helping the student writers develop more ideas and questions about issues related to the issues that Rodriguez and hooks, and now they themselves have written about. Next, they move on to a more complete, formal essay.

The writing assignment begins by asking them to repeat the process they used in responding to hooks, only this time they add the excerpt from "Public and Private Language" to the mix. Once they have done that, they are asked to evaluate each writer's essay and claims, discussing their value for an audience of college-age readers. The return in the reading of and written responses to Rodriguez and hooks, as well as other texts they want to discuss and the re-reading of and writing about the student's own experiences and knowledge, moves them from instant of the glance recognition of ideas and events to a time for understanding them in a complex and contextual manner. The writing of a final essay provides evidence to the students that they have moved beyond the surface, two-dimensional view of their own lives to that the point of separation between intellectual deprivation and enlightenment that begins their journey within the realm of higher learning.[7]

MARITZA'S REFLECTIONS ON LITERACY EXPERIENCES

Maritza, who had just graduated from high school, was taking an Upward Bound section of Introduction to College Writing when she wrote in response to the assignment described above. Her essay, "My True Identity," is not only an insightful response to Rodriguez and hooks, as well as Sandra Cisneros (1984), who we had read earlier in the semester, but also a powerful testimony to issues of identity that I have raised in this chapter.

Maritza begins her essay by describing how her "culture, language, and economic status" helped to shape her identity. She writes of the expectations of her Mexican-American family regarding females.

"Women had to behave like ladies, and many strict rules were set upon us." She notes that growing up in the United States created "conflicts" between those expectations and the kind of young woman she grew up to be. She cites an excerpt from Cisneros' "A House of My Own" from *The House on Mango Street*, in which the speaker declares independence from Mexican macho expectations. "Women are supposed to be housewives and do every thing their husbands' request." Maritza writes, "I want to be a career-woman who does not depend on a man to stand on both feet." She joins Cisneros, Rodriguez, and hooks in writing of conflicts in the realm of the private and public, the home and community in regard to ethnicity, and hooks and Cisneros in the realm of gender. By beginning to compose an identity in the discourse of higher learning, in the context of writers who have published similar identity experiences, Maritza is becoming aware of what was once unconscious—her state of being.

Next, Maritza moves on to the issue of language, for as surely as she is influenced by American culture, she recognizes that her identity is also "influenced by the English."

She describes how her experience parallels that of Rodriguez: growing up in a home where her "parents [like his] speak Spanish fluently," so that she "was raised speaking Spanish." Like Rodriguez, she begins school speaking only Spanish and learns English without the benefit of bilingual education. She writes of being proud of that accomplishment and of the benefit of being able to write in two languages. She also writes of the loss that accompanies that gain:

> As portrayed by Richard Rodriguez, once you learn something new it is hard to share it with your parents. "The family's quiet was due to the fact that as we children learned more and more English, we shared fewer and fewer words with our parents" (Rodriguez 70). Once I spoke English fluently, the dialogue between my parents and myself decreased. As I learned more English and got an education, I had less things to talk about with them.

Maritza's writing of identity also echoes bell hooks:

> My education has influenced my identity a great deal. Going to school and gaining knowledge has shaped the person that I am today. As I mentioned earlier, I was brought up to believe certain things, I was influenced by my parents. For example, I was raised to believe that homosexuality is wrong. Yet as I got older and went to school I learned more about the subject. I started to have my own believes [*sic*] and ideas, most of them always contradicted either my parent's or cultures [*sic*] believes [*sic*]. As

bell hooks states in "Keeping Close to Home: Class and Education": "Like many working-class folks, they feared what college education might do to their children's minds even as they unenthusiastically acknowledged the importance." (hooks 1998, 76)

In order to illustrate the point, Maritza tells the story of attending Chicago's Gay Pride Parade:

> I went with one of my best friends because I wanted to support him and let him know that I accept him the way he is. My parents did not approve much of me attending the parade . . . My parents feel that homosexuality is wrong, that it is a sin in God's eyes. Yet I think differently.

The reason for thinking "differently," according to Maritza is the influence of "teachers, writers, and philosophers" that she has encountered throughout her education. Class conflict does not only manifest itself in a conflict of morality with her parents. Maritza writes of a culture clash with other relatives.

> In my family not many people have gotten an education. Now that I am going away to college and try to get an education, my relatives (aunts, uncles, cousins, etc.) do not speak to me. They think that I am a "sell-out" [and] they claim that I have forgotten about my culture and that I am trying to be American. I really do not argue back because it would only be a waste of time because they would still not understand me. The thing with my relatives is that they are conformists, and I am not. I actually want to change and strive for a better life.

It is clear in her writing that Maritza recognizes the loss/gain production of the process of identity composition in literacy acquisition and acculturation. Reading and writing about the ways that others have confronted these issues helps her recognize and validate her own experience in a way that aims her toward her desire of the success of self-realization, or, as hooks puts it, "to define and determine alternative standards, to decide the nature and extent of compromise" of private and public life, of her past present and future. She ends her essay by expressing that desire:

> Throughout my life I have had to deal with many changes. Now my life is heading in a totally different direction than that from my family. I am going to go to college, graduate, and eventually attend Law School and become a well-respected attorney. All of these changes will eventually

separate me from my family, because I will start a new life. After college I see myself taking up on the identity of a responsible, studious, focused young woman. I have always set goals in my life and so far I have accomplished all of them. I always finish what I start, and I started getting an education and I will finish it.

All of my identities have been partially influenced but they have also been my creation, because I am happy with myself and with what I have accomplished. As I mentioned before my parents, culture, and language have and will always play an important role in my identities. They have all become part of my daily life and personality.

PRIVATE AND PUBLIC IDENTITIES AND LITERACIES

I began by noting that those of us in Rhetoric and Composition have been addressing issues of literacy acquisition and acculturation and assimilation for decades. In "Rhetorical Sovereignty: What Do American Indians Want from Writing?" Scott Lyons (2000) writes that "Indians generally do *not* want . . . stereotyping, cultural appropriation, exclusion, ignorance, irrelevance, rhetorical imperialism. . . rhetorical sovereignty requires above all the presence of an Indian voice, speaking or writing in an ongoing context of colonization [the discourse of the university and capitalism] and setting at least some of the terms of debate" (462). While Lyons' concern is aimed at Indians themselves putting an end to the "Indian problem," the lessons that he teaches are valuable to all practitioners and teachers of writing. For, as he writes, "rhetorical sovereignty requires of writing teachers more than a renewed commitment to listening and learning; it also requires a radical rethinking how and what we teach as the written word at all levels of schooling, from preschool to graduate curricula and beyond" (460). Lyons then cites Hawaiian nationalist Haunani-Kay Trask: "Language, in particular, helps to decolonize the mind . . . Thinking in one's own cultural referents leads to conceptualizing in one's own world view which, in turn, leads to disagreement with and eventual opposition to the dominant ideology" (462).

All of our students have the right to their own language, their own voices. Within each one of their own identifications, they have the right to private language and intimate life. They also have the right to a public language and a public identity, based upon, in Lyons' words, "the inherent right and ability of peoples to determine their own communicative needs and desires in the pursuit of self-determination" (450). The inherent right to pursue "self-determination" not only requires, but demands literacy. The world's business increasingly is dominated by the university discourse structure, a discourse that disseminates knowledge in reference to political and cultural biases and stereotypes. Paradoxically, because it is the universal discourse of politics, law, business, and religion, it affords the only means for addressing and changing the biases and stereotypes perpetuated by its use. It is the discourse in which students are expected to pursue the life of the mind, which might be said to be a locus or temporality providing a breathing space. While in this space, we may think through and examine the sources of our instantaneous judgments, reflect upon where we have been, where we are now, and where we wish to go. In this locus, we may discover our own point of view and develop a voice to bear witness to our vision.

In working with the language of writers confronting "stereotyping, cultural appropriation, exclusion, ignorance, irrelevance, [and] rhetorical imperialism," Maritza writes of her experience in developing a voice of her own. In the process of writing, she finds herself in a position of choice and self-determination, able "to define and determine alternative standards, to decide the nature and extent of compromise" within the cultures that define her. Such self-definition, composition of identity if you will, is necessary if one is to direct one's own course rather than yield this duty to another. Samson Occom was only one the first to learn this lesson in America. And literacy within the dominant discourse structure constitutes the first step toward countering its constricting effects.

PART III

Identity Outside the Institutional Walls

10

MIGRATORY AND REGIONAL IDENTITY

Robert Brooke

Imagine with me Cedar Bluffs, Nebraska, population 591. We've driven up from Lincoln, the University town, and it's evening, early summer, our Mid-Plains air heavy with moisture and the scent of milo. The two-lane runs mostly straight north, and every rise in elevation is matched by a corresponding drop a quarter mile further. We've passed through grass and crops, alongside the steel snakes of center pivot irrigation, by farmsteads ringed with trees. But mostly there's earth and late day sun, and the wide second landscape of prairie sky.

We're in the gym at Cedar Bluffs School, the one shared by the elementary and secondary students, around twenty to a grade. Of course now it's evening and the gym is redefined as a community place. This is the night, after all, that the fourth graders show off their Me Museums—trifold boards displaying pictures and writing, placed on tables behind artifacts from their lives and heritage. The tables sport Czech flags and World War II knapsacks and military medals donated by grandparents, corn shuckers and kerosene barn lanterns from mid-century farms, photos of younger siblings, passports from immigration ancestors, religious symbols, 4-H ribbons. The idea of these Me Museums is to represent to school and community what each child sees as important about them, in this place. Ms. Laughridge's fourth graders have been working toward these Me Museums all year. Now these fourth graders are ready, well-groomed and fidgeting with excitement, while they escort community adults to their seats, check the video-camera they've set up, and then run back to their personal displays to readjust that one picture that keeps slipping.

We're here because the Nebraska Writing Project is sponsoring the fourth graders. Their teacher, Virginia Laughridge, (Ginger to her friends) has been working with us for the past five years, and is part of a growing team of teachers, preschool through college, exploring what we call "place-conscious education." The idea of place-conscious education is simple: learning should be integrated into local place, and should guide students in developing the intellectual, civic, and democratic abilities necessary to help shape the future of their place. In its emphasis on local context, place conscious educators draw on a tradition that stretches at least back to Dewey (1916), believing that people learn best when learning is immediately relevant. But beyond that, place-conscious educators share a commitment to a particular definition of citizenship, a citizenship that recognizes, in Paul Theobald's words (1997), each human community's *intradependence*. Theobald writes,

> Intradependence means "to exist by virtue of necessary relations *within a place*." Throughout most of human history, people lived their lives in a given locality and were highly dependent on the place itself and on those others with whom the place was shared. It has only been since the seventeenth century or so that intradependence of this sort has eroded and people have begun to think of themselves as unencumbered by the constraints of nature or community. (7)

In our place-conscious work, we quote Wallace Stegner (1992), who says,

> Migratoriness has its dangers. I know about this. I was born on wheels. I know the excitement of newness and possibility, but I also know the dissatisfaction and hunger that result from placelessness. Some towns that we lived in were never real to me. They were only the raw material of a place, as I was the raw material of a person. Neither place nor I had a chance of being anything until we could live together for a while. (200–201)

We quote Robert Manley (1997), who says,

> Heritage is the story of us; history is the story of them. The part of history we must know best is the story of ourselves and our families.

And we quote Wendell Berry, who says (quoted in Stegner 1992),

> You don't know *who* you are until you know *where* you are. (199)

Since 1997, the kindergarten-through-college teachers in the Nebraska Writing Project network have been exploring how we might teach from such a commitment to place-conscious education. Part of this exploration has been formal teacher research. In 1997–2000, a team of eight rural Nebraska secondary/elementary teachers and I participated in the National Writing Project's Rural Voices, Country Schools teacher research program, joining teams from Arizona, Louisiana, Michigan, Pennsylvania, and Washington in documenting what is good in rural education. These teacher researchers found that place-conscious teaching is at the heart of what is good in rural schools, and their ongoing work has provided key leadership for our whole state network. (See our book, *Rural Voices: Place-Conscious Education and the Teaching of Writing,* Brooke 2003, for fuller description of this program.) But another part of this exploration has been our Rural Institute program, through which teachers and community members from one rural place come together for an extended examination of what place-conscious teaching might mean in that community.

Nebraska Writing Project Rural Institutes are three-week institutes for twelve to twenty-four teachers and community members that immerse participants in place conscious education. In structure, they are modeled on the Invitational Summer Institutes that are core programs at all 175 National Writing Project sites across the country. Participants are admitted only after an application process that assures they are leaders in their local schools and communities. During the institute, each participating teacher presents an especially effective unit or lesson or project from their own classroom, insuring that the pedagogy shared comes directly from successful teachers' practice rather than from theory-blinded academics at some years' distance from public schools. Every day, all participants immerse themselves in their own writing, and in collective inquiry into the study of writing. All of these items are common to National Writing Project Invitational Summer Institutes.

ATTENTION TO PLACE-CONSCIOUS EDUCATION

To these items, our Nebraska Writing Project Rural Institutes have added direct attention to place-conscious education. Rather than treat writing as something at once hopelessly general (as, for instance, a general skill necessary for all academic study), or individually peculiar (as, for instance, the creative passion of this one teacher), the Rural Institutes explore writing through local place and our relationship to it. All of the features of the National Writing Project Invitational Summer Institute are adapted to this exploration. We select participants from schools and communities surrounding a single host school—the participants all come from the same part of the state, and usually half come from the host community itself. We coach participants to choose teaching presentations that emphasize their connections to their community (such as oral history projects from interviews with town elders, or studies of local political issues, or "adopt a building" projects where fourth graders learn the histories of edifices on Main Street). Daily writing in the Rural

Institutes is of course chosen by the individual participants, but we offer invitations to writing that might include "I am from" poems, renderings of place or family or heritage, and essays that probe the meaning of place. Much of this writing is supported by reading. For the research and inquiry portion of the institute, we draw attention to writing manuals immersed in place (Georgia Heard (1995), *Writing Towards Home;* Denis LeDoux (1993), *Turning Memories into Memoirs*) and we offer many essayists' meditations on the meaning of place (for instance, Kim Stafford (1986), *Having Everything Right;* Lisa Knopp (1996), *Field of Vision;* Paul Gruchow (1995), *Grassroots: The Universe of Home;* Scott Russell Sanders (1993), *Staying Put*). In addition, many afternoons we take writing field trips to local resources. We might, for example, visit the local cemetery with the second grade teacher and write from the stories we find there of the host town's earliest settlers. Or we might visit the local prairie preserve in the company of the high school biology teacher to learn what can be described about the past and present ecology of place. Or we might visit a successful local entrepreneur to imagine the writing and vision necessary to create livelihood in this regional setting. Overall, all the elements of the National Writing Project Invitational Summer Institute are given a place-conscious twist. The consequence is a richly embedded sense of the possible connections of writing curriculum to local place. Such connections, we hope, are not merely parochial but spiral out, incorporating regional and national history, economics, politics, and biology. In the Rural Institutes, we explore how (in Paul Theobald's words 1997)

> the school's place allows educators to take what is artificial out of the schooling experience. . . . With skillful pedagogical guidance, the school's place allows children to develop the intellectual flexibility needed to see history as a force in their lives rather than as an exercise in the acquisition of names and dates. All of the traditional "subjects" can reap the same intellectual rewards through a focus on place. (138)

Imagine now the Cedar Bluffs gym, where the fourth graders have set up their Me Museums. As the culminating project of the fourth grade year, the Me Museums are a rich example of place-conscious education in practice. Ms. Laughridge's social studies curriculum is strictly Nebraska history—the standard curricular material that includes Stephen Long (the explorer who called the Plains "the Great American Desert"), the Union Pacific Railroad, the Oregon and Mormon trails, the sod busters. But because she is a place-conscious teacher, and seeks intradependent citizenry as much as historical knowledge, Ms. Laughridge located these curricular mandates in students' own explorations.

These explorations start early in the term. For instance, to make real the immigrant and dispossession experiences surrounding the Euro-American settlement of the plains, Ms. Laughridge asked her fourth graders to gather moving stories. Each student asked a family member or neighbor for a story of a time they had to move their home. These family/community interviews turned up origin stories of coming to settle in Nebraska, choice of life stories from parents who selected rural over urban communities, and dispossession stories of individuals who had to leave home to start anew in a different place. The fourth graders wrote their versions of these stories, initially to share with each other, later to add to their Me Museums. These collected moving stories make the experience of emigration locally real and communal in a way text-book history is not, since every family has a moving story. At the end of the unit, in a blatant connection to the standard history curriculum, students designed advertisement posters of the sort distributed through-out Europe by the Union Pacific Railroad to lure economically poor Europeans to Nebraska. What sort of broadside, asked Ms. Laughridge, might have brought your family to this place?

Also, to connect the sweep of Plains history to her students, Ms. Laughridge has her fourth graders conduct heritage interviews. Ginger takes her students on guided tours of Pahuk Hill (a prairie preserve and sacred site to the Pawnee just four miles north of town) and to the home of a local woman who has preserved a stretch of actual prairie in a landscape dominated by agricultural redevelopment. After these visits, hearing these stories and seeing some of the artifacts, Ms. Laughridge asks students to gather their own heritage stories. Can they find, from grandparents or great-grandparents, or (given Cedar Bluffs' changing demographics) from neighborhood "old-timers" important to the child, stories and artifacts that explain something of their personal past?

These fourth graders don't know they are working toward their Me Museums as they do these early assignments. They don't know they are engaged in place-conscious education as they listen to old-timers tell about the 1930s swimming pool, the biggest in Nebraska at that time, dug with horses and an implement one town elder calls a "slide" right by the current Boy Scout camp, or when they gather seeds from prairie mallow to plant in their own home gardens, or when they have their picture taken with a grandparent next to a 1950s tractor. But now it's spring, and the Cedar Bluffs gymnasium is full of tables and trifolds and

Figure One: Fourth Grade Me Museums from Cedar Bluffs School.

family artifacts, full of pictures and writing and proud children, full of community members who have some ownership over the learning of this one class.

Imagine we're there, standing in the back while the children give their presentations and the community adults applaud. I'm in my tie and jacket, the university sponsor, and you're wearing whatever professional uniform is right to mark your place as visiting dignitary. When Ms. Laughridge introduces us around, we shake the smiling hands of parents and community officials, all of us pleased with this fourth grade celebration of local culture.

But we also see the strain in those smiles and handshakes. While we know this moment is celebratory, with a community's children and adults honoring who they are and where they are from, you and I know we are not ourselves part of this community. And so there is strain. It's not just the strain of being the outsiders, the ones everyone knows will, at the end of the evening, travel in that rusted blue Volvo back to Lincoln.

It's something else.

Something systemic.

At some level, every adult who has chosen Cedar Bluffs as a home community must worry about our presence—as they must worry about Ms. Laughridge and the rest of her teaching colleagues. As educators, all of us are implicated in the destruction of small communities—even those of us who work with place-conscious education. For education, as a national system, clearly has different aims than the creation of a place-conscious citizenry. Throughout this century, American education has functioned to create a migratory personal identity, an identity not linked to a specific place, community or region, but instead to an identity of the skilled laborer, equipped with the general cultural and disciplinary knowledge that will enable the person to work wherever those skills are required. What education really teaches, says Paul Gruchow (1995), is "How to Migrate 101."

ACADEMICS AND MIGRATORY PERSONAL IDENTITIES

Lisa Knopp (1996), in her essay "Local Geography," captures the emotional burden of our educational system. Of her schooling in Burlington, Iowa, she writes,

> Gradually, I saw Burlington [Iowa] as the end of the world where nothing ever happened or ever would. Certainly, what I learned in school reinforced, perhaps created, this attitude. American history never happened

in my part of America; world history never happened in my part of the world. Since local history wasn't valued and thus wasn't taught (or vice versa), I learned little about where I was from and what it meant to be shaped by such a place. I started imagining ways to become something other than I was. I studied [my teacher] Mrs. Ament, who was *in* Burlington but not *of* it. I studied television programs set in New York or Los Angeles, from which I learned of commuter trains, muggings, and apartments reached by elevators . . . Isaiah predicted that his people would go into exile for "want of knowledge": because they had not made the stories they heard *mean deeply* . . . Neither did I understand that stories about home were stories about me . . . If I had internalized the stories before my decision-making time, I would have been more ingenuous and receptive; I would have found a way to stay where I belong. (7–9)

Lisa Knopp's story is, I think, resonant, especially for successful academics. Very few of us now live and work in our community of origin. In fact, at the 2002 Watson conference from which this collection of essays emerged, Kurt Spellmeyer asked the attendees at the first general session how many of them now taught in their home town. According to various reports, either one person or three people from all of those attending raised their hands. (Of course, we might be able to extend Spellmeyer's question, and ask as well "How many of you know how to belong to the region in which you now live?" To that question, we might receive much more complicated responses. But that's a question for another essay.)

I think of my own history here as symptomatic of the way American education promotes migration. For instance, I know more about national trends in composition scholarship than I know about my local place. The people I converse with daily dwell elsewhere, and I reach them primarily through electronic means, in the strange conversation that is e-mail. In my English Department, only one professor of over 40 tenure-track lines grew up in Nebraska. Most of us mark our professional identities through conferences, to which we travel in order to network in the placeless environs of well-equipped conference centers. Professionally, our home community of scholars is an abstract, placeless community.

And when I think further about the place I live in—the Great Plains surrounding Lincoln, Nebraska—I realize I have a vexed relationship with that place. I know more about it than most of my departmental colleagues because of my work with good teachers like Ms. Laughridge, but in many ways after 18 years here I am still struggling to make it my own.

I still get lost when directions come with compass points (I'm used to turning right or left instead of North or South). I don't get Big Red football. I make mistakes, when I write about our region, in simple things like the appropriate uses of farm equipment (one of my rural teachers told me I don't know a harvester from a hole in the ground.)

Yet I know more about this adopted place than I know about my region of origin. I grew up in Denver, Colorado, in the rain shadow of the Rockies, and part of me still feels most at home in a landscape edged with mountains. Yet I am near clueless about Colorado's history or politics or educational issues, and must admit that my feeling for the mountains is primarily nostalgia.

I am, in short, a product of the migratory educational system that Knopp describes. Some part of me believed the message of my high school education, that the life of the mind was a placeless life, centered elsewhere. Another part of me believed the message of college and graduate school, that the intellectual and rhetorical skills I was developing were ones that would serve me *anywhere*. I learned to write, as have you, in the nuanced, decontextualized prose that is immediately accessible to any academic compositionist, whether they're from Texas or upstate New York or even New Zealand. I followed my undergraduate advisor's recommendations and went to the graduate school that gave me the best support; I followed my dissertation advisor's advice that "academics can't choose where they live" and came to Nebraska because the university chose me, rather than the other way around.

Imagining the children standing in the gym in Cedar Bluffs, I think about my personal history versus the personal histories of these fourth graders, awash tonight in the excitement of their Me Museums. I think about my own enculturation as a migratory academic versus the regional understanding this community celebrates. I can almost see the pattern that will force these young people, in their next eight-to-twelve years of education, to choose versions of the same kind of migratory life I lead.

Education is a part of that pattern. But there are other parts.

Economics, for instance. If, as I'm suggesting, we might see life in a small rural community as the clearest example of an alternative to migratory identity, then we have to address economics head on. It is hard to make a living in rural America. Contrary to the national media focus on urban poor, the most poverty-stricken areas of our nation are rural. The most recent census data for per capita income shows that only one county among the poorest 50 counties in America is urban. 10 of the poorest 20 counties in America are located in the rural Great Plains of Nebraska and South Dakota. The average income in Loup County, Nebraska, ranked number one on the poverty chart, is $6,606 a year (Center for Rural Affairs 2002). So many things follow from such stark economic facts: access to housing, healthcare, jobs; the increasing trend for rural communities to become bedroom communities for the closest big city; the difficulty of young persons imagining themselves as professionals while at the same time living in a small community.

IMAGINING REGIONAL IDENTITIES

When I think about the economic, imaginative, and educational forces that push us all toward migratory identities, I worry that any alternative may be beyond us, at this point in cultural history. And yet, increasingly, I think that alternatives are exactly what we need. As a culture, and certainly as educators, we need ways to imagine *regional identities* for ourselves and for our students.

How might we imagine regional identity? Toni Haas and Paul Nachtigal (1998), the co-directors of the Annenberg Rural Challenge, have offered an initial starting place in their short pamphlet, *Place Value*. Writing of what might be required to live well in contemporary rural America, Haas and Nachtigal suggest educators replace the traditional five physical senses with five new "senses" that form the core of rural citizenship:

1. A sense of place, or of living well ecologically: According to Haas and Nachtigal, part of living well involves developing a sustainable relationship with the natural world in which one's community is located. Understanding the biology of one's region, how that biology connects to local industry and agriculture, and the consequent biological issues that impact one's community is thus a fundamental aspect of regional identity.

2. A sense of civic involvement, or living well politically: A second part of living well involves an understanding of government, broadly defined as the range of institutional ways communities make decisions that affect their members. Individuals with a strong regional identity will know what the local issues are, and will know how to participate in public forums that decide those issues.

3. A sense of worth, or living well economically: The phrase "making a living" captures this sense of living well. To participate fully in a community, individuals need a livelihood. Individuals should know the options for livelihood available to them in their

region, about the skills, knowledge, and experience necessary
to sustain those livelihoods, and about the place of such work in
the regional, national, and international economics. They will
need to understand how businesses are formed and sustained,
how to identify skills and resources they can offer personally, and
how to locate markets they can tap. Otherwise, upon graduation
individuals will have no real choice but to join the stream of able
youth migrating toward America's cities.

4. A sense of connection, or living well spiritually: A fourth aspect
   of living well involves discerning connections to one's place on
   earth, that is, understanding and articulating the meaning of living one's life in a given place. Haas and Nachtigal unabashedly
   call this aspect spirituality. For them, spirituality is primarily a
   person's way of understanding the connections and relationships
   that form a life, whether or not that understanding is based in
   any given institutionalized religion.

5. A sense of belonging, or living well in community: "Community,"
   Haas and Nacthigal write, "is how we together create a story
   about our place" (26). This final aspect of living well involves
   the collective meaning in which one locates one's life, along a
   continuum of heritage to imagined future that one shares with
   others. Part of having a regional identity is thus knowing the stories about the past that shape life in this area, yet an equal part
   is involving oneself in the community creation of the stories that
   will guide the future.

Haas and Nachtigal's five senses offer, I believe, an initial starting
point to begin imagining regional identity. Though they are especially
aimed at rural America, I suspect the senses of place, civic involvement,
worth, connection, and belonging might prove a useful rubric for imagining regional identity in any place.

But the task of imagining regional identity must, by definition, always
be local labor. Looking around the Cedar Bluffs gym, I realize this community and its school is hard at work on its own version of regional
identity. Over by the Me Museums, for instance, talking with the older
sister of one of the fourth-graders is secondary teacher Robyn Dalton.
Ms. Dalton grew up in central Nebraska, traveled to Lincoln for college
and graduate school, but instead of joining the migratory pipeline that
travels I-80 east to Chicago or west to Denver, she sought out a teaching job in the state. Now, as part of her English curriculum, she guides

juniors through a career unit that helps them define what livelihoods are possible here. She has her students research a career of interest to them, spend at least a day "job shadowing" a local person in that career, and give a multimedia presentation on the career's local, regional, and national prospects. (See Robyn Dalton's chapter in the *Rural Voices* collection, "Career Education: Creating Personal and Civic Futures Through Career Discernment".) Ms. Dalton is also in regular contact with rural Nebraska schools like Mead and Albion that have made entrepreneurial education part of the secondary curriculum. She would like her students, by graduation, to have experience running their own businesses. While Robyn is ceaselessly devoted to excellence (her speech and drama teams regularly place in the state's top ten), she wants her students to understand that choosing an excellent career doesn't necessarily require leaving the region. Regional identity, for Robyn Dalton, isn't opposed to professional identity. It means, instead, seeking the professional training that will allow students to craft a livelihood in their region of choice. Regional identity, in short, becomes an identity of civic leadership, of responsibility for the economic well-being of the community in which one chooses to live.

Next to Robyn is Millie Beran, the Consumer Science and Art teacher, who has a different emphasis for regional identity. She wants to connect learning in so-called vocational education to the generations-deep practices of her community. For some years, she has had her quilting and cooking classes work across school levels with community sponsors (sixth graders and eleventh graders work alongside the county Quilters Association, for example). As Ms. Beran has become involved in Nebraska Writing Project Rural Institutes, she has added writing to this mix, helping to create a community writing group that spans elementary students to octogenarians. If you have worked with Foxfire, you may recognize the version of regional identity Ms. Beran espouses: regional identity involves real knowledge of the human heritage of the community and region—the crafts, art, agriculture, practical knowledge that make a way of life.

Ginger Laughridge has a vision of regional identity too. Imagine her taking the stage, since it's finally time to start the Me Museum program. Her introductory remarks focus on her fourth graders and the community support they've received in putting together their Me Museums. But I notice how gently Ms. Laughridge models the kind of work she values. She speaks of her love for the Plains and its history, and reads from a piece she wrote about her grandmother, a Kansas pioneer. She speaks of the need to value what we have around us, and tells how she has taken both her students and her university sponsors to visit Pahuk Hill, the preserve and sacred Pawnee grounds a few miles north along the abandoned train tracks that pass just west of the school building. She hopes we'll listen to the students' stories tonight with a similar sense of wonder and value. Listening to Ginger Laughridge, I think I see stewardship as a form of regional identity, in the care and preservation she exudes and passes on.

Civic leadership, knowledge of heritage, stewardship: these may well be the most important aspects of regional identity, as a possible alternative to the migratory identity so prevailingly fostered by American education. We stand in the back of the gym while the children take the stage, some so painfully shy we can't make out what they say, others exuberant in the family stories they share. It's hard not to think about the future as we hear their young voices. How will they imagine themselves, their regions, and their responsibilities in eight years when they graduate, or in thirty years when they reach our age and find themselves standing in the back of some other gymnasium, watching other children perform?

The road back to Lincoln from Cedar Bluffs passes by the same farmhouses, the same crops, the same ring of trees. Except now it's night, the weak moon clouded, the stars thick as Junebugs. On the prairie, the only constant is an ancient wind, and in its grasp my Volvo wagon rocks and drifts, rocks and drifts, as did another kind of wagon a century ago, as will some other kind of craft a century hence. In that future, this wind will still be here, as will these hills and all these stars. And I suspect someone will be driving then as well across these endless plains, if not on this road then another, though whether toward a local home or just passing through, this wind alone may guess.

11

SOME TROUBLE WITH DISCOURSES

What Conflicts between Subjects and Ethnographers Tell Us about What Students Don't/Won't/Can't Say

Sally Chandler

Embedded within Beth Roy's (1994) ethnography, *Some Trouble with Cows: Making Sense of Social Conflict,* is an exploration of methods for studying how individuals remember and reconstruct contested, emotionally charged events. Roy suggests that close attention to subjects' patterns for remembering and reporting can help ethnographers understand the discourses which individuals, groups, and cultures use to construct the "realities" they report. Roy's work is not unique in using what subjects say and do to theorize culture; what is unusual is that Roy does not focus on discovering what is verifiable or true in her subjects' accounts. Rather, she focuses on what and how they remember. Through analyzing the discourses which produced both the (unverified) accounts and the processes for recollection Roy is able to infer information about the unstated relationships, assumptions, values, and beliefs which drive the conflicts she is studying. This essay uses a version of Roy's method to theorize a conflict central to teaching composition: the often unconscious difficulties students encounter as they struggle to represent themselves in standard academic discourses.

Language researchers tell us that identities are generated through discourse; they also tell us that discourse is political and that when talk places us outside dominant discourses, we are judged as "wrong," "abnormal," or otherwise unacceptable. "Each Discourse protects itself by demanding from its adherents performances which act as though its ways of being, thinking, acting, talking, writing, reading, and valuing are right, natural, obvious, the way good and intelligent and normal people behave" (Gee 1996, 190–91). Taken together, these observations predict the landscape of difficulties encountered by students as they move from home discourses to standard academic discourses. Because writing is implicitly bound to conceptions of self, changing the way one writes generally challenges the self engendered by the discourse marked for "correction" (Smitherman 2000). As a result, even when speakers of "nontraditional" Englishes consciously contemplate what is gained and what is lost through the use of academic discourses, making the changes necessary to produce "good" writing can engender intense, internal conflicts (DiPardo 2001). These conflicts are highly personal and generally remain embedded in individual psychology and identity development (Herrington and Curtis 2000). At the same time, so long as these conflicts remain covert, they will be poorly understood, and student development as academic writers will be vexed by resistance and failure which may feel baffling both to students and to teachers.

Because psychological processes cannot be directly observed, the details of what, why, and how of students negotiate discourse change must be inferred. One approach to making accurate inferences about student processes would be to assume that individuals faced with structurally similar conflicts will respond in ways similar to students negotiating discourse change. If researchers select observable, interpersonal interactions with strong, rich parallels to the representational difficulties faced by students, the analysis of these overt processes could suggest—by analogy—patterns for students' internal, inarticulate processes.

In this essay I analyze conflicts associated with student moves from marginalized, home discourses to standard academic discourses through an analogy to patterns through which ethnographic subjects resist, evade, and appropriate the discourses ethnographers use to represent them. Specifically, I draw from work by Richard Handler (1993), Dona Davies (1993), and myself (2001) to provide a detailed account of how subjects challenge, revise, and evade representations set forward by ethnographers. Using methods suggested by Roy, I then develop an analysis of student reactions to being "taught" standard academic discourses. I conclude by considering how further study of ethnographic work, including reflective and methodological studies, might suggest possibilities for valuing and supporting student use of home discourses as they build a relationship to academic writing.

ETHNOGRAPHIC SUBJECTS, STUDENT WRITERS, AND CONFLICTS WITH DOMINANT DISCOURSES

A primary advantage to recasting students' *internal* conflicts in terms of conflicts between ethnographers and subjects is that, what in the case of students remains fused and inarticulate, bifurcates and becomes overt within the interpersonal, complexly articulated conflicts between ethnographers and their subjects. Even richly descriptive case studies of student confrontations with academic discourse rarely provide the details of students' internal processes. For example, Anne DiPardo (2001) offers the following description of reflections by Fannie, a student writer whose first language and culture is Navajo.

> Fannie pointed to the high drop-out rate among young Navajos as the primary reason for her people's poverty, and spoke often of the need to encourage students to finish high school and go on to college. And yet, worried as she was about the growing loss of native language and traditions, Fannie also expressed concerns about the Anglicizing effects of schooling. Education is essential, she explained, but young Navajos must also understand its dangers.
>
> "I mean like, sometimes if you get really educated, we don't really want that. Because then, it like ruins your mind and you use it, to like betray your people, too. . . . That's what's happening a lot now." (354)

DiPardo presents Fannie's misgivings from two separate perspectives, but even this rich description provides a limited window on the assumptions, strategies, and values which drive Fannie's conflict. In contrast, the conflicts between ethnographers and their subjects described in this essay are interpersonal, observable, extended, and—as in the case of Richard Handler's conflicts with the Quebecois nationalists he studies—articulated in writing.

Perhaps more important, the structure and nature of negotiations between subjects' resistance to ethnographers have strong parallels to student conflicts with the wish to remain aligned with home discourses and the conflicting wish to master academic writing. The positions of ethnographic subjects and students are parallel in that the power to analyze or evaluate the validity or worth of a discourse falls almost exclusively to the dominant discourse, and assessments of the authority or truth of a discourse is almost always constituted through the application of its own logic, values, and assumptions (Lemke 1995). Because of this, efforts by both ethnographic subjects and students to argue the truth of home discourses generally meet with either incomprehension or refutation.

Though these two conditions present compelling similarities, the two negotiations differ in that while ethnographic subjects may draw support from their home community when taking ethnographers to task, student writers are enlisted as the authors of their own (mis)representation. That is, to the extent to which they "want" to learn academic discourse, they "betray" their home discourse by (implicitly) joining in the academy's devaluing and rejection of the truths and values their home discourses engender. Discussion in the final section of this essay returns to this difference; the following sections use descriptions from three different case studies to develop parallel analyses of conflicts faced by ethnographic subjects and students.

FIELDWORK IN QUEBEC: SOME TROUBLES WITH DISCOURSES

In *Nationalism and the Politics of Culture in Quebec*, Handler (1988) deconstructs the "reality" of Quebecois nationalist cultural identities, ideologies, and practices by arguing that culture is not bounded and cannot be characterized by a fixed set of isolated features. He asserts that Quebecois nationalism, like all nationalistic ideologies, is in fact unbounded, multiple, and complex in form and expression. He points out that folk dances and other "pure" identifiers of Quebec culture are never separate from the larger cultural frames for performance. He characterizes nationalist rhetoric as embedded in naturalistic or biologistic metaphors which present the nation as a living entity and portray Quebec history in terms of life, death, survival, and pollution. His argument stresses that "such metaphors [are] metaphors, that is, a way of imagining social realities but not neutral statements of fact" (69).

Quebecois nationalists did not agree with Handler's analysis and protested his characterizations of their culture in various reviews and articles. In response to what he perceived as an unfair reaction to his book, Handler published an article in a collection of essays on how and why ethnographers and subjects confront and negotiate their different worldviews. In this essay, Handler states that reviews from ". . . French-language Quebec universities were uniformly negative," and he identifies the most striking feature of these reviews as their "uncritical recapitulation of the very ideology that the book deconstructed. . . [Reviewers] neither state [the book's] arguments in recognizable terms nor develop counterarguments . . ." and ". . . these reviews are not constructed as the rational consideration of ideas that is normal for the academic world" (69). Within the series of examples Handler provides, the Quebecois' argument does seem to offer an "uncritical recapitulation" of the ideology he deconstructs. At the same time, Handler's argument is only convincing if readers share Handler's investment in discourses for the "rational consideration of ideas that [are] normal for the academic world." In other words, Handler's critique of the Quebecois nationalist rebuttal of his argument is valid only if we assume the assumptions and values of academic discourse rather than those of the home discourse of Quebecois nationalists. Within the breakdown in communication between Handler and his subjects both "sides" remain invested in their home discourse, such that neither will (can?) interpret the arguments of the other as valid or reasonable.

For example, Handler offers Nicole Gagnon's (1989) review of his book as an illustration of writing that discredits his arguments without analyzing their errors. Handler writes,

> As Nicole Gagnon puts it, "[Handler's] analysis of nationalist thought is neither a description, nor an explication, nor a deconstruction, nor an interpretation: it is a false translation." Gagnon then quotes several passages from the book and summarily dismisses them without argumentation: "Is there any need to specify that these paralogisms . . . are the author's invention and that one would search in vain to find them in the discourse claimed to illustrate them?" (70)

While Handler dismisses Gagnon's argument because of its use of unexplicated paralogisms, *his* dismissal of these parallels as unexplicated seems to arise from the very "false translation" Gagnon cites as the book's failure. That is, Gagnon's examples (written in French but presented by Handler in English) invoke insider-knowledge which would allow the examples themselves to provide implicit analysis of what Handler has "mistranslated" (Gagnon 1989). Without knowledge of the argument implicit to the example, the reader cannot accurately comprehend Gagnon's point. What is more, because Handler believes it is not possible "to evaluate critically the values that one studies without legitimating one's critique by an appeal to scientific authority" (73) it seems unlikely he would find Gagnon's implicit argument made by analogy as persuasive. Rather, as suggested in his argument against the validity of Quebecois nationalists' self-representations, Handler seems to believe both that "neutral statements of fact" are possible and that such statements constitute a truth "more true" than what might be constituted metaphorically.

Within this particular discussion, ethnographic subjects face a dilemma. If they argue in terms of their home discourse, their arguments will not be valued or even heard. Then again, if they argue in terms of dominant discourse's rhetoric and form, their "truth" might still be denied since it would not concur with dominant discursive assumptions. It is as if, within this particular conflict, dominant discursive argument *forgets* that multiple (conflicting) perspectives containing diverse logics, assumptions, and truth values constitute not just cultural phenomena such as nationalism, but also the paradigms that would analyze and theorize those same phenomena. That is, it forgets that truth might be represented not only in different forms, but also that it might be conceptualized and theorized through different assumptions and paradigms of analysis.

Though discourse theorists almost unanimously assert that all languages are "equal" (Lemke 1995), in general, arguments to articulate these positions appear in forms replicating the explicit coherence, consistency, and linear logics used by Handler, rather than the indirect, allusive, metaphoric argument set forward by Gagnon. So, it seems that even though academic discourses endorse the validity of different patterns for creating meaning, the fact that scholarship is almost always written in dominant academic discourses gives a somewhat different message. In other words, the validating features of academic arguments—including this one—remain rooted in the standards for consistency, coherence, closure, and linear either/or logic which are used to deconstruct discourses which do not necessarily endorse or even value these standards.

This suggests yet another similarity between the representational conflicts faced by ethnographic subjects and student writers. In both instances, academic discourse perceives itself as able to describe and theorize the discourse of the Other, while at the same time remaining unable to comprehend the Others' descriptions of themselves. This situation reiterates the ongoing contradiction that while the academy ostensibly pledges to respect diverse voices within its community, in practice, standard academic discourses continue to privilege dominant (white, middle-class) discourse (Smitherman 2000).

One final and critically important parallel between the experiences of students and ethnographic subjects can be seen in how the power to author texts perpetuates both representational forms and discursive patterns which sanction those representations (Lemke 1995). By virtue of being the "author," the ethnographer—like the writing instructor—is empowered to select and edit not only the words of subjects, but also the conventions through which those words will be interpreted.

SUBJECTS' NEGOTIATION OF ETHNOGRAPHERS' REPRESENTATIONS

In "No Kinda Sense," Lisa Delpit (2002) describes how the academy's fundamental disdain for discourses other than its own contributes to student experiences speaking and writing in standard academic discourses. Upon observing her daughter, Maya's, seemingly effortless move from academic discourses taught at her former school (and spoken in her home) to the Ebonics of classmates in her new school, Delpit wonders how her daughter, a middle-class, African American child whose first language is a close relative of academic discourses, was able to acquire a second language in less than a semester while writing teachers struggle for years to teach students to write in standard academic English. She offers her answer in terms of Stephen Krashen's (1982) work on second-language acquisition. According to Delpit, Krashen found that the unconscious, "picking up" of a language in social settings was much more effective than rule-based instruction. He also found that, in some cases, individuals developed what he called affective filters which created effective mental blocks to learning. Delpit reports Krashen as stating that

> . . . the filter operates "when affective conditions are not optimal, when the student is not motivated, does not identify with the speakers of the second language, or is overanxious about his performance. . . ." (40)

In other words, unless learners identify with speakers of a second language (or discourse) and unless they expect that their representations will be heard—an affective filter will present obstacles to learning. This unconscious, affective response is both parallel to ethnographic subjects' response to ethnographers, and central to individual students' struggles with standard academic discourses. The following analyses of my work with an elder women's writing group and Dona Davies' work with residents of Grey Rock Harbour in Cape Breton illustrate the processes through which ethnographic subjects negotiate, resist, and appropriate ethnographers' representations of their lives.

To understand "writing group talk" it is necessary to understand both the context of my study and the ethos of writing groups. My research focused on a group of women who were both professional writers and my friends. I was a member of the group for several years before I asked them to consider being subjects for my dissertation research. They consented both out of a personal commitment to me, and out of a sense that writing about what they did at their group was important. Both these reasons reflect writing group ethos: an abiding commitment to supporting individual group members, and a firm belief in the importance of each participant's writing.

During the two years I collected data, attendance varied, but always a core membership of six women—Pam, Bonnie, Joan, Marty, Amy, and Beth—attended every meeting. Though only two of these participants belonged to the original group from 1975, all women except for me were over fifty, and several were in their eighties. All participants were either married or widowed, and all had adult children so that talk about family, particularly children, was an expected feature of every meeting.

Talk focused on our work: the conception, revision, and placement of various writing projects. At the same time, all conversation had deep roots in our personal lives, and was governed by the rules of connection, feeling, and indirection characteristic of women's private discourses (Hall and Buckholtz 1995; Tannen 1993). The first hour of every meeting was explicitly devoted to talk about family, personal crisis and triumphs, health, travel, work, and social events, and this talk generally set "themes" for our ensuing talk about writing. While it was impossible to determine whether writing brought for discussion colored the selection and interpretation of anecdotes raised in "pre-meeting" discussions—or the other way around—discussions of writing were always interspersed with personal anecdotes and reflective observations in resonance with the content and focus of introductory talk. Elizabeth Long's (1993) study of book groups notes similar patterns among talk and "work" in book group talk. According to Long, book group talk tends to use talk about books and the interpretation of books to generate "equipment for living" (199). That is, by focusing on plotlines and characters from books, discussants explore personal aspects of their lives and who they are becoming.

Almost all of the women's objections to my representations in the dissertation draft centered on the section on Ernest Gaines's novel, *A Lesson before Dying* (1994). Gaines's book focuses on racism in a rural community in Louisiana in the 1940s. Events are narrated by a school teacher, Grant Wiggins, who has returned to his home town and is torn between a wish to fight against the racism, poverty, and hopelessness of the community where he grew up, and a wish to leave it all behind. Conversations about Gaines' novel contained exactly the kinds of personal narratives and reflective analyses Long describes, and subject material bore a logical and emotional connection to material in surrounding conversations in ways which generated exactly the kind of "equipment for living" observed by Long. Immediately preceding the Gaines discussion, Pam told a story about an older friend with bipolar disorder (115–24). In this story, the friend's self-representation is not "heard" by the doctor until Pam intervenes. Talk surrounding this anecdote included two additional stories where older women were not listened to, including a story about an older woman who had her breast removed in unnecessary surgery. While stories about the mistreatment of mentally ill and older women are not generally accorded equal standing with stories of oppression connected to race, the women's talk suggests that the discussion of Gaines' novel provided a way for them to reflect on and rethink injustices in their own lives.

Marty introduced *A Lesson before Dying* by recounting the plot and commenting on the story's transformative power. After several somewhat less enthusiastic comments by other participants, Pam said that although—"looking at it simply from the writing style. . . I thought he (Gaines) did a successful job of getting me engaged, and me really being there, but [in the end] I didn't care" because "in the end it's the ubiquitous story of the poor . . . black victim who is being railroaded to death by a white, and the white red-necked sheriff, and I mean you know . . . that kind of bothers me because it's the same story" (121). In conversation that followed the women pointedly discussed how telling "the same story"—a story of racism and resistance where victims resist with dignity but nonetheless are put to death—presents a problem in that transformation is internal and personal, and therefore does not change power structures that perpetrate the injustice. Pam suggested, with some heat, that buying into such stories perpetuates exactly the kind of injustice the victims are portrayed as resisting.

What is noteworthy in this discussion is that these older, white, middle-class women, in the privacy of their writing group, ventured into a domain that dominant cultural discourses designate as outside of their authority. "Good, intelligent, and normal" speakers are not generally permitted to challenge or criticize insiders' stories of resistance with respect to experiences with racial injustice. There are conventions that allow "outsiders" —usually professionals such as social scientists, theologians, or language theorists—to offer alternative interpretations, but acceptable forms of speaking on behalf of a racial group almost always invoke some form of academic discourse for validation.

In this conversation, writing group women not only challenged wider cultural valuing of stories of inner-transformation and martyrdom, they did so in the language of *feeling*. Talk about the book was articulated almost exclusively in terms of personal responses; as Pam put it, the use of this same story "kind of bothers her." She sets up her critique by stating "I felt" and follows with a description of the text and an assessment of how that section of text functioned within the story. This pattern of using felt impressions as a basis for analysis is the women's most common analytic structure. While such talk is in keeping with women's talk in general and the ethos of their writing group in particular, it violates larger cultural conventions both for what the women are allowed to say *and* how logical arguments are supposed to be formulated.

To my surprise, objections to the representation of this conversation in my dissertation chapter did not dispute the accuracy of what was reported. Rather the women maintained that because this was a private conversation; they had said things they would not have said in quite the same way for a wider audience. They did not want the conversation to be interpreted as "offensive" or to reflect badly on the group. While, at least in my mind, certain remarks might best be interpreted as harsh or unsympathetic, the language the women wanted removed did not strike me as overtly racist. In many ways, the women's concern about how an outsider might understand what was said was a quintessential illustration of the group's ethos. Such a concern reflects writing groups' efforts to ensure comfort both for individual participants and for the group as a whole, and to value feeling in a way that sometimes overrode establishing the "truth."

Although I can characterize what the women wanted removed, I can't give examples because I promised not to attribute the deleted material to them in any way. Fortunately Dona Davies' essay on how her subjects responded to her book, *Blood and Nerves: An Ethnographic Focus on Menopause*, offers many illustrations of exactly the kind of objections raised by my subjects. Davies did her fieldwork in 1977. When Davies returned to the site ten years later she found residents had come to believe she wrote a "bad" book. Similar to me, she found her subjects distressed by not her interpretations or the accuracy of what she reported but by her alleged inclusion of particular words, phrases, and facts. For example, Davies related subject displeasure with a story, that

> . . . described how women had a great deal of power as individuals if their domestic domain was intruded upon. Grey Rock Harbour is a fishing village and in this story, there was a decision by village men to divert village water to a herring boat temporarily moored in the harbor that interfered with the women's after-dinner cleaning. One local woman, fed up with this, took an axe down to the pump and axed the connecting hose and threatened the men. Pointing with her axe to the cement base of the pump, she warned that they would all end up with their asses in cement if they ever tried to reconnect that hose at dinner time. (30–31)

Although when this story was told locally it always included the word "asses" as an important rhetorical element, when the main actor read the account, she was greatly put out and wanted it removed.

Writing group women also wanted me to change or delete particular words or phrases which they felt the larger culture might judge unfavorably. According to Davies, the Grey Rock Harbour women wanted words taken out that might cause them to be interpreted as "crude" or "ignorant" or "backward" (30). The conundrum here is that while conceding to discursive restrictions about the ways "good" women talk, neither group wished to revise *content* transgressing and extending cultural stories about what "good" women do. That is, while the heroine at the pump didn't want to be represented as using the ungenteel word "asses," she did not want to remove the story of her resistance. In the same vein, while writing group women did not want to be represented as talking bluntly or unsympathetically about characters or events in *Lessons before Dying*, they wished to let stand both their "felt" logic and their disesteem for stories conflating martyrdom and heroism.

So, in both cases, these different sets of ethnographic subjects resorted to strategic compliance with dominant discursive norms (regarding polite talk) in order to create stronger, more credible resistance. While this is certainly at least partially true of student negotiation of academic discourses, it does not explain conflicts described by Delpit—where students who learn Ebonics in a few months cannot learn standard academic English in twelve years. Rather, it implies that some part of the negotiation process, both for students and ethnographic subjects, is unconflicted, and the unconflicted part seems to be a wish to represent home discourse values in a way that will be received and valued by dominant discourse.

PATTERNS FOR RESISTING DOMINANT DISCOURSES

At the writing group, the standard practice was to review very long manuscripts by circulating a single copy; each participant offered written comments and within several weeks the manuscript would be returned. Because my dissertation was a very long manuscript, I circulated the draft beginning in September. Because of my teaching schedule, I had to stop attending in October and as a result I did not know that participants engaged in heated discussion of the Gaines chapter throughout fall and winter. I did not figure out that things had gone wrong until I received a call from Pam, in February. She told me that that the group "had problems" and suggested changes which the group had agreed upon. I was later told that the text circulated through about half the group, but then a particular reader held on to it and no one else read it. Because of this, discussion of "what should be changed" took place in a group where less than half the members had read the entire manuscript.

Before Pam's call, no one had spoken or written to me about what needed to be changed or why. During the conversation in February, Pam made clear that all women had "agreed" to the proposed changes, even though it was also true that every woman in the group had "compromised." The women felt strongly that everyone should feel comfortable with what was written about them *and* that I should have permission to use material which would produce a strong dissertation. Changes were negotiated without my input and directed by the values of caring (rather than values of justice) typical of both women's groups and writing groups. In many ways, the list of changes represented a radical "circling of the wagons" through which the women protected themselves from me (the academy's representative). Pam's mediated the final version and I did not speak with the group as a whole about the changes until after the dissertation was turned in. In the end, I was assured the group felt comfortable with the final version.

Contention over *Blood and Nerves* followed similar patterns. Even though Davies sent manuscripts and chapters to residents throughout composing and revising, and despite assurances that "we knew it was to be about menopause, and all you said was true, so who can complain?" many residents were unhappy (30). As with the writing group, discussion of what Davies wrote and why it needed changing was carried out in a group where many of the discussants had not read the manuscript. Also as at the writing group, individuals did not talk directly to Davies, rather, as Davies put it, they talked "behind my back." Rumors included that she had written that men of Grey Rock were good for nothing and the women were crazy. Davies explains this by observing that the year of her return was very bad for the inshore fishery and "most fishermen and all plant workers were living on unemployment." As a result, she suggested that ". . . [m]y book became a kind of mythological 'Rorschach' onto which all their worst contemporary fears about themselves were projected" (32).

These negotiations, along with the exchanges between Handler and his disgruntled subjects, suggest four generalizations about how:

- Subject resistance is generally articulated in home discourses rather than dominant discourses. That is, subject's state objections to "misrepresentations" in terms of the rhetoric, values, and assumptions of home discourses and in that way enact the very "faults" dominant discourses identify as discrediting their arguments.

- Ethnographic subjects are keenly aware that dominant discourses devalue their home discourses and wish to present themselves so as to receive favorable judgments; that is, they have an accurate understanding of dominant discursive values, and are willing to concede to revisions to "surface" features by revising particular words or phrases; at the same time, they do not want to change "deep" features associated with home discourse identities and values.
- When subjects feel pressed, they withdraw from conversation with ethnographers and dig deeper into the values, truths, and forms of home discourse and turn to their home community for support.
- Subjects (and ethnographers) sometimes project concerns about shortcomings, inconsistencies, and other problems within home discourse communities as judgments imposed upon them by some "outside" discourse.

While Delpit's central observation that " . . . [facility] acquiring an additional code comes from identifying with the people who speak it" (2002, 39) remains uncontestable, these four observations offer possibilities for articulating some specifics regarding *how* to help students connect to aspects of academic discourses which they may want to "own."

If parallels between students and ethnographic subjects are valid, the generalizations suggest that even as students enact standardized academic discourses' judgments and demands, they remain clearly identified with home discourse. At the same time, as stated in the introduction, students' position is different in that they have a double investment as participants in both academic and home discourses. This creates a skewed, double positioning where home discourse becomes an "interpreter" of academic discourses such that if student feelings about writing in academic discourses become "high stakes"—and practices for evaluation and grading often seem to guarantee that this will be the case—Krashen's "affective barriers" may well take the form of the tautological miscommunication between Handler and his subjects. That is, to the degree that students feel excluded or devalued, academic discourses will be perceived through and distorted by the particular metaphors, values, and logics of the home discourses.

This distortion complicates the second observation—which suggests that students have a general cultural understanding of the benefits and form of academic discourses, that they know it judges them as lacking, and that, as evidenced by their presence in the classroom, they are committed to learning it. Reflections by students like Fannie, who want to become educated without betraying their home communities, indicate that while students and ethnographic subjects both struggle to retain home discourse identities, students cannot comfortably position themselves within one discourse or the other. If we think about this difference in light of research into classroom negotiations of identity and difference, we can reinterpret the four generalizations about ethnographic subjects in ways which bear upon how teachers can best work with students to effect the unique, personal negotiations necessary to craft comfortable relationships between home and academic discourses.

RACE IDENTITY, DIFFERENCE, AND DISCOURSES IN THE CLASSROOM

In work on applying race identity theory in the classroom, Beverly Daniel Tatum (1992) observes that issues connected to race, class, and/ or gender often generate "powerful emotional responses in students" and if left unaddressed these responses can result in "student resistance to oppression-related content areas" that ". . . can ultimately interfere with understanding and mastery of the material" (1–2). Requiring students to articulate their ideas and identities in standard academic discourses implicitly injects issues of race, class, and gender into every assignment within the writing classroom. Tatum explains that if "affective and intellectual responses are acknowledged and addressed, [the] level of understanding is greatly enhanced." Educator activist Helen Fox (2001) states that race identity development can help educators place the struggles "both whites and people of color go through" within a predictable frame where the emotions and positions that arise with respect to difference become "in some sense 'normal'" (86).

In general, educators such as Tatum (1992) and Fox (2001) cite work by researchers of race identity development such as Janet Helms (1990) and W. E. Cross (1991) to assert that a positive sense of one's self as a member of one's group is important for psychological health (Phinney 1990). Helms defines race identity as "a sense of group or collective identity based on one's perception that he or she shares a common racial heritage with a particular racial group"; this identity includes shared belief systems, assumptions, and patterns of communication (9). These systems shape patterns in student writing. According to Helms and Cross, race identity development takes place in a series of stages, each of which can be characterized by particular patterns for defining self with relation to an identity group, as well as patterns for maintaining psychological comfort within that definition. In all models, individuals' progress from earlier to later stages takes place through recursive movement among intermediate stages.

Because of strong connections between race identity, home discourse, and patterns observed in student writing, much of what race identity researchers point out with respect to student negotiations of interpersonal issues within the classroom can be applied to student negotiations of standard academic discourses. In terms of race identity development, the "circling of the wagons," or forming close, exclusive bonds with one's identity group in order to define and explore self—observed when ethnographic subjects find themselves "misrepresented"—is characteristic of the Immersion/Emersion stage within Black race identity development (Cross 1991) and of the Contact and Reintegration stages in White identity development (Tatum 1992). For people of color, this stage ". . . is characterized by the simultaneous desire to surround oneself with visible symbols of one's racial identity and an active avoidance of symbols of Whiteness" (11). For whites, Fox notes that "[s]ometimes whites in this stage feel they have 'tried and failed' to reach out across the racial divide. . . and will need encouragement and help to move beyond [Reintegration]" (91). Both educators emphasize that students need role models to move on to a place where they can embrace a "multicultural, multiracial America" (92).

Integrating this work with the generalizations about ethnographic subjects' relationships to home discourses suggests that understanding race identity theory and knowing where individual students are with respect to identity development will be crucial for instructors to respond appropriately to students' "affective responses" to learning standardized academic discourses. What is more, subject/student distortions of dominant discourses suggest that for effective communication ethnographers/instructors will need to "hear" and respect subject/student perspectives in terms of home—not academic—discourses.

With these general observations in mind, we can formulate specific classroom practices. For example, the observation that effective communication within both Davies' work and my own was generally achieved through a spokesperson from a home community suggests that instructors might work with student writers of nonacademic discourses through combinations of group work and mediated talk. Groups should be composed of individuals with shared home discourses so that spokespersons (who may be in a more "advanced" stage with respect to acceptance of nonhome discourses) can negotiate "corrections" to student writing both with the instructor, the home discourse group, and student authors. Such a strategy would empower individual student authors through aligning them with a group and by ensuring that their work will be represented by a speaker who understands both the home and academic discourses. Such representation would ensure that "translation" of student ideas and forms could be explained to speakers of both discourses. Such a process could help instructors understand home discourses rather than simply "correcting" them.

FURTHER POSSIBILITIES

Because this essay primarily focuses on developing a theoretical model for student conflicts, it does not even begin to explore pedagogical practices which might derive from further study of ethnographic theory and practice. I have focused on a particular problem within ethnographic study as it applies to a single pedagogical problem. As a result, this essay cannot claim to fully explore all that ethnography might tell us about student struggles to master standard academic discourses. At the same time, compositionists who explore theoretical ethnographic works or even particular ethnographies will find rich, useful overlap between ethnographic study and the complexities of teaching writing.

For example, both Michel de Certeau's classic *The Practice of Everyday Life* (1984) and Kathleen Stewart's *A Space on the Side of the Road: Cultural Poetics in an "Other" America* (1996) describe how subjects live within both home and dominant discourses. These works shed light both on what students already do with their writing and on what they might be encouraged to do more of as they negotiate their double commitment to academic and home discourses. Certeau's discussion of the routine subversions of dominant cultural forms within everyday life suggests multiple models for students to own home identities within standard academic discourses; and Stewart's appropriation of the liars' tale, a form for exchanging information and signaling group membership, is a specific example of how home discourse can retain its identity and power within academic writing. Embedded within these and other ethnographic works are strategies which, to paraphrase Fannie, students can use to become educated without betraying their home communities. Creative reflection on issues common to ethnographic and composition research can invigorate both disciplines.

12

COMPOSING (IDENTITY) IN A POSTTRAUMATIC AGE

Lynn Worsham

The philosophy one has does not depend solely on the kind of person one is. It depends more essentially on the time in which one lives and, above all, the way in which one belongs to the time.

—Ernst Bloch[1]

The events of September 11, 2001 and its aftermath would seem to provide all the corroboration necessary to substantiate the claim that this is a "posttraumatic culture"—the idea, in other words, that the twenty-first century has begun the way the twentieth century ended: as an especially catastrophic age characterized by unprecedented historical trauma that has produced a pervasive and generalized mood corresponding to posttraumatic stress disorder.[2] To claim that we are living in a posttraumatic age does not mean, of course, that everyone is equally traumatized or suffers in quite the same way. This diagnosis of our social psychology calls attention to a collective sense of profound historical shock, to a sense that we live out our individual lives, more or less consciously, in the overwhelming shadow cast by the unspeakable atrocities of war, genocide, mass murder, and terrorism.[3] Identifying what he calls "a new form of historical reality," Hayden White (1992) points to "a profound sense of the incapacity of our sciences to *explain*, let alone control or contain" the events that constitute our epoch, and "a growing awareness of the incapacity of our traditional modes of representation to *describe* them adequately" (52). White's examples include "the phenomena of Hitlerism, the Final Solution, total war, nuclear contamination, mass starvation, and ecological suicide." I would also include the daily agonies caused by imperialism, racism, sexism, poverty, and crime that have been endured by generations of a vast number of the world's population. This history implicates us all. Indeed, as Cathy Caruth (1996) argues, "History, like trauma, is never simply one's own"; history is "precisely the way in which we are implicated in each other's traumas" (24). In a post-9/11 world, in a world that seems more than ever to spin threateningly out of control, our every effort to wrest meaning from senselessness only serves to bring the specter of social death, if not our own literal death, too frighteningly near (see Farrell 1998, 2, 15).

In this catastrophic age, the concept of trauma offers a diagnosis for both an individual and a social reality. Yet, trauma is also a trope, as Kirby Farrell (1992) argues, similar to the Renaissance figure of the world-as-stage. In his view, trauma serves as an enabling fiction and an explanatory tool for "managing unquiet minds in an overwhelming world" (7). In a catastrophic age, the focus on trauma has become, in other words, a "radical form of terror management." To be sure, the concept of trauma may have explanatory power precisely because we increasingly feel, or are prepared to feel, traumatized and wounded. Representations of trauma in postmodern art, popular culture, and the news media contribute to creating what Mark Seltzer (1997) calls a "wound culture"—a culture that is preoccupied with (if not addicted to) suffering, woundedness, and trauma, preoccupied with its own suffering and sense of injury (both physical and psychic). In this context, the term *trauma* applies not only to those who *directly* suffer traumatic events but also to those who suffer *with* victims of trauma, or *through* them, or *for* them and thus live their lives as survivors of a traumatic history that *is* and *is not* their own (see Laub 1992, 57–58). In a wound culture, life is lived not as life but as survival. This culture, Seltzer reminds us, is in a very real sense both deeply traumatized *and* profoundly pathological. It is therefore in immediate need of the curative promise of both political critique and psychiatric intervention (3–5).

In this broad sense, trauma arguably forms the most fundamental rhetorical situation in which we operate as scholars and teachers of composition. I employ the term *composition* here in the familiar sense to designate the field of inquiry into writing, literacy, and discourse as well as to the product and process of writing. In this disciplinary sense, one that is more or less consciously aware of the time to which composition belongs, we may be increasingly drawn to an examination of the relationship between writing and healing; we may be increasingly drawn to pedagogies of self-disclosure and personal narrative for the curative power that they claim to bestow. I argue, however, that pedagogies of disclosure (and the concepts of identity, experience, and narrative that inform them) may serve less effectively as tools for gaining access to and integrating the unspeakable truth of traumatized subjects than as strategies of managing our own terror in an overwhelming world—or, if not terror, exactly, then a kind of free-floating anxiety that cannot be easily traced to a particular source or cause, whether personal or public.[4]

As I will suggest, the concept of trauma cannot be easily factored into existing epistemological and pedagogical projects in composition studies, for trauma presents a fundamental challenge—indeed, I would say a *fatal* challenge, as it were—to some of the field's most cherished concepts, concepts that continue to inform what is taken for granted as the common sense of composition. In fact, I would go so far as to say that the concept of trauma itself *traumatizes* concepts that authorize epistemological and pedagogical work in the field—in particular, concepts of identity, experience, and narrative.[5] The concept of trauma displaces these concepts and in so doing displaces us from a conceptual terrain that many compositionists might want to call "home." What's more, traumatic history represents a fundamental challenge to the very project of epistemology and historiography, for, as many trauma theorists routinely observe, we have no concept of knowledge or history that is adequate to understanding and representing the events that constitute our epoch (see Caruth 1996; White 1992; Bernard-Donals and Glejzer 2003). This situation implicates us not only as scholars and teachers of writing but also as subjects of our time: as subjects *in* and *of* trauma.

For this reason, I also want to employ *composition* in the broadest possible sense to designate the primary task or project of human existence. Here, *composition* refers to the effort to compose a life, a sense of identity, place, and purpose—in other words, the effort to wrest meaning from senselessness. As Toni Morrison (1998) puts it, "We die. That may be the meaning of life. But we *do* language. That may be the measure of our lives" (22). How we "do language"—or what Morrison calls "word-work"—is what individualizes each of us; it is the groundless ground of identity and the very principle of individuation. For each of us, word-work will give us all we will ever know of substance, identity, boundary, location, relation, and purpose. And word-work will serve as the measure by which each individual life will be judged and the agency through which we will belong to our time. In this context, I ask you to consider what language, word-work, can *do* in a catastrophic age—what it means to compose identity, community, and culture if our history is to be understood as the history of massive trauma. This history implicates each and every one of us, not first of all as scholars and teachers of writing, but as subjects *in* and *of* trauma.

TRAUMA: EVENT, EXPERIENCE, IDENTITY

In the original Greek, *trauma* referred to a wound or injury inflicted on the body. In much of the medical and psychiatric literature of the late nineteenth and twentieth centuries, trauma is understood as a wound that may be inflicted on the body, but the greater injury occurs to the mind. In contrast to physical and psychological trauma, which focuses on a devastating wound to an individual, *cultural trauma* refers, as Ron Eyerman (2001) explains, to an overwhelming wound to identity and meaning, a sundering of the social fabric, that affects a group of people that has achieved some sense of identity and cohesion as a group (2–5; see also Sztompka 2000, 449). Cultural trauma does not necessarily affect or afflict everyone in a community in quite the same way; nor is it necessarily experienced directly by any or all. In a catastrophic age, the "experience" of cultural trauma is highly mediated through news agencies and popular culture; thus, it has undergone, Eyerman explains, a process of selective construction and (re)presentation by professionals who have made at least some rudimentary decisions about how the traumatic event should be (re)presented. Cultural trauma, therefore, always involves what Jeffrey Alexander calls a "trauma process" that itself involves a crisis of individual and collective identity and, in his words, a "meaning struggle" over, for example, the nature of the wound, the identity of the victims, the attribution of responsibility, and the way in which these elements will be narrativized (qtd. in Eyerman 2001, 3). (For example, since September 11, 2001, the Bush administration arguably has been quite adept at managing the trauma process so as to shore up a narrative of nation and nationalistic identity and thereby to place us right where it wanted the United States before 9/11: in a second war with Iraq.) I want to focus briefly on some of the common elements of individual and cultural trauma, foregrounding those that are most consequential for composition, construed in both its narrow (disciplinary) and broad (cultural) senses.

In its most general and contemporary definition, *trauma* refers to an overwhelming, catastrophic event, one that occurs too unexpectedly to be consciously assimilated and known. Trauma is not "locatable," as Caruth (1996) puts it, "in an individual's past, but rather in the way that its very unassimilated nature—the way it was precisely *not known* [and experienced] in the first instance—returns to haunt the survivor later on" (4). A traumatic event is one that, in its unexpectedness and horror, overwhelms every resource that the individual or community has to understand and make sense of the event, leaving one or both feeling utterly helpless in the face of a force that is perceived to be psychically, if not also physically, life-threatening. Trauma overwhelms existing schemes of knowledge and interpretation, leaving the individual or community without the means to make the event intelligible, control-lable, and communicable. Thus, the traumatic event cannot be assimi-lated or experienced fully at the time of its occurrence, but only belat-edly, in its repeated possession of the one who has been overwhelmed by trauma (see Caruth, 1995). Holocaust survivor and psychoanalyst Dori Laub (1992) explains,

> The traumatic event, although real, took place outside the parameters of "normal" reality, such as causality, sequence, place and time. The trauma is thus an event that has no beginning, no ending, no before, no during and no after. This absence of categories that define it lends it a quality of "otherness," a salience, a timelessness and a ubiquity that puts it outside the range of associatively linked experiences, outside the range of com-prehension, of recounting and of mastery. Trauma survivors live not with memories of the past, but with an event that could not and did not pro-ceed through to its completion, has no ending, attained no closure, and therefore, as far as its survivors are concerned, continues into the present and is current in every respect. (69)

To be traumatized, then, is paradoxically to be possessed by an event that one cannot take possession of through existing frames of intelligi-bility, such as narrative. To be traumatized is to be possessed by a past experience that was never fully experienced as it occurred. To be trau-matized is to be claimed by an experience that cannot be fully claimed and subjectivized.

The immediate response to a traumatic event may include terror, loss of control, and an overwhelming fear of annihilation. Long-term residu-al effects may include any of the symptoms associated with posttraumatic stress disorder: panic, a heightened startle response, sleep disorders, depression, numbing, an inability to concentrate, dissociation, chronic dread, and death anxiety (see Herman 1992; Farrell 1998, 11–12; Brison 2002, 39–40). Although the definition of posttraumatic stress disorder continues to be debated, most descriptions of it focus on the disorder as a delayed response to an overwhelming event, a response that takes the form of repeated, intrusive thoughts, emotions, behaviors, or dreams that stem from the event. As Judith Herman (1992) explains, trauma so overwhelms and disorganizes the individual's system of self-defense that each component of "the ordinary response to danger, having lost its utility, tends to persist in an altered and exaggerated state long after the actual danger is over."

Traumatic events produce profound and lasting changes in physiological arousal, emotion, cognition, and memory. Moreover, traumatic events may sever these normally integrated functions from one another. The traumatized person may experience intense emotion but without clear memory of the event, or may remember everything in detail without emotion. . . . Traumatic symptoms have a tendency to become disconnected from their source and take on a life of their own. (34)

In his own effort to explain psychic responses to trauma, Freud suggested that there is a protective shield or psychic skin that, under normal conditions, regulates the flow of stimuli and information, a skin that maintains bodily and psychic integrity (1961, 29–30). This protective skin is overwhelmed and even shattered by traumatic events. While there is undoubtedly a neurological component involved in forming and maintaining this psychic skin, Eric Santner argues that it is primarily composed of symbolic materials that function as a boundary between "inside" and "outside" and that serve as a rudimentary interpretive filter for incoming information. This protective "skin" is primarily *textual*, Santner (1992) argues; it is a "culturally constructed and maintained organization"—in other words, a composition of sorts—that provides the ground for constructing individual and collective identity (152). It is the text and texture of expectations and associations that make up the parameters of the "normal"; it is a composition of associations, images, expectations, dispositions, and knowledge that forms one's sense of trust in others and in the world. In short, it is ideological through and through.

In the wake of trauma, not only identity but this psychic skin must be constructed entirely anew and in the context of posttraumatic suffering. In *Aftermath: Violence and the Remaking of a Self*, feminist philosopher Susan Brison (2002) recounts her own experience of rape and attempted murder. She explains that the person she was before the incident was annihilated one sunny morning in France. As she puts it, she has "outlived" herself. Trauma, she observes, "unravels whatever meaning we've found and woven ourselves into"; it cancels every effort to stitch the "before" and "after" together into one coherent identity, into one coherent narrative (58). For Brison, survival confronts her with the impossible task of mourning a life—her own life—that has been annihilated by trauma; recovery requires that she undertake the impossibly difficult and consuming work of constructing another sense of boundary, identity, relation, and location, one that somehow weaves the traumatic event into the fabric of a new existence.

What's more, the traumatic event, at its most extreme, fixes the individual in what Caruth (1996) calls the oscillation of a double crisis: between the crisis of death and the crisis of survival, between the unbearable nature of the event and the unbearable nature of its survival. Caruth asks, "Is the trauma the encounter with death, or the ongoing experience of having survived it?" (7). She explains, "for those who undergo trauma, it is not only the moment of the event, but of the passing out of it that is traumatic; . . . *survival itself*, in other words, *can be a crisis*" (1995, 9). Holocaust survivor and poet Charlotte Delbo figures this paradoxical in-between state in these words: "I died in Auschwitz, but no one knows it" (qtd. in Brison 2002, 37). About her life after Auschwitz, Delbo writes, "life was returned to me / and I am here in front of life / as though facing a dress / I cannot wear" (47). Caught between the crisis of death and the crisis of survival, the subject in and of trauma is inextricably tied to what cannot be fully experienced, narrated, or subjectivized and thus takes up the task of existence as an "unfinished becoming," as a radicalized process of composing that which finally cannot be composed. The subject in and of trauma is, as Petar Ramadanovic (1998) argues, "culturally and politically a diasporic subject, *en route* toward subjectivity" (55).[6]

TRAUMA: RHETORIC, NARRATIVE, MOURNING

While trauma arguably forms, in some fundamental sense, the rhetorical situation in which we find ourselves today, there may be nothing more apparently arhetorical or antirhetorical than the phenomenon of trauma, for it designates an expressive limit: the unspeakable event; the event that cannot be fully claimed and experienced; the experience that cannot, will not be put into words or woven into an existing narrative; the event that cannot, will not be communicated to another; the event that language can *do nothing* with. Writing about his own experience of the Jewish Holocaust, Primo Levi (1985) remarks, "Our language lacks words to express this offense, the demolition of a man" (9). Yet, trauma is preeminently rhetorical. It places the one it claims in a paradoxical situation: on the one hand, the traumatized subject is left in profound silence without the motivation or resources to construct a narrative; on the other, the traumatized subject is left with an overwhelming need to "tell what seems untellable" and to tell it to someone who is able to listen and *hear* (Culbertson 1995, 170; see also Brison 2002, 50). "There is, in each survivor," Laub (1992) explains, "an imperative need to *tell* and thus to come to *know* one's story, unimpeded by ghosts from the past against which one has to protect oneself. . . . Yet no amount of telling seems ever to do justice to this inner compulsion. There are never enough words or the right words, there is never enough time or the right time, and never enough listening or the right listening to articulate the story that cannot be fully captured in *thought, memory* and *speech*" (78).

Perhaps this pure rhetoricity—the occasion defined by the imperative to express and represent that which eludes expression and representation—is what attracts, and will attract, those who, especially at this moment in our history, want to articulate a close relation between writing and healing; those who quite rightly want to proceed with the confidence that their pedagogy arises from and addresses the rhetorical situation of our time. Perhaps this desire, in retrospect, accounts for the enduring attraction in the discipline of composition studies to pedagogies of self-disclosure and personal narrative. Yet, the text of trauma cannot speak through the very concepts of experience, identity, and narrative that inform most of these pedagogies. Specifically, I mean a concept of experience (or "lived experience") as the "ground" of and authority for knowledge; a concept of identity that, however much it may gesture toward social constructionism, postmodernism, or Bakhtinian dialogism, nonetheless remains resolutely tied to liberal humanist notions of self, agency, and authentic self-expression; and a concept of narrative that is invested with the authority and appeal of "the personal" and "personal voice" as the ultimate and original frame of intelligibility. In the discipline of composition, these concepts form what I will call, following Freud, a protective shield, as it were, that undoubtedly constitutes and preserves a limited disciplinary vitality (and identity) but at great cost to the vitality of composition, understood here in its broadest possible sense. That is to say, this conceptual shield provides the very terms through which we misrecognize—and, more seriously, disavow—the crucial work that words must do in a catastrophic age.

That work is the work of mourning, which is one of two responses to trauma that Freud explores. The other is narrative fetishism.[7] The distinction between these two modes of symbolic behavior—mourning and narrative fetishism—complicates the relation between narrative and healing in ways that are critically important for the project of composition. Let me explain.

Narrative fetishism refers to the construction of a narrative that is consciously or unconsciously designed to purge the traces of the trauma that calls the narrative into being in the first place. Freud contrasts the use of narrative as fetish to what he calls the work of mourning—or, that arduous process of "working through," of elaborating and integrating the reality of the traumatic event into consciousness. Narrative fetishism, in contrast, results from an inability or, more likely, a refusal to mourn that protects the psyche by emplotting trauma in a way that disavows the very need for mourning. In particular, narrative fetishism substitutes for the painful work of mourning the *pleasure* of narrative, the pleasure that this genre provides through its power to compose—and, indeed, impose—a sense of order, sequence, causality, coherence, and completion. This power allows us to imagine we have mastered an event that has occurred entirely outside the parameters of narrative meaning. When narrative becomes fetishized, narrative offers a way of avoiding the residue of traumatic events, and the emphasis shifts to the economy of pleasure that narrative provides. Once fetishized, narrative serves as a symbolic strategy for undoing the need for mourning by simulating a condition of wholeness, often by locating the site or origin of trauma elsewhere (see Santner 1992, 144). (Here, it is helpful to keep in mind that one can acknowledge that a traumatic event happened and yet, through dissociation, disavow the traumatic impact of that event.) Narrative fetishism offers a way of "managing" trauma that does not demand—indeed, that disavows the need for—the kind of "working through" that true mourning entails. Narrative, in this case, does not lead to recovery or healing. Quite the contrary, it releases one from the burden, as Santner suggests, of having "to reconstitute one's self-identity under 'posttraumatic' conditions" (144).

Mourning also involves the construction of a narrative—actually, the reconstruction of a history, and, in Dori Laub's (1992) words, the "re-externalizing of the event": "This re-externalization of the event can occur and take effect only when one can articulate and *transmit* the story, literally transfer it to another outside oneself and then take it back again, inside" (69). Mourning involves an effort to integrate a traumatic event that so overwhelmed the individual or social psyche that it could not be integrated as it occurred. Most importantly, the story that is transmitted to another in the work of mourning bears witness not to the *meaning* of the event but to *the truth of the event*—the fact that it actually happened—and to *the truth of its incomprehensibility*, to the impossibility of constructing a comprehensible story and an adequate representation of the event (see Caruth, 1995, 153–55; Bernard-Donals and Glejzer 2003, 13). The truth of trauma, in other words, is that it transports us to the very limit of signification and understanding, to a woundedness that defies all healing" (Laub 1992, 73). Let me offer an example that may clarify the distinction between these uses of narrative.

Toni Morrison's *Beloved* is arguably a work *of* mourning and a narrative that opens up the space *for* mourning by confronting readers with the truth of an unspeakable event *and* the truth of its incomprehensibility—as Barbara Christian (1997) puts it, the unspeakable truth of "the four-hundred-year holocaust that wrenched tens of millions of Africans from their Mother, their biological mothers as well as their Motherland, in a disorganized and unimaginably monstrous fashion" (364). *Beloved* was published at a time (1987) when this unspeakable event had, as Christian argues, "practically disappeared from American cultural memory for reasons having as much to do with the inability on the part of America to acknowledge that it is capable of having generated such a holocaust, as well as with the horror that such a memory calls up for African Americans themselves" (364). While Christian does not frame her comments in terms of the distinction between mourning and narrative fetishism, her argument suggestively points to the fact that throughout its history this nation has engaged in countless acts of narration—to be found in official histories as well as in art, popular culture, and politics—that have worked together to ensure the collective disavowal and forgetting of the individual and cultural trauma of American slavery and the Middle Passage. *Beloved* together with other contemporary neo-slave narratives represent efforts to disrupt this field of discourse by proposing what is needed at this time: a "fixing ceremony"—that is, a ceremony arising from African cosmology that serves as "an act of remembrance that initiates the healing of a psychic wound that was originally inflicted by an individual and collective act of forgetting" (Christian). *Beloved* explicitly stages just such a ceremony, not only for Sethe but potentially for every reader who is willing to undertake this work (*Beloved* 101). The novel confronts readers with the fact that the work of individual and collective mourning of the Middle Passage and American slavery has yet to begin, that history is precisely the way that Americans, regardless of racial heritage, remain implicated in the history of this trauma, that we are indeed subjects *in* and *of* trauma. The novel ultimately poses a question as simple as it is consequential: How will we belong to this time?

The distinction between mourning and narrative fetishism compels us to grapple with the proposition that there is no natural or intrinsic relation between narrative and healing, even though much of the literature in composition studies on personal narrative too often suggests otherwise.[8] Let me mention just a couple of examples.[9] In *Teaching Lives*, published almost a decade ago, Wendy Bishop (1997) examines the therapeutic promise of expressive writing and personal narrative, recommending that we investigate the "personal," "therapeutic," and "affective" aspects of our field—as if these terms ("the personal," "the therapeutic," and "the affective") were coextensive with one another (143). She writes, "The analogies between writing instruction and therapy have something to offer me and something I need to offer to the teachers I train." In their introduction to *Writing and Healing: Toward an Informed Practice*, Charles Anderson and Marian MacCurdy (2000) seek to deepen and solidify the correlation between writing and healing. They place trauma at the center of their own pedagogy and urge us to do likewise, arguing that writing about trauma "transforms stories that have never been told into texts that bear witness to lived experience; [that writing about trauma] opens confusion and pain to the possibilities of wholeness" (16). Not only do their remarks suggest the fantasy of wholeness that characterizes narrative fetishism, their remarks also suggest that traumatic experience presents itself in narrative form, that "bearing witness" is a relatively simple matter of telling that story publicly (see also MacCurdy 2000). They also suggest that listening to the text of trauma requires no more skill than the empathy the "average" college student or teacher may be presumed to possess.[10]

Yet, if we understand composition in the broadest possible sense, we must confront a few difficult questions: How can teachers of writing know that a personal narrative about traumatic experience fosters the work of mourning rather than substituting for this important word-work the pleasure of storytelling? Are we certain that in inviting students to construct narratives of their own traumatic experience we are not merely inviting them to fetishize narrative—thereby exacerbating their woundedness—rather than truly mourning their losses? Are we certain that we should ask or encourage our students to undertake the work of mourning in required writing courses? Is the temporal structure of the pedagogical encounter (the class meeting, the conference, the typical semester-long course) sufficiently open and enduring to make such word-work even possible? Are writing instructors sufficiently trained to be "therapeutic" listeners who are able to truly bear witness to traumatic experience, and do we have sufficient time, patience, energy, and expertise to train students to listen and bear witness to each other in appropriate and productive ways? Is our disciplinary investment in personal narrative "innocent"; or is that investment a product of a wound culture that would have us (students and instructors alike) narcissistically pre-occupied with and distracted by our own individual injuries rather than engaged in questioning the many ways in which we are already consti-tuted as subjects in and of trauma in a catastrophic age?

As scholars and teachers of composition (in both the broad and narrow senses that I have given that term), we have an obligation to make ourselves and our students aware of our situatedness within a posttraumatic culture. As scholars and teachers, we must become aware of how we are positioned within a wound culture, and we must adopt as a professional ethic, "First, do no (further) harm." In other words, we must be careful not to do more harm than good by encouraging students to reinvest uncritically in an economy of narrative pleasure, an economy that is indisputably one of the central forces at work in a cul-ture dominated by the military-entertainment complex. This economy ensures that the everyday realities of racism, sexism, and economic disenfranchisement—what I might call the "macropolitics" of traumatic experience—go unrecognized for what they are. "Narrative is one of the principal ways we absorb knowledge," as Morrison (1998) observes, and it is "radical, creating us at the very moment it is being created (7, 27). Yet, what kind of knowledge is created and absorbed through a narrative that disavows the work of mourning and substitutes for it the pleasure of the text? What kind of subject? This question, and its answer, returns us to the question motivating my remarks: How will we belong to our time?

13

CONCLUSION
Working Bodies: Class Matters in College Composition

Min-Zhan Lu

This is a partial reading of the collection, so let me start with an account
of the how-why-what of the questions framing my response. Summer of
2005. I'm putting together a graduate course titled "Class Matters: The
Information Age," a project aimed at examining composition scholarship on the relations between matters of class, writing, and teaching
from the perspective of social-economic-geopolitical-technological shifts
in the United States in the last three decades. I'm working on a talk for
the 5th Biennial International Feminism(s) and Rhetoric(s) Conference
with the hope of approaching the conference theme, "Affirming
Diversity," from positionalities which are co-constitutive of but yet often
obscured by my lived experiences as the bearer of various visible markers of my identity, such as my aging body, foreign accent, skin color,
facial features, wedding ring. The June issue of *CCC* arrives in the mail.
In its "Summary and Critique" section, I encounter Richard Fulkerson's
(2005) survey of "Composition at the Turn of the Twenty-first Century."
Fulkerson groups "feminist composition," "critical pedagogy," and
"cultural studies" under the rubric of "social theories" for their shared
"focus on having students read about systemic cultural injustices" and
"the empowering possibility of rhetoric," on educating students "to
'read' carefully and 'resist' the social texts that help keep some groups
subordinated" (659). He maintains that the aim of composition courses
taking the "social theories" turn "is not 'improved writing' but 'lib-
eration' from dominant discourse" (660). And he portrays the turn to
"social theories" as "inappropriate" for college composition along three
lines, including his concern that such courses will not leave room for
any actual teaching of writing and are likely to turn into "leftist political indoctrination" while "showing open contempt for their students'
values" (665). The "survey" turns up the volume of the voice of an Arch-
"Angel in My House of Composition" with which I see myself, along with
all the writers whose work appears in this collection and all its potential
readers, as having to wrestle continuously (Lu, "Essay").

Angel: *Essay after essay argues that the nation's college first-year students show unprecedented levels of academic and political disengagement (Durst, Smith). Three-quarters of the students surveyed planned to major in pre-professional fields and list "being very well off financially" as an essential goal. Students are not interested in social-political analysis of identity-difference. They aspire to become professionals rather than academics or social activists. Composition needs to focus on the teaching of writing that matters to the students—writing matters that can help them achieve their financial security and career success.*

Reply: *I too, want to take seriously students' expressed interest in financial and career success. I too, see student writing as the focus of college composition. But Identity Papers reminds me of the necessity to ask: How are we defining writing? What happens to individual students, their writing, careers, and lives when efforts to learn writing in a discourse—academic or professional—are treated as separate and separable from how they shape their past, present, and future relations with peoples whose discursive practices are marked "nonacademic" or "unprofessional" in college classrooms?*

In "Composing (Identity) in a Post Traumatic Age," Lynn Worsham urges us to define composition as "efforts to compose a life, a sense of identity, place, and purpose"—"to wrest meaning from senselessness" (171). Worsham thus marks "familiar" concerns of composition such as "the field of inquiry into writing, literacy, and discourse as well as to the product and process of writing" (171), as inseparable from the "broader" concerns of how "word-work will give us all we will ever know of substance, identity, boundary, location, relation, and purpose" (172). These questions define writing and learning as bodily work conducted by, through, and on material bodies, *Bodies that Matter*, as Judith Butler puts it in the title of her 1993 book. I read Worsham to join critics such as Judith Butler, Janice Haraway, and David Harvey in defining the material body (self, identity or subjectivity) of individual teachers and students as relational and in process as "unfinished projects" shaped by and shaping "a spatiotemporal flux" of processes—metabolic, ecological, political, social, psychological, cultural, economical (Harvey 1998, 402–4, 413). Different social processes, including processes of learning and writing, "produce" radically different kinds of bodies on both the epistemological and ontological levels. "Class, racial, gender and all manners of other distinctions are marked upon the human body by virtue of the different socio-ecological processes that do their work upon that body" (Harvey "Body" 403). At the same time, the human body is active and transformative in relation to the processes that produce, sustain, and dissolve it.

Worsham puts "writing" and the "teaching of writing" in the context of a "catastrophic age characterized by unprecedented historical trauma" (170): a time and place where "the text and texture of expectations and associations that make up the parameters of the 'normal'" (175) are shattered, life is lived as "survival." I interpret her use of the term "survival" as referring in part to the intensive labor individual writers put into the survival, termination, or transformation of all the relationships critical to materializing of their body and life as they learn to enact a process of writing to produce the kind of writing products deemed acceptable in college classrooms. I note the same insistence on the materiality of writing and learning permeating the other articles: a concerted effort to treat common notions of what constitutes "academic" or "professional" ways of writing, thinking, learning, or succeeding as material forces constraining how students go about working their bodies, including their sense of identity and their relations with others and the world.

In an article titled "The Body as an Accumulation Strategy," Harvey (1998) re-reads Marx's account of "how the laws of motion of capital impinge upon differentially positioned bodies and so transform their internalized subjectivities." He does so by broadening the focus of the "conventional Marxian definition of class" (which fixates attention solely on individual workers' positionality in relation to property rights over the means of production) to examining "positionality in relation to capital circulation and accumulation" (405). Using the Marxian distinction between "the laborer (qua person, body, will), and labor power (that which is extracted from the body of the laborer as a commodity)," and the notion of "variable capital" (the sale or purchase and use of labor power), Harvey poses the question of what happens to the bodies (persons and subjectivities) of the individual persons at different moments of the circulation of variable capital: the process in which individual workers sell labor power (a commodity extracted from the body of the worker) "to use in the labor process in return for a money wage which permits [them] to purchase capitalist-produced commodities in order to live in order to return to work. . . " (405). Read from the perspective of the circulation of variable capital, most of the accounts of the educational experiences of composition teachers and/or students we encounter in this collection seem to touch on the ways in which the work of composition participates in the circulation of variable capital: constraining how individual teachers and students push the limits of one's body, its capacities, and possibilities (407) in the process of extracting from it (or, producing out of it) a specific commodity—labor power: a set of "academic or professional skills" promising to secure "career successes" and "financial securities" in a given market. More specifically, these accounts call attention to composition's official role in disciplining individual teachers and students to deem a particular set of thinking, writing, and learning skills (labor power-commodity) as more valuable than other ways of thinking, writing, and learning and to labor over only those activities and relations which promise to facilitate the extraction-production of such market over-valued skills while atrophying all other capacities and relations, including ones critical to "nonacademic" or "unprofessional" aspects of our past, present, and future lives. At the same time, these accounts can serve as a reminder that learning to extract the same set of "academic" thinking, writing, learning skills—the set promising the most financial security-career success on a given market—often poses different challenges for and brings different consequences to differently situated working bodies. Attention to the ways in which the everyday realities of racism, sexism, economic disenfranchisement, homophobia, and agism mediate the materializing of the bodily projects of individual teachers and students is a necessary part of composition, if and especially when financial security and career success seem to be the primary goal of a majority of the incoming students.

For instance, in "'Who Are *They* and What Do They Have to Do with What I Want to Be?' The Writing of Multicultural Identity and College Success Stories of First-year Writers," Jim Ottery urges us to use accounts of the literacy education of students from "oppressed," "exploited" racial and ethnic groups, such as that of his ancestral cousin, Samson Occom, an educator and the founder of Brothertown Indians, to help students reflect on the transformation of the mind and heart required of anyone making the journey from the land of the "unschooled" to that of "higher learning," a universe (university) where students are made to extract-reduce their literacy skills to the dictates of "Christianity, the market, and the law" (127). In "She Toiled for a Living: Writing Lives and Identities of Older Female Students," Mary Hallet examines the bodily labor required of older, working-class, female students. She argues that students bearing such physical markers are often labeled as "not university material" because they are perceived as bearers of a textured toughness associated with reproductive labor, women's work, or working-class work—as bearers of capacities othered by and thus resistant to the extraction-production of "academic" labor power (86). In "Migratory and Regional Identity," Robert Brooke uses his own educational and professional experiences as a case in point to illustrate the particular form of labor power "America education" aims to extract from the body of individual teachers and students: a set of intellectual and rhetorical skills which is "placeless," enabling one to work wherever those skills are in demand, and thus be "in" a particular place but "not of" it. The ideal state of being for the person with a "college" trained labor power puts at a disadvantage students from rural America, who are facing stark economic conditions such as lack of access to housing, healthcare, jobs, and daily struggling to "make a *living* in" small, rural communities (149, my emphasis).

In "Speaking from the Borderlands: Exploring Narratives of Teacher Identity," Janet Alsup extends this line of inquiry to the training of secondary school teachers. Using data collected from a longitudinal, qualitative, interview-based research she conducted from January 2002 to spring 2003, Alsup maps the cultural script for the body of the secondary school teachers: one that is "intellectually neutral" and "academically rigorous" but culturally defined as white, female, middle-aged, politically conservative, and heterosexual (117). Alsup recounts the tension some pre-service teachers experience when trying to "place [themselves] in the 'body' of the teacher." Alsup concludes that teacher training needs to move past its "familiar" focus ("simple imitation of classroom practices") by helping students address the tension they experience between their sense of who they are prior to and outside of their vocational training and the standardized script of who they have to become to function as secondary school teachers of English (120). In other words, we need to treat the "simple imitation" of established ways of "teaching" as material forces constraining how individual teachers and students extract "educational" labor power from their material bodies—pressuring them to devalue or reject ways of thinking, writing, living critical to their lives prior to and outside their "vocational training."

In "When 'Ms. Mentor' Misses the Mark: Literacy and Lesbian Identity in the Academy," Tara Pauliny conducts a survey of professional advice literature to argue that queer female faculty are expected to play the part of a dutiful spouse: take primary responsibility for the care of "difficult" children by performing un- or under-paid labor and functioning as "silent commodities" (commodities valued for their diversity but relegated to shadows") (73). I read Pauliny as joining Hallet in calling attention to the ways in which signs of sexuality as well as race, ethnicity, age, and gender are used as external measures of what individual members of diverse social collectives are capable of doing and permitted to do at various moments of the circulation process, as extractors, exchangers, and-or users of a particular kind of labor power.

In "Social Class as Discourse: The Construction of Subjectivities in English," James Zebroski argues that individual students' sense of their self and life before, during, or after college are in large measure shaped by the particular discourse(s) of class available to the student. Using as a point of departure the challenges he faces when negotiating the "working-class discourse" of home and the "middle-class discourse" of the Parents Confidential Financial Statement (a bureaucratic document required of anyone applying for financial aid and the securing of which was his only hope for actually going to Ohio State), Zebroski argues that "the clash of social class discourses" often made students from working-class backgrounds face the "extremely difficult" task of "translating across these discourses" while risking becoming invisible to not only their family and old friends but also their professors and new middle-, upper-class friends (20). I read Zebroski to join others in arguing that, by "just teaching writing," composition classrooms are not only "exposing" students to a specific—"academic" (and often "new" or "alien")—process-product of writing but always also constraining how students go about mobilizing their capacities and potentials, pressuring them to submit their sense of what capacities (discursive or otherwise) to develop (and put to use) and which to deskill or reject according to the logic of the job market and the given commodity value of a particular kind of "academic" labor power. This kind of training in turn impinges on their decisions on how to rework—terminate, sustain, change, strengthen—those social relations cogent to their lives prior to and outside the academy but devalued by standardized notions of academic or professional thinking, writing, and learning skills.

However, the articles in the collection can also be read as reminders that the working bodies of individual teachers and students are neither docile nor passive but rather the extractors and bearers of the commodity of labor power as well as "the bearer of ideals and aspirations concerning, for example, the dignity of labor and the desire to be treated (and to treat others) with respect and consideration as a whole living being" (Harvey 1998, 414). They are attentive to the needs and capacities of individual teachers and students to address the potential contradictions between their concerns to become a bearer of the commodity of labor power promising to secure them the economic returns to make them feel "financially secure" and "successful" in their aspired "career" and their desires to pursue ideals, interests, and social relations devalued on a given market but critical to their sense of the kind of person they were, are, or would like to be in areas of life outside "higher education" and one's chosen "profession."

For instance, Jim Ottery posits writing prompts aimed at helping students bridge the gap between the limit points of where they have been, where they are now, and where they wish to go (132). Hallet urges us to following Mauk's call to design writing assignments, such as a "working diary" (89), which prompt students to "make meaning out of the people-places that constitute their daily lives," that is, to "flesh out" those social relations, experiences, and desires "flattened out" by the "academic" skills they are trying to extract from their bodies, including their experiences with housework and low-paying clerical work (90–91). Robert Brooke poses a "place-conscious education" (a pedagogy emerging from the ongoing efforts of the Nebraska Writing Project) which asks students to put their concern to "liv[e] well economically"—to amass the "intellectual" skills and knowledge that promise to bring the most economic return "everywhere" (else but the shrinking rural communities)—in the contexts of their and their family members' interests in, knowledge of, and capacity to live well ecologically, politically, spiritually, and in community, thus exploring options for alternative livelihoods in their region (151–52).

In "Excellence is the Name of the (Ideological) Game," Patricia Harkin joins Worsham, Brooke, and others to locate decisions over what particular forms of labor power are to be extracted from composition teachers and students in the specificity of the material where-when of individual efforts of writing and teaching-learning. Harkin defines composition researchers and teachers not merely as "persons who raise questions about how to define writing so that we can teach it" but also as persons working in global capitalism (under the logic of multinational corporations): a "grant culture" pressuring us to do work that can secure corporate funding rather than to look for funding for work that we see as necessary and/or interesting (30). Harkin urges us to counter the pressure to extract from ourselves only the corporate-valued labor power of "grantsmanship" by complicating our desire for financial security and career success as a "tenure-line professional" and to do so by keeping rather than losing sight of the "questions that we ourselves raise as a consequence of actual problems we encounter in the classroom, library, or culture"—aspects of our lives devalued and undervalued by the logic of global capitalism (33).

In foregrounding the bodily work of individual teachers and students in a globalizing capitalist market, the articles in this collection pose a cogent rebuttal to the tirade of the Angel (of my House of Composition) that composition can and should teach "just writing." They remind us that, when making the writing of our students the focus of composition classrooms while taking seriously their expressed financial and career concerns, composition teachers and researchers need to become more reflective of the market pressures we encounter during different points of our academic-professional lives and more attentive to the material consequences of forgetting that we, like all our students, are simultaneously also the bearers of "nonacademic," "unprofessional" interests, desires, capacities, and relations which are critical to other areas of our lives in the past, present, and future. These articles can in turn help us re-view how and why the teaching and learning of a specific set of writing processes and products can never be separate from interrogation into its relation to the formation of the individual bodies (self, subjectivity, identity) under capitalism, especially when the students' primary, fully articulated purpose for taking a composition course is to amass the set of skills that is most likely to secure "financial security" and "career success" in a given labor market. They can also help us re-view the possibilities of making composition a material space for students to use writing and learning as processes for addressing rather than ignoring the potential conflict they experience between their desire to qualify as "having" the most valued forms of labor power at a given market and to sustain, build, and initiate intimate relations with peoples marked as de-, un-, or under-skilled by the logic of capital.

At the same time, the recurring move to ground the efforts of individual students and teachers in specific, historical-social contexts, also cautions us against the tendency to attribute an absolute uniformity and continuity to capitalism and thus, overlook the shifts in its spatio-temporal order throughout its history and especially in what Harvey terms "the neo-liberal hegemony" since the 1970s (Harvey 2003, 62). Harvey argues that the United States has moved since the 1980s from an industrial toward a renter economy in relation to the rest of the world and a service economy at home (66). Technological rents continue to flow from the rest of the world into the U.S. economy, since much of the world's research and development is still done in the United States (221). U.S.-based manufacturing corporations repatriate substantial profits from their overseas ventures (223). However, most of the return flow pumped from the rest of the world does not compensate for job losses within the United States because it benefits the already wealthy, making the rest of the population even more dependent on the consumption habits of the upper-income brackets while doing, mostly without benefits, low-paying service jobs that cannot be moved offshore (223). Furthermore, technologically induced increases in productivity, in bringing costs down, do not necessarily improve the quality of daily life for the working and middle class. Rather, it sets in motion a chronic problem of unemployment and job insecurity (224). The logic of capital circulation pressures the laborer to channel her efforts solely to the end of increasing disposable income so as to increase her power of consumption of ever newer commodities such as objects, lifestyles, pleasures, services, trainings, skills (Harvey 1998, 411). Relentless U.S. consumerism generates a consumer market giving the United States a substantial advantage in bilateral trade deals (Harvey 2003, 224). But the recent bout of U.S. consumerism is debt-financed and class-biased. The habit of spending beyond one's means is more and more fueled by necessity, the need of working people to cash in mortgages to pay for the rising costs of health care, medical insurance, and education. The current stage can also be characterized by the increasing volume and speed but also range of goods and services in world trade, unprecedented levels of finance and capital flows in "a global electronic economy" geared toward money that exists only as digits in computers (Giddens 1999, 27; Harvey, 2003, 62). Any fluctuation in the financial market can destabilize seemingly rock-solid local economies as well as the value of whatever money we may have in our pockets or bank accounts (Giddens 1999, 28).

I recite the account of these shifts in the capitalist spatio-temporal order informing my reading of the collection to remind myself and other readers of this collection of the danger of turning any account of the educational experience of a particular student (in literacy autobiographies by individual composition teachers-researchers and students or ethnographic research) and any account of capitalism (especially those written during and about the U.S. society-economy of the period between World War II and the 1970s that have played instrumental roles in the work some of us have produced) into some sort of a master narrative (or commonplace) for cleansing the specificity of the actual material conditions of the writing and learning of individual students in the 2000s, even and especially when these accounts seem to be written by, about, and in the interests of composition teachers and researchers bearing markers of class, race, ethnicity, age, gender, and sexuality similar to the students one is most interested in reaching. We need instead to approach all accounts of literacy training and U.S. society-economy, including the ones emerging from the articles in this collection and my invested reading of these articles in light of David Harvey's work, with these questions in mind: What are the hearing systems we've developed through the years when approaching verbal articulations of "financial" and "career" concerns? How might such hearing habits hinder my ability to listen, carefully and respectfully, to the specificity of the material conditions informing individual students' writing and learning?

In "Manufacturing Emotions, Tactical Resistance in the Narratives of Working-Class students," Janet Bean (2003) poses a way of listening that attends to the "languages of the particular, of the body, and emotion": a way of attending to details in students' writing that "poach" various master narratives by "insinuating" into them heterogeneity and ambivalence (111, 103–4). I think Bean's advice on how composition teacher-researchers might best make sense of student writings which appear to reproduce clichés of individualism and meritocracy applies equally well to how we best go about making sense of writings by ourselves and our students appearing to reproduce "seminal" accounts of literacy training and U.S. capitalism informing our work at different points of our training as composition teacher-researchers. If learning to listen to individual students' account of their experience living through "the death and rebirth of Akron" (the uncertainties during the downturn of the late 1970s-1980s when Akron lost 35,000 manufacturing jobs, eliminating virtually all major rubber production in a city that once manufactured two-thirds of the nation's tires and half of the world's rubber goods and Akron's ascent by 2001 to be one of the top ten "new tech" cities of the United States for its preeminence in polymer engineering) is critical to Bean's understanding of how and why each of her students approached their "financial" and "career" concerns in a specific way in a particular text, then learning to break our confidence in our ability to know-hear the challenges students face when "writing and learning in a capitalist society" is equally critical (Bean 2003, 101–2). This kind of learning involves intense labor of the heart, body, and the mind because it is a form of work which brings home the limitations of the kind of labor power we have worked so hard to "possess," sell and "make a living out of" (Lu, "Redefining"). *Identity Papers* offers ample food for us to ponder how and why listening (rather than merely voicing and hearing) remains such a central and challenging task for composition researchers and teachers, myself included, a decade after Jacqueline Royster (1996) made the call in "When the First Voice You Hear is Not Your Own."

NOTES

CHAPTER 2 (ZEBROSKI)

1. Perhaps the most important resource for the scholar interested in working class studies is the Center for Working Class Studies (CWCS) at Youngstown State University. They hold regular conferences, publish a newsletter, do community service, and support the scholarly investigation of class and the working class. The website of CWCS is http://www.as.ysu.edu/~cwcs. We are not alone.

CHAPTER 5 (PAULINY)

1. This column, dated January 11, 2005, addresses questions asked by four academic women ("Doreen," "Eileen," "Kathleen," and "Maureen"), all of whose queries circulate around issues of professional mistreatment. To provide a fuller sense of Ms. Mentor's response to these women, I quote her here at length: "Ms. Mentor's sage readers will note that all of this month's letters come from faculty women—who, like clerical staff, and maintenance women, are overworked and underappreciated. Even Ms. Mentor, in all her majesty, is not sufficiently worshipped. As for her correspondents, Doreen, in the classic minority bind, finds that she's expected to represent everyone who is 'other,' and devote her time to 'otherness' instead of to the research and writing that feed her. [...] Someone's also playing with Eileen, whose schedule mysteriously was 'changed.' And now her job, apparently, is to rise above it all, do without rest or money, be several places at once, and be cheery ('collegial') at the same time. Ms. Mentor doubts that anyone could do that without serious drugs."

2. See her full-length advice text, *Ms. Mentor's Impeccable Advice for Women in Academia* for more examples of heteronormativity, including her suggestion to a job candidate that she keep her homosexuality private (36), and her comment that coming out is only appropriate as a post-tenure activity (200).

3. Once again, I quote Ms. Mentor's response (from her February 6, 2004 column) at length here to offer a more comprehensive sense of her perspective: "Ms. Mentor sighs and recalls the sage counsel drummed into all her agemates, during that late Victorian era: 'Don't do it in the road. You'll frighten the horses.' This month's subject is really discretion: What to share with whom, and whether your private life should be public news. While doing her daily deletion of e-mailed ads for nude celebrities, Ms. Mentor observes sourly that sex has become the most public subject in American life—yet one with the fewest clear rules."

4. Within this essay, I use "queer" not simply to denote the identities "lesbian" or "gay," but rather to mark a particular kind of critical view. To borrow from Kathy Rudy's definition, for my purposes here, I understand the term queer not as referencing the "matter of being gay [...] but rather [as] being committed to challenging that which is perceived as normal" (Rudy 2001, 197).

5. In my Introduction to Fiction course, for example, I often taught Dorothy Allison's *Two or Three Things I Know for Sure*, which overtly discusses her experiences as a lesbian feminist. As well, I sometimes organized my Second-Level Writing class around sexuality, and asked students to read such articles as Adrienne Rich's "Compulsory Heterosexuality and Lesbian Existence," Judith Halberstam's "Drag

Kings: Masculinity and Performance," and Cheryl Chase' "Hermaphrodites with Attitude: Mapping the Emergence of Intersex Political Activism."

6. For a list of some of these, please see the References section of this essay.

7. Although not an advice text per se, Linda Garber's collection, *Tilting the Tower: Lesbians Teaching Queer Subjects* (1994), does offer numerous suggestions to lesbian faculty members. It advises readers about how and when to come out, discusses the pitfalls and possibilities inherent in overtly discussing one's sexuality in a professional setting, and comments on how queer politics can collide with the more hegemonic and heteronormative principles of academic institutions. So although the text was compiled in order to "extend the conversation about the institutionalization of lesbian and gay studies and the need for a forum in which teachers can share their pedagogies and strategies for professional survival and success," it also elucidates the absences contained in the many texts compiled explicitly for the purpose of providing advice (ix).

8. For more on this connection, see the essays by Ronald Strickland and Robyn Wiegman cited in the References section of this piece.

CHAPTER 7 (CARPENTER AND FALBO)

1. This argument has been made over the careers of these scholars; however, the following work is most relevant to our discussion in this paper: David Bartholomae, "Inventing the University" (2001); Mariolina Salvatori, "Toward a Hermeneutics of Difficulty" (1988); Min-Zhan Lu, "Professing Multiculturalism: The Politics of Style in the Contact Zone" (1999).

2. Literacy narratives by Maya Angelou, Frederick Douglass, and Lorene Cary are frequently taught at Lafayette, so some Writing Associates will have encountered these texts.

3. Nancy Sommers (2003), in her recent CCCC talk observed that her undergraduate writers, at the end of a FY writing course, did not "improve" in ways that could be perceived on the page. And for this reason, she argues, assessment of the students' performance in writing at the end of a FY writing course is not very useful.

4. This is not a possibility Bartholomae excludes, but rather one that has been muted as a result of the ways in which his argument has come to be associated with the situation of the basic writer.

5. It is worth noting as an aside, perhaps, that we see ourselves in this image: though our education histories are different (private vs. public institutions) we both identified ourselves (because our teachers so identified us) as "good" writers, and yet we often found ourselves, like Colton, crossing our fingers and hoping for the best.

6. In his essay, Bartholomae cites Flower's distinction between "reader-based" and "writer-based" prose (514).

CHAPTER 9 (OTTERY)

1. My use of "the university discourse" in this case is based upon Jacques Lacan's topological mapping of discourse structure in *Seminar XX*. An excellent discussion of the cause and deadly effects of this university discourse is Ellie Ragland's "Editorial: L'envers de la Psychanalyse." In the university discourse, a master signifier is the production of intellectual exchange. But since a master signifier is always already in place, in the so-called exchange of university discourse, no real meaning or knowledge is created. The discourse becomes one of mindless repetition of what has become platitude—a staple or commodity that one "*buys*" into." The example that appears in Ragland's discussion is: "1) no one feels inclined to learn anything from a [real] leader (master, teacher, [elder], etc.); 2) the referent for group knowledge itself becomes the discourse of opinion, indeed, the word of the strongest ('might makes right')" (3). The "bought into" opinion, like any other popular commodity,

becomes the costliest desire that determines the value of the currency in—in the case of the university and similar institutions—the "marketplace of ideas." American Indians had little choice other than "buying into" the Westernized discourse of Christianity. The only option was a quicker death.

2. Will and Rudi Ottery, 30 and 21. They cite Francis Jennings (*The Invasion of America: Indians, Colonialism, and the Cant of Conquest*) and Roderick Nash (*From These Beginnings: A Biographical Approach to American History*) as she writes of one cause of belief (that existed/exists and was/is expressed in language) that places Christians in a place of superiority over the indigenous people they converted or killed:

    > Although the Massachusetts Bay Colony Puritans have been portrayed as a superior, chosen people with completely noble motives, this perspective is somewhat misleading. They did have this self-perception and their charter did indicate a missionary purpose, but their colonization was a commercial venture and their objectives included power, wealth, and land. . . As Puritans, they believed that everyone was destined for damnation except for God's chosen few—and they were this chosen group of saints. Their government and church were one, so only church members could vote. To be a church member required convincing both one's peers and self that one was a regenerated, elected and saved saint. Anyone who disagreed with Puritans was not only wrong, but in league with evil.

3. Will and Rudi Ottery, 27 and 28. "Varying reports of the Pequot casualties range from 300 to 700. Two English were killed and one of these was killed by a colonist. Twenty English were wounded, and of these some complained they had been shot by other colonists. [Captain John] Mason and his men apparently shot at everything that moved."

4. Lyons (2000) writes, "Sovereignty is the guiding story in our pursuit of self-determination, the general strategy by which we aim to best recover our losses from the ravages of colonization: our lands, our languages, our cultures, our self-respect. . . . Attacks on our sovereignty are attacks on what it enables us to purse; the pursuit of sovereignty is an attempt not to revive our past, but our possibilities. Rhetorical sovereignty is the inherent right and ability of *peoples* to determine their own communicative needs and desires in this pursuit, to decide for themselves the goals, modes, styles, and languages of public discourse."

5. I'm indebted to E. L. Doctorow's (2002) "Ultimate Discourse" for this idea that "What we call fiction [myths, traditions] is the ancient way of knowing, the total discourse that antedates al the special vocabularies of modern intelligence."

6. One cannot help but notice the parallel between Malcolm learning that "he himself was the byproduct of an ancestral rape, the mother of his mother having been raped by a white man . . . a knowledge, always already there within his consciousness" and Occom's own ancestral story, the massacre of his mother's people at Mystic River.

7. Jacques Lacan's formulation of "the modulation of time" in "the instant of the glance, the time for comprehending, and the moment of concluding" is found in "Logical Time and the Assertion of Anticipated Certainty: A New Sophism." *Newsletter of the Freudian Field*, 22, (Fall 1988), 4–22.

CHAPTER 12 (WORSHAM)

1. As quoted in Ball (2002) who references the quotation as appearing in Zipes (1998).

2. *Post-traumatic Culture* is Farrell's (1998) term, employed to signify both a clinical and cultural syndrome. See also Felman (1992), "Education," who calls the twentieth century a "posttraumatic century," and LaCapra (2001), who calls ours a "time marked by trauma."

3. This article was originally composed in the spring of 2002 and thus very much in the context of the events of September 11, 2001.

4. Jameson (1984) identifies the postmodern condition with this kind of free-floating anxiety and dread.

5. See Ball (2000), Mowitt (2000), and Caruth (1995), all of whom make this same point (or something close to it) about the power of the concept of trauma to disrupt and call into question our notions of epistemology and historiography.

6. See also Bernet (2000), who argues, rather convincingly, that subjectivity is always already traumatized and that the notion of a substantial subject is a fiction. He argues that subjectivity can only be constituted and maintained through "surviving the dramas that ceaselessly menace its existence." What menaces existence are events that are "nonappropriable and, in consequence, traumatizing": "Being a subject would thus be a matter of being a subject by virtue of losses of identity and subsequent attempts to reconstitute a subjectivity, this subjectivity being henceforth no more than a vulnerable subjectivity, a wounded *cogito*" (160).

7. See Santner (1992) for a lucid discussion of the distinction between mourning and narrative fetishism. In the context of this distinction, see also Eng and Kazanjian (2003), who provide an understanding of the politics and ethics of mourning. Their discussion of Walter Benjamin's distinction between historical materialism and historicism is especially relevant to an understanding of mourning and narrative fetishism. They argue that historical materialism provides the means by which we may productively (and hopefully) mourn the remains of lost histories and histories of loss, while historicism and, by implication, narrative fetishism, precipitate despair and hopelessness.

8. The literature on the relationship between narrative and healing written by psychotherapists and medical doctors is fairly extensive. See, for example, White and Epston (1990). The literature about "the personal," personal narrative, experience, and healing is also extensive in composition studies. See, for example, Anderson and MacCurdy (2000), Berman (2002), Borrowman (2005), Brandt et al. (2001), Read (1998), and Spellmeyer (1996). For a more carefully nuanced treatment of the concept of experience, see, for example, Scott (1994), Horner and Lu (1996), and my own effort at "working through," via personal narrative, experiences of personal and professional loss. Since this article was composed, *JAC* has published two special issues on trauma, rhetoric, and writing.

9. I received a copy of the most recent effort to link writing and healing, Borrowman's (2005) *Trauma and the Teaching of Writing*, just before this article went to press; therefore, I could not include it in this discussion. However, I note that only one of thirteen articles in this collection draws on, or even mentions, what is now an extensive body of scholarship on trauma and its pedagogical implications. I note this fact because it suggests to me the kind of willed ignorance that sustains the protective shield constituting the discipline of composition and that supports the way in which "narrative" and "experience" are fetishized in the field. This willed ignorance corresponds to the limited vitality that I note in my discussion here of the discipline of composition.

10. Laub, for example, provides a useful discussion of the hazards of listening to the text of trauma.

REFERENCES

Aisenberg, Nadya and Mona Harrington. 1988. *Women of Academe: Outsiders in the Sacred Grove.* Amherst: University of Massachusetts Press.

Alcoff, Linda and Elizabeth Potter. 1993. "Introduction: When Feminisms Intersect Epistemology." In *Feminist Epistemologies.* Edited by Linda Alcoff and Elizabeth Potter. New York: Routledge. 1–14.

Alsup, Janet. 2005. *Teacher Identity Discourses: Negotiating Professional and Personal Spaces.* Mahwah, NJ: Lawrence Earlbaum.

Althusser, Louis. 1971. *Lenin and Philosophy and Other Essays.* Trans. Ben Brewster. New York and London: Monthly Review Press.

Alvermann, Donna E. 2001. "Reading Adolescents' Reading Identities: Looking Back to See Ahead." *Journal of Adolescent and Adult Literacy* 44: 676–90.

Anderson, Charles M. and Marian M. MacCurdy. 2000. *Writing and Healing: Toward an Informed Practice.* Urbana, IL: NCTE.

Ball, Karyn. 2000. "Trauma and its Institutional Destinies." *Cultural Critique* 46: 1–44.

Ball, Karyn. 2002. "Wanted, Dead or Distracted: On Ressentiment in History, Philosophy, and Everyday Life." *Cultural Critique* 52: 235.

Barale, Michèle Aina. 1994. "The Romance of Class and Queers: Academic Erotic Zones." In *Tilting the Tower: Lesbians Teaching Queer Subjects.* Edited by Linda Garber. New York: Routledge. 16–24.

Bartholomae, David. 2001. "Inventing the University." In *Literacy: A Critical Sourcebook.* Edited by Ellen Cushman et al. Boston, MA: Bedford/St. Martin's. 511–24.

Barton, David and Mary Hamilton. 1998. *Local Literacies: Reading and Writing in One Community.* London: Routledge.

Bawarshi, Anis and Stephanie Pelkowski. 2003. "Postcolonialism and the Idea of a Writing Center." In *The St. Martin's Sourcebook for Writing Tutors,* 2nd edn. Boston, MA: St. Martin's. 80–95.

Bean, Janet. 2003. "Manufacturing Emotions: Tactical Resistance in the Narratives of Working-Class Students." In *A Way to Move: Rhetorics of Emotion and Composition Studies.* Edited by Dale Jacobs and Laura R.Micchiche. Portsmouth, NH: Boynton/Cook. 101–12.

Berman, Jeffrey. 2002. *Risky Writing: Self-Disclosure and Self-Transformation in the Classroom.* Amherst: University of Massachusetts Press.

Bernard-Donals, Michael and Richard Glejzer. 2003. "Representations of the Holocaust and the End of Memory." In *Witnessing the Disaster: Essays on Representation and the Holocaust.* Edited by Michael Bernard-Donals and Richard Glejzer. Madison, WI: University of Wisconsin Press. 3–19.

Bernet, Rudolf. 2000. "The Traumatized Subject." *Research in Phenomenology* 30: 160–79.

Bishop, Wendy. 1997. *Teaching Lives: Essays and Stories.* Logan, UT. Utah State University Press.

Blackmore, Jill. 1999. *Troubling Women: Feminism, Leadership, and Educational Change.* Philadelphia, PA: Open University Press.

Bleich, David and Deborah Holdstein. 2001. *Personal Effects: The Social Character of Scholarly Writing.* Logan, UT: Utah State University Press.

Bloom, Leslie Rebecca. 1998. *Under the Sign of Hope: Feminist Methodology and Narrative Interpretation.* Albany, NY: SUNY Press.

Bloom, Lynn. 1996. "Freshman Composition as a Middle-Class Enterprise." *College English* 58: 654–75.

Boquet, Elizabeth H. 2002. *Noise from the Writing Center.* Logan, UT: Utah State University Press.

Borrowman, Shane, ed. 2005. *Trauma and the Teaching of Writing.* Albany, NY: SUNY Press.

Brandt, Deborah et al. 2001. "The Politics of the Personal: Storying Our Lives Against the Grain." *College English* 64: 41–62.

Brison, Susan J. 2002. *Aftermath: Violence and the Remaking of a Self.* Princeton, NJ: Princeton University Press.

Britzman, Deborah P. 1991. *Practice Makes Practice: A Critical Study of Learning to Teach.* Albany, NY: SUNY Press.

Britzman, Deborah P. 1998. *Lost Subjects, Contested Objects: Toward a Psychoanalytic Inquiry of Learning.* Albany, NY: SUNY Press.

Brooke, Robert, ed. 2003. *Rural Voices: Place-Conscious Education and the Teaching of Writing.* Columbia, NY: Teachers College Press.

Brooks, Jeff. 1991. "Minimalist Tutoring: Making the Students Do All the Work." *Writing Lab Newsletter* 15: 1–4.

Brownworth, Victoria. 1997. "Life in the Passing Lane: Exposing the Class Closet." In *Queerly Classed: Gay Men and Lesbians Write About Class.* Edited by S. Raffo. Boston, MA: South End Press. 67–78.

Brueggemann, Brenda Jo and Debra Moddelmog. 2002. "Coming-Out Pedagogy: Risking Identity in Language and Literature Classrooms." *Pedagogy: Critical Approaches to Teaching Literature, Language, Composition, and Culture* 2: 311–35.

Bruner, Jerome. 1986. *Actual Minds, Possible Worlds.* Cambridge, MA: Harvard University Press.

Bruner, Jerome. 1991. "The Narrative Construction of Reality." *Critical Inquiry* 18: 1–21.

Bruner, Jerome. 1996. *The Culture of Education.* Cambridge, MA: Harvard University Press.

Bruner, Jerome. 2002. *Making Stories: Law, Literature, Life.* New York: Farrar, Straus and Giroux.

Bruno, R. 1999. *Steelworker Alley: How Class Works in Youngstown.* Ithaca, NY: Cornell University Press.

Bryson, Mary and Suzanne de Castell. 1997. "Queer Pedagogy?!: Praxis Makes Im/Perfect." In *Radical Interventions: Identity, Politics, and Difference/s in Educational Praxis.* Edited by Suzanne De Castell and Mary Bryson. Albany, NY: SUNY Press. 269–93.

Bulloughs, Robert. 1987. "First Year Teaching: A Case Study." *Teachers College Record* 89: 39–46.

Butler, Judith. 1993. *Bodies That Matter: On the Discursive Limits of "Sex."* New York: Routledge.

Caplan, Paula J. 1993. *Lifting a Ton of Feather: A Woman's Guide to Surviving in the Academic World.* Toronto: University of Toronto Press.

Carroll, James. 1996. An American Requiem: God, My Father, and the War That Came Between Us. Boston, MA: Houghton Mifflin.

Carroll, Lee Ann. 2002. *Rehearsing New Roles: How College Students Develop as Writers.* Carbondale, IL: Southern Illinois University Press.

Caruth, Cathy. 1995. *Trauma: Explorations in Memory.* Baltimore, MD: John Hopkins University Press.

Caruth, Cathy. 1996 *Unclaimed Experience: Trauma, Narrative, and History.* Baltimore, MD: John Hopkins University Press.

Center for Rural Affairs. 2002. "New Data on Rural Poverty." *Center for Rural Affairs Newsletter*, September.

Chandler, Sally. 2001 "Theorizing Interpretation in Context: A Feminist Ethnographic Study of an Elder Women's Writing Group." Ph.D. Dissertation, Wayne State University, Detroit.

Chinn, Sarah. 1994. "Queering the Profession, or Just Professionalizing Queers?" In *Tilting the Tower: Lesbians Teaching Queer Subjects.* Edited by Linda Garber. New York: Routledge. 243–50.

Christian, Barbara. 1997. "Fixing Methodologies: Beloved." In *Female Subjects in Black and White: Race, Psychoanalysis, Feminism.* Edited by Elizabeth Abel, Barbara Christian, and Helene Moglen. Berkeley, CA: University of California Press. 363–70.

Cisneros, Sandra. 1984. "A House of My Own." *The House on Mango Street.* New York: Vintage Books.

Code, Lorraine. 1995. *Rhetorical Spaces: Essays on Gendered Locations.* New York: Routledge.

Collins, Lynn H., Joan C. Chrisler, and Kathryn Quina, eds. 1998. *Career Strategies for Women in Academe: Arming Athena.* Thousand Oaks, CA: Sage.

Cooper, Marilyn M. 2001. "Really Useful Knowledge: A Cultural Studies Agenda for Writing Centers." In *The Allyn and Bacon Guide to Writing Center Theory and Practice.* Edited by Robert Barnett and Jacob Blumner. Boston, MA: Allyn and Bacon. 335–40.

Cross, William E. 1991. *Shades of Black: Diversity in African-American Identity.* Philadelphia, PA: Temple University Press.

Culbertson, Roberta. 1995. "Embodied Memory, Transcendence, and Telling: Recounting Trauma, Re-establishing the Self." *New Literary History* 26: 169–95.

Danielewicz, Jane. 2001. *Teaching Selves: Identity, Pedagogy, and Teacher Education.* Albany, NY: SUNY Press.

Davies, Bronwyn. 2000. *A Body of Writing: 1990–1999.* Oxford, England: Rowman and Littlefield.

Davies, Dona L. 1993. "Unintended Consequences: The Myth of 'The Return' in Anthropological Fieldwork." In *When They Read What We Write: The Politics of Ethnography.* Edited by Caroline B. Brettell. Westport, CT: Bergin and Garvey. 27–37.

de Certeau, Michel. 1984. *The Practice of Everyday Life.* Berkeley, CA: University of California Press.

Deats, Sara Munson and Lagretta Tallent Lenker, eds. 1994. *Gender and Academe: Feminist Pedagogy and Politics.* Boston, MA: Rowman and Littlefield.

Delpit, Lisa. 2002. "No Kinda Sense." In *The Skin that We Speak: Thoughts on Language and Culture in the Classroom.* Edited by Lisa Delpit and Joanne Kilgour Dowdy. New York: New Press. 33–48.

Denzin, Norman K. 1987. *Sociological Methods.* New York: McGraw-Hill.

Dewey, John. 1916. *Democracy and Education: An Introduction to the Philosophy of Education.* New York: Macmillan.

Dews, B. and C. Law, eds. 1995. *This Fine Place So Far From Home: Voices of Academics from the Working Class.* Philadelphia, PA: Temple University Press.

DiPardo, Anne. 1993. *A Kind of Passport: A Basic Writing Adjunct Program and the Challenge of Student Diversity.* Urbana, IL: NCTE.

DiPardo, Anne. 2001. "'Whispers of Coming and Going': Lessons from Fannie." In *The Allyn and Bacon Guide to Writing Center Theory and Practice.* Edited by Robert Barnett and Jacob Blumer. Boston and London: Allyn and Bacon. 350–68.

Dixon, J. 1991. *A Schooling in 'English': Critical Episodes in the Struggle to Shape Literary and Cultural Studies.* Philadelphia, PA: Open University Press.

Doctorow, E. L. 2002. "Ultimate Discourse." *The Conscious Reader,* 8th edn. Edited by Caroline Shrodes, Harry Finestone, and Michael Shugrue. Boston, MA: Allyn and Bacon.

Domhoff, G. W. 1998. *Who Rules America? Power and Politics in the Year 2000.* New York: Simon and Schuster.

Downing, D., C. M. Hurlbert, and P. Mathieu, eds. 2002. *Beyond English Inc.: Curricular Reform in a Global Economy.* Portsmouth, NH: Boynton/Cook.

Dunn, Patricia. 2000. "Marginal Comments on Writers' Texts: The Status of the Commenter as a Factor in Writing Center Tutorials." In *Stories from the Center: Connecting Narrative and Theory in the Writing Center.* Edited by Lynn Craigue Briggs and Meg Woolbright. Urbana, IL: NCTE. 30–42.

Durst, Russel. 1999. *Collision Course: Conflict, Negotiation, and Learning in College Composition.* Urbana, IL: NCTE.

Ebert, Teresa. 1996. *Ludic Feminism and After: Postmodernism, Desire, and Labor in Late Capitalism.* Ann Arbor, MI: University of Michigan Press.

Eng, David L. and David Kazanjian. 2003. "Mourning Remains." In *Loss: The Politics of Mourning.* Edited by David L. Eng and David Kazanjian. Berkeley, CA: University of California Press. 1–25.

Ernest, John. 1998. "One Hundred Friends and Other Class Issues: Teaching Both In and Out of the Game." In *Coming to Class: Pedagogy and the Social Class of Teachers.* Edited by Alan Shepard, John McMillan, and Gary Tate. Portsmouth, NH: Boynton/Cook. 23–36.

Eyerman, Ron. 2001. *Cultural Trauma: Slavery and the Formation of African American Identity.* Cambridge: University of Cambridge Press.

Farrell, Kirby. 1998. *Post-traumatic Culture: Injury and Interpretation in the Nineties.* Baltimore, MD: John Hopkins University Press.

Feiman-Nemser, Sharon. 1983. "Learning to Teach." In *Handbook of Teaching and Policy.* Edited by L. S. Shulman and G. Skyes. New York: Longman. 150–70.

Felman, Shoshana. 1992. "Education and Crisis, or the Vicissitudes of Teaching." In *Testimony: Crises of Witnessing in Literature, Psychoanalysis, and History.* Edited by Shoshana Felman and Dori Laub. New York: Routledge. 1–56.

Flax, Jane. 1989. *Thinking Fragments: Psychoanalysis, Feminism, and Postmodernism in the Contemporary West.* Berkeley, CA: University of California Press.

Fleckenstein, Kristie. 1991. "Writing Bodies: Somatic Mind in Composition Studies." *College English* 61: 281–306.

Forno, Dawn M. and Cheryl Reed. 1999. *Job Search in Academe: Strategic Rhetorics for Faculty Job Candidates.* Sterling, VA: Stylus.

Foucault, Michel. 1972. *The Archaeology of Knowledge.* Translated from the French by A. M. Sheridan Smith. New York: Pantheon.

Fox, Helen. 2001. *When Race Breaks Out: Conversations about Race and Racism in College Classrooms.* New York: Peter Lang.

Freedman, Diane, Olivia Frey, and Frances Murphy Zauhar. 1993. *The Intimate Critique: Autobiographical Literary Criticism.* Durham, NC: Duke University Press.

Freire, Paulo. 1970. *Pedagogy of the Oppressed.* New York: Continuum.

Freud, Sigmund. 1961. *The Ego and the Id. The Standard Edition of the Complete Psychological Works,* vol. 19. Trans. James Strachey. London: Hogarth.

Fulkerson, Richard. 2005. "Composition at the Turn of the Twenty-first Century." *College Composition and Communication* 56: 654–87.

Gagnon, Nicole. 1989. Review of *Nationalism and the Politics of Culture in Quebec,* by Richard Handler. *Recherches Sociographiques* 30: 125–27.

Gaines, Ernest. 1994. *A Lesson Before Dying.* New York: Vintage Books.

Garber, Linda, ed. 1994. *Tilting the Tower: Lesbians Teaching Queer Subjects.* New York: Routledge.

Garger, Stephen. 1995. "Bronx Syndrome." In *This Fine Place So Far From Home.* Edited by Carolyn Leste Law and C.L. Barney Dews. Philadelphia, PA: Temple University Press. 41–53.

Gee, James. 1996. *Social Linguistics and Literacies: Ideology in Discourses,* 2nd edn. London: Taylor and Francis, 190–91.

Gee, James. 1999. *An Introduction to Discourse Analysis: Theory and Method.* New York: Routledge.

George, Diana Hume. 1994. "'How Many of Us Can You Hold to Your Breast?': Mothering in the Academy." In *Listening to Silences: New Essays in Feminist Criticism.* Edited by Elaine Hedges and Shelley Fisher Fishkin. New York: Oxford University Press. 225–44.

George, Diana, ed. 1999. *Kitchen Cooks, Plate Twirlers, and Troubadours: Writing Program*

Administrators Tell Their Stories. Portsmouth, NH: Boynton/Cook.

Gergen, Kenneth J. 1994. *Realities and Relationships: Soundings in Social Construction.* Cambridge, MA: Harvard University Press.

Gergen, Kenneth J. and Mary M. Gergen. 1986. "Narrative Form and the Construction of Psychological Science." In *Narrative Psychology: The Storied Nature of Human Conduct.* Edited by Theodore R. Sarbin. New York: Praeger. 22–44

Gibson, Michelle, Martha Marinara, and Deborah Meem. 2000. "Bi, Butch, and Bar Dyke: Pedagogical Performances of Class, Gender, and Sexuality." *College Composition and Communication* 52: 69–95.

Giddens, Anthony. 1999. *Runaway World: How Globalisation Is Reshaping Our Lives.* New York: Routledge.

Gilyard, Keith, ed. 1999. *Race, Rhetoric, and Composition.* Portsmouth, NH: Boynton/Cook.

Goodburn, Amy and Carrie Shively Leverenz. 1998. "Feminist Writing Program Administration: Resisting the Bureaucrat Within." In *Feminism and Composition Studies: In Other Words.* Edited by Susan C. Jarratt and Lynn Worsham. New York: MLA. 276–90.

Goodson, Ivor F., ed. 1992. *Studying Teachers' Lives.* New York: Teachers College Press.

Gordon, S. P. 1991. *How to Teach Beginning Teachers to Succeed.* Alexandria, VA: Clearinghouse.

Grant, Carl A. and Kenneth Zeichner. 1981. "Inservice Support for First-Year Teachers: The State of the Scene." *Journal of Research and Development in Education* 14: 99–111.

Grimm, Nancy Maloney. 1999. *Good Intentions: Writing Center Work for Postmodern Times.* Portsmouth, NH: Boynton/Cook.

Gruchow, Paul. 1995. *Grassroots: The Universe of Home.* Minneapolis, MN: Milkweed.

Haas, Toni and Paul Nachtigal. 1998. *Place Value: An Educator's Guide to Good Literature on Rural Lifeways, Environments, and Purposes of Education.* Charleston, WV: ERIC Clearinghouse on Rural Education and Small Schools.

Hall, Kira and Mary Buckholtz. 1995. *Gender Articulated: Language and the Socially Constructed Self.* New York: Routledge.

Hall, Stuart. 1994. "Cultural Identity and Diaspora." In *Colonial Discourse and Post-colonial Theory.* Edited by P. Williams and L. Chrisman. New York: Columbia University Press. 392–403.

Hall, Stuart. 1996. "On Postmodernism and Articulation: An Interview with Stuart Hall." In *Stuart Hall: Critical Dialogues in Cultural Studies.* Edited by David Morley and Kuam Hsing Chen. London: Routledge. 131–50.

Handler, Eric. 1988. *Nationalism and the Politics of Culture in Quebec.* Madison, WI: University of Wisconsin Press.

Handler, Eric. 1993. "Fieldwork in Quebec, Scholarly Reviews, and Anthropological Dialogues." In *When They Read What We Write: The Politics of Ethnography.* Edited by Caroline B. Brettell. Westport, CT: Bergin and Garvey. 67–75.

Harding, Sandra. 1996. "Feminism, Science, and the Anti-Enlightenment Critiques." In *Women, Knowledge, and Reality: Explorations in Feminist Philosophy,* 2nd edn. Edited by Ann Garry and Marilyn Pearsall. New York: Routledge. 298–320.

Hart, Elva Treviño. 1999. *Barefoot Heart: Stories of a Migrant Child.* Tempe, AZ: Bilingual Press.

Havey, David. 1998. "The Body as an Accumulation Strategy." *Environment and Plan D: Society and Space* 16: 401–21.

Harvey, David. 2003. *The New Imperialism.* Oxford: Oxford University Press.

Heard, Georgia. 1995. *Writing Towards Home: Tales and Lessons to Find Your Way.* Portsmouth, NH: Boynton/Cook/Heinemann.

Heath, Shirley Brice. 1983. *Ways With Words: Language, Life and Work in Communities and Classrooms.* Cambridge: Cambridge University Press.

Helms, Janet. 1990. "Introduction: Review of Racial Identity Terminology." In *Black and*

White Racial Identity: Theory, Research, and Practice. Edited by Janet E. Helms. New York: Greenwood Press. 3–4.

Herman, Judith Lewis. 1992. *Trauma and Recovery.* New York: Basic.

Hermans, Hubert. M., T. I. Rijks, J. G. Harry, and Harry J. G. Kempen. 1993. "Imaginal Dialogue in the Self: Theory and Method." *Journal of Personality* 61: 207–36.

Herrington, Ann J. and Marcia Curtis. 2000. *Persons in Progress: Four Stories of Writing and Personal Development in College.* Urbana, IL: NCTE.

Higgins, J. J. 1999. *Images of the Rust Belt.* Kent, OH: Kent State University Press.

Hindman, Jane. 2001. "Making Writing Matter: Using the "Personal" to Recover(y) an Essential(ist) Tension in Academic Discourse." *College English* 64: 88–108.

Hocking, Brent, Johnna Haskell, and Warren Linds, eds. 2001. *Unfolding Bodymind: Exploring Possibility Through Education.* Brandon, VT: Foundation for Educational Renewal.

hooks, bell. 1998. "Keeping Close to Home: Class and Education." In *Learning Dynamics.* Edited by Marjorie Ford and Jon Ford. Boston, MA: Houghton Mifflin.

hooks, bell. 1996. "Choosing the Margins as a Space of Radical Openness." In *Women, Knowledge, and Reality: Explorations in Feminist Philosoph,* 2nd edn. Edited by Ann Garry and Marilyn Pearsall. New York: Routledge. 48–55.

hooks, bell. 1994. *Teaching to Transgress: Education as the Practice of Freedom.* New York: Routledge.

hooks, bell. 1989. *Talking Back: Thinking Feminist, Thinking Black.* Boston: South End Press.

Horner, Bruce. 1996. "Discoursing Basic Writing." *College Composition and Communication* 47: 199–222.

Horner, Bruce, Kelly Latchaw, Joseph Lenz, Jody Swilky, and David Wolf. 2002. "Excavating the Ruins of Undergraduate English." In *Beyond English, Inc.: Curricular Reform in a Global Economy.* Edited by David Downing, Claude Mark Hurlbert, and Paula Matthieu. Portsmouth, NH: Heinemann Boynton/Cook. 75–92.

Huizinga, Johann. 1950. *Homo Ludens: A Study of the Play Element in Culture.* Boston, MA: Beacon Press.

Huling-Austin, L., S. Odell, P. Ishler, R. Kay, and R. Edelfelt. 1989. *Assisting the Beginning Teacher.* Reston, VA: Association of Teacher Educators.

Jameson, Fredric. 1981. *The Political Unconscious: Narrative as a Socially Symbolic Act.* Ithaca, NY: Cornell University Press.

Jameson, Fredric. 1984. "Postmodernism, or the Cultural Logic of Late Capitalism." *New Left Review* 146: 53–92.

Jameson, Fredric. 1991. *Postmodernism, or the Cultural Logic of Late Capitalism.* Durham: Duke University Press.

Jarratt, Susan C. and Lynn Worsham, eds. 1998. *Feminism and Composition Studies: In Other Words.* New York: MLA.

Jolliffe, David. 2001 "Discourse." In *Routledge Encyclopedia of Postmodernism.* Edited by V. Taylor and C. Winquist. New York: Routledge.

Knopp, Lisa. 1996. *Field of Vision.* Iowa City, IO: Iowa University Press.

Knowles, J. Gary and Diane Holt-Reynolds. 1991. "Shaping Pedagogies Through Personal Histories in Preservice Teacher Education." *Teachers College Record* 93: 87–113.

Krashen, Stephen D. 1982. *Principles and Practices in Second Language Acquisition.* New York: Pergamon.

Lacan, Jacques. 1998. "Logical Time and the Assertion of Anticipated Certainty: A New Sophism." *Newsletter of the Freudian Field* 2(2). 4–22.

Lacan, Jacques. 1975. *Seminar XX: Encore.* Edited by Jacques-Alain Miller. Paris: Seuil.

LaCapra, Dominck. 2001. *Writing History, Writing Trauma.* Baltimore, MD: John Hopkins University Press.

Laub, Dori. 1992. "Bearing Witness, or the Vicissitudes of Listening." In *Testimony: Crises of*

Witnessing in Literature, Psychoanalysis, and History. Edited by Shoshana Felman and Dori Laub. New York: Routledge. 57–74.

LeDoux, Denis. 1993. *Turning Memories into Memoirs: A Handbook for Writing Llife Stories*. Lisbon Falls, ME: Soleil.

Lemke, Jay L. 1995. *Textual Politics: Discourses and Social Dynamics*. London: Taylor and Francis.

Levi, Primo. 1985. *If Not Now, When?* New York: Penguin.

Lieblich, Amia, Rivka Tuval-Mashiach, and Tamar Zilber. 1998. *Narrative Research: Reading, Analysis, and Interpretation*. Thousand Oaks, CA: Sage.

Lindquist, J. 2002. *A Place to Stand: Politics and Persuasion in a Working Class Bar*. New York: Oxford University Press.

Lipka, Richard P. and Thomas M. Brinkthaupt, eds. 1999. *The Role of Self in Teacher Development*. Albany, NY: SUNY Press.

Long, Elizabeth. 1993. "Textual Interpretation as Collective Action." In *The Ethnography of Reading*. Edited by Jonathan Boyarnin. Berkeley, CA: University of California Press. 180–212.

Lortie, Dan. 1975. *Schoolteacher: A Sociological Study*. Chicago, IL: University of Chicago Press.

Love, W. DeLoss. 2000. *Samson Occom and the Christian Indians of New York. 1899*. Syracuse, NY: Syracuse University Press.

Lu, Min-Zhan and Bruce Horner. 1998. "The Problematic of Experience: Redefining Critical Work in Ethnography and Pedagogy." *College English* 60: 257–77.

Lu, Min-Zhan. 1994. "Redefining the Legacy of Mina Shaughnessy: A Critique of the Politics of Linguistic Innocence." In *The Writing Teacher's Sourcebook*, 3rd edn. Edited by Gary Tate, Edward Corbett, and Nancy Meyers. New York: Oxford University Press. 327–37.

Lu, Min-Zhan. 1999. "Professing Multiculturalism: The Politics of Style in the Contact Zone." In *Representing the "Other": Basic Writers and the Teaching of Basic Writing*. Edited by Bruce Horner and Min-Zhan Lu. Urbana, IL: NCTE. 166–90.

Lu, Min-Zhan. 1999. "Redefining the Literate Self: The Politics of Critical Affirmation." *College Composition and Communication* 51: 172–94.

Lu, Min-Zhan. 2004. "An Essay on the Work of Composition." *College Composition and Communication* 56: 16–50.

Lyons, Scott Richard. 2000. "Rhetorical Sovereignty: What do American Indians Want from Writing?" *College Composition and Communication* 51: 447–68.

Lyotard, Jean-François and Jean-Loup Thébaud. 1985. *Just Gaming*. Trans. Wlad Godzich. Minneapolis, MN: University of Minnesota Press.

MacCurdy, Marian M. 2000. "From Trauma to Writing: A Theoretical Model for Practical Use." In *Writing and Healing: Toward an Informed Practice*. Edited by Charles M. Anderson and Marian M. MacCurdy. Urbana, IL: NCTE. 158–200.

McBride, James. 1996. *The Color of Water: A Black Man's Tribute to His White Mother*. New York: Riverhead.

Mah, Adeline Yen. 1997. *Falling Leaves: A True Story of an Unwanted Chinese Daughter*. New York: Wiley.

Malcolm X and Alex Haley. 1995. "Coming to an Awareness of Language." In *Language Awareness*, 6th edn. Edited by Paul Eschholz, Alfred Rosa, Virginia Clark. New York: St. Martin's.

Malinowitz, Harriet. 1995. *Textual Orientations: Lesbian and Gay Students and the Making of Discourse Communities*. Portsmouth, NH: Boynton/Cook.

Manley, Robert. 1997. *Classroom Handout for Visiting Speaker Presentation*. Henderson, NE: Henderson Schools.

Mark, Rebecca. 1994. "Teaching from the Open Closet." In *Listening to Silences: New Essays in Feminist Criticism*. Edited by Elaine Hedges and Shelley Fisher Fishkin. New York:

Oxford University Press. 245–59.

Maslow, Abraham. 1962. *Toward a Psychology of Being*. Princeton, NJ: Van Nostrand.

McAdams, Dan P. 1993. *The Stories We Live By: Personal Myths and the Making of the Self*. New York: William Morrow.

Mauk, Jonathon. 2003. "Location, Location, Location: The 'REAL' (E)states of Being, Writing, and Thinking in Composition." *College English* 65: 368–88.

Mayberry, Katherine J. 1996. *Teaching What You're Not: Identity Politics in Higher Education*. New York: New York University Press.

Menon, Vilas. 2001. "WA Reflection." *Writing Matters: The Newsletter of the Lafayette College Writing Program* 2.2.

Mentor, Ms. 2004. "Should Your Life Be Public News?" *The Chronicle of Higher Education*. February 6, 2004. C3.

Mentor, Ms. 2005. "Don't Be Docile." *The Chronicle of Higher Education*. January 11, 2005. http://chronicle.com/jobs/2005/01/2005011101c.htm

Message, Kylie. 1998. "Mum's Got a Whirlpool: Abject Bodies and the Regulation of Maternity." *Journal of Australian Studies* 147: 147–53.

Miller, Richard. 1996. "What Does It Mean to Learn?: William Bennett, the Educational Testing Service, and a Praxis of the Sublime." *JAC* 16: 41–60.

Morley, Louise and Val Walsh, eds. 1995. *Feminist Academics: Creative Agents for Change*. London: Taylor and Francis.

Morrison, Toni. 1998. *The Nobel Lecture in Literature and Speech of Acceptance, 1993*. New York: Knopf.

Morrison, Toni. 2004. *Beloved*. New York: Vintage.

Mowitt, John. 2000. "Trauma Envy." *Cultural Critique* 46: 272–97.

Mutnick, Deborah. 1996. *Writing in an Alien World: Basic Writing and the Struggle for Equality in Higher Education*. Portsmouth, NH: Boynton/Cook.

Newkirk, Thomas. 1997. *The Performance of Self in Student Writing*. Portsmouth, NH: Boynton/Cook.

North, Stephen M. 1984. "The Idea of a Writing Center." *College English* 46: 433–46.

Oliver, Mary. 1992. "Singapore." *New and Selected Poems*. Boston, MA: Beacon Press.

Olsen, Tillie. 1978. *Silences*. New York: Dell.

Ottery, Rudi. 1989. *A Man Called Sampson: 1580–1989*. Camden, Maine: Penobscot Press.

Palmer, Parker J. 1998. *The Courage to Teach: Exploring the Inner Landscape of a Teacher's Life*. San Francisco, CA: Jossey-Bass.

Phelps, Louise Wetherbee. 1995. "Becoming a Warrior: Lessons of the Feminist Workplace." In *Feminine Principles and Women's Experiences in American Composition and Rhetoric*. Edited by Louise Wetherbee Phelps and Janet Emig. Pittsburgh: University of Pittsburgh Press. 289–340.

Phinney, Jean S. 1990. "Ethnic Identity in Adolescents and Adults: Review of Research." *Psychological Bulletin* 108: 3. 499.

Polkinghorne, Donald E. 1991. "Narrative and Self Concept." *Journal of Narrative and Life History* 1: 135–54.

Poovey, M. 2001. "The Twenty-First Century University and the Market: What Price Economic Viability." *Differences: A Journal of Cultural Studies* 12: 1–16.

Ragland, Ellie. 1992. "Editorial: L'envers de la Pychanalyse." *Newsletter of the Freudian Field* 6: 1–2.

Ramadanovic, Petar. 1998. "When 'to Die in Freedom' is Written in English." *Diacritics* 28: 54–67.

Rankin, Susan R. 2003. "Campus Climate for Gay, Lesbian, Bisexual, and Transgender People: A National Perspective." New York: The National Gay and Lesbian Task Force Policy Institute. www.ngltf.org

Read, Daphne. 1998. "Writing Trauma, History, Story: The Class(room) as Borderland." *JAC* 18: 105–21.

Readings, Bill. 1996. *The University in Ruins*. Cambridge, MA: Harvard University Press.

Rich, Adrienne. 1980. "Compulsory Heterosexuality and Lesbian Existence." *Signs* 5: 631–60.

Rodriguez, Richard. 1983. *Hunger of Memory: The Education of Richard Rodriguez*. New York: Bantam Books.

Rodriguez, Richard. 1998. "Private and Public Language." In *Learning Dynamics*. Edited by Marjorie Ford and Jon Ford. Boston, MA: Houghton Mifflin.

Rogers, Dwight L. and Leslie M. Babinski. 2002. *From Isolation to Conversation: Supporting New Teachers' Development*. Albany, NY: SUNY Press.

Rose, Shirley K. 1998. *Situated Stories: Valuing Diversity in Composition Research*. Portsmouth, NH: Boynton/Cook.

Roy, Beth. 1994. *Some Trouble with Cows: Making Sense of Social Conflict*. Berkeley, CA: University of California Press.

Royster, Jacqueline Jones. 1996. "When the First Voice You Hear Is Not Your Own." *College Composition and Communication* 47: 29–40.

Rudy, Kathy. 2000. Queer Theory and Feminism. *Women's Studies* 29: 195–216.

Ryan, Kevin. 1970. *Don't Smile Until Christmas: Accounts of the First Year of Teaching*. Chicago, IL: University of Chicago Press.

Salvatori, Mariolina. 1988. "Toward a Hermeneutics of Difficulty." In *Audits of Meaning: A Festschrift in Honor of Ann E. Berthoff*. Edited by Louise Smith Portsmouth, NH: Boynton/Cook. 88–95.

Sanders, Scott Russell. 1993. *Staying Put: Making a Home in a Restless World*. Boston, MA: Beacon Press.

Santner, Eric L. 1992. "History Beyond the Pleasure Principle: Some Thoughts on the Representation of Trauma." In *Probing the Limits of Representation: National-Socialism and the "Final Solution."* Edited by Saul Friedländer. Cambridge, MA: Harvard University Press. 143–54.

Schell, Eileen. 1997. *Gypsy Academics and Mother-Teachers : Gender, Contingent Labor, and Writing Instruction*. Portsmouth, NH: Boynton/Cook

Scott, Joan W. 1994. "Evidence of Experience." In *Questions of Evidence: Proof, Practice, and Persuasion across the Disciplines*. Edited by James K. Chandler, Harry Harootunian, and Arnold I. Davidson. Chicago, IL: University of Chicago Press. 363–87.

Seltzer, Mark. 1997. "Wound Culture: Trauma in the Pathological Public Sphere." *October* 80: 3–26

Shepard, Alan, John McMillan and Gary Tate, eds. 1998. *Coming to Class: Pedagogy and the Social Class of Teachers*. Portsmouth NH: Boynton/Cook.

Shevin, D. and L. Smith, eds. 1996. *Getting By: Stories of Working Class Lives*. Huron, OH: Bottom Dog Press.

Showalter, English, Howard Figler, Lori G. Kletzer, Jack H. Schuster, and Seth Katz, eds. 1996. *The MLA Guide to the Job Search: A Handbook for PhDs and PhD Candidates in English and Foreign Languages*. New York: MLA.

Simeone, Angela. 1987. *Academic Women Working Towards Equality*. South Hadley, MA: Bergin and Garvey.

Slack, Jennifer Daryl. 1996. "The Theory and Method of Articulation in Cultural Studies." In *Stuart Hall: Critical Dialogues in Cultural Studies*. Edited by David Morley and Kuam Hsing Chen. London: Routledge. 112–30.

Smitherman, Geneva. 2000. *Talkin that Talk: Language, Culture and Education in African America*. New York: Routledge.

Sommers, Nancy. 2003. "The Undergraduate Writing Experience: A Longitudinal Perspective." Paper Presented at the Conference on College Composition and Communication. New York. March 20, 2003.

Spellmeyer, Kurt. 1996. "After Theory: From Textuality to Attunement with the World."

College English 58: 893–913.

Stafford, Kim. 1986. *Having Everything Right: Essays of Place.* Seattle, WA: Sasquatch.

Stegner, Wallace. 1992. "The Sense of Place." *Where the Bluebird Sings to the Lemonade Springs: Living and Writing in the West.* New York: Random House. 199–206.

Sternglass, Marilyn S. 1997. *Time to Know Them: A Longitudinal Story of Writing and Learning in the College Level.* Mahwah, NJ: Lawrence Earlbaum.

Stewart, Kathleen. 1996. *A Space by the Side of the Road: Cultural Poetics in an "Other" America.* Princeton, NJ: Princeton University Press.

Street, Brian V. 1995. *Social Literacies: Critical Approaches to Literacy in Development, Ethnography, and Education.* New York: Longman.

Street, Brian V. 2001. "Introduction." In *Literacy and Development: Ethnographic Perspectives.* Edited by Brian Street. London: Routledge. 1–18.

Strickland, Ronald. 2002. "Gender, Class, and the Humanities in the Corporate University." *Genders* 35. http://www.genders.org/g35/g35_strickland.html

Sztompka, Piotr. 2000. "Cultural Trauma: The Other Face of Social Change." *European Journal of Social Theory* 3: 449–66.

Tannen, Deborah. 1993. *Gender and Conversational Interaction.* New York: Oxford University Press.

Tatum, Beverly Daniel. 1992. "Talking about Race, Learning about Racism: The Application of Racial Identity Development Theory in the Classroom." *Harvard Educational Review* 61: 1–25.

The Chilly Collective, eds. 1995. *Breaking Anonymity: The Chilly Climate for Women Faculty.* Waterloo, Ontario, Canada: Wilfred Laurier University Press.

The Midwife's Tale. Writ. and Prod. Laurie Kahn-Levitt. PBS Home Video, 1998. Based on the book, *The Midwife's Tale,* by Laurel Thatcher Ulrich.

Theobald, Paul. 1997. *Teaching the Commons: Place, Pride, and the Renewal of Community.* Boulder, CO: Westview.

Tobin, Lad. 1993. *Writing Relationships: What Really Happens in the Composition Class.* Portsmouth, NH: Boynton/Cook.

Toth, Emily. 1997. *Ms. Mentor's Impeccable Advice for Women In Academia.* Philadelphia, PA: University of Pennsylvania Press.

Trauma and Rhetoric: Part One. 2004. Spec. Issue. *JAC* 24.

Trauma and Rhetoric: Part Two. 2004. Spec. Issue. *JAC* 24.

Ulrich, Laurel Thatcher, 1990. *The Midwife's Tale.* New York: Alfred A. Knopf.

Villanueva, Jr., Victor. 1997. "Considerations for American Freireistas." In *Cross-Talk in Comp Theory.* Edited by Victor Villanueva, Jr. Urbana, IL: NCTE. 621–38.

White, Hayden. 1992. "Historical Emplotment and the Problem of Truth." In *Probing the Limits of Representation: National-Socialism and the "Final Solution."* Edited by Saul Friedländer. Cambridge, MA: Harvard University Press. 37–53.

White, Michael and David Epston. 1990. *Narrative Means to Therapeutic Ends.* New York: Norton.

Wiegman, Robyn. 1994. "Queering the Academy." In *The Gay '90s: Disciplinary and Interdisciplinary Formations in Queer Studies.* Edited by Thomas Foster, Carol Siegel, and Ellen E. Berry. New York: New York University Press. 3–22.

Williams, Bronwyn T. 2003. "The Face in the Mirror, The Person on the Page." *Journal of Adolescent & Adult Literacy.* 47: 178–83.

Worsham, Lynn. 1998. "After Words: A Choice of Words Remains." In *Feminism and Composition Studies: In Other Words.* Edited by Susan C. Jarratt and Lynn Worsham. New York: MLA. 329–56.

Wortham, Stanton. 2001. *Narratives in Action: A Strategy for Research and Analysis.* New York: Teachers College Press.

Wright, E. O. 1985. *Classes.* London: Verso.

Zipes, Jack. 1998. "Ernst Bloch and the Obscenity of Hope." *New German Critique* 45. 3–8.

Zweig, M. 2000. *The Working Class Majority: America's Best Kept Secret.* Ithaca, NY: ILR Press of Cornell University Press.

CONTRIBUTORS

BRONWYN T. WILLIAMS is an associate professor of English at the University of Louisville. He writes and teaches about issues of literacy, identity, popular culture, and cross-cultural communication. His books include *Tuned In: Television and the Teaching of Writing* and *Popular Culture and Representations of Literacy* with Amy A. Zenger. He also writes a column on issues of literacy and identity for the *Journal of Adolescent and Adult Literacy*.

JANET ALSUP is an associate professor of English education at Purdue University. In addition to articles and book chapters, she has written two books, *But Will it Work with Real Students? Scenarios for Teaching Secondary English Language Arts* and *Teacher Identity Discourses: Negotiating Personal and Professional Spaces*.

ROBERT BROOKE is a professor of English at the University of Nebraska–Lincoln, where he directs the Nebraska Writing Project and edits the Studies in Writing and Rhetoric series. His book, *Rural Voices: Place-Conscious Education and the Teaching of Writing*, is related to this article.

WILLIAM J. CARPENTER is an assistant professor of English and the WAC Consultant at Chapman University in Orange, California. He is the co-editor of *The Allyn & Bacon Sourcebook for Writing Program Administrators* and has published essays on style and information literacy. He teaches courses in discourse analysis, rhetoric, and creative writing.

SHANNON CARTER is an assistant professor of English at Texas A&M University–Commerce, where she directs the Writing Center and the Basic Writing Program and teaches basic writing and graduate-level courses in composition theory. She has recently completed *The Way Literacy Lives: New Literacy Studies and the "Basic" Writer*, currently under review.

SALLY CHANDLER is an assistant professor of English at Kean University where she teaches college composition. Her research interests include the study of communication across difference, and the exploration of ethnographic and feminist methods for collaborative research. Her work has appeared in *Feminist Teacher*, *Generations*, and *Oral History*.

BIANCA FALBO is an assistant professor of English and assistant director of the College Writing Program at Lafayette College. Her scholarship focuses on the institutionalizing of literacy practices since the turn of the nineteenth century in a range of cultural sites including school books, periodicals, editions of "literary" texts, and student writing. Her articles have appeared in *Reader* and *Composition Studies*.

MARY HALLET has her PhD in composition and literature from the University of New Hampshire and is writing director at Long Island University–Brooklyn. She studies student papers about death, grief, and violence; the writing and literacy challenges of nontraditional and learning disabled students; and the rhetorics of popular documentaries.

PATRICIA HARKIN teaches English and communication studies at the University of Illinois, Chicago. She is author of *Acts of Reading*, editor of a special issue of *Works and Days* celebrating the work of Richard Ohmann, and co-editor of *Configuring Virtual Worlds: Teaching with Virtual Harlem* and *Contending with Words: Composition and Rhetoric in a Postmodern Age*. Her work has appeared in *College English, College Composition and Communication, Rhetoric Review* and she has served on the executive committees of the National Council of Teachers of English, the Conference on College Composition and Communication, and the Society for Critical Exchange.

MIN-ZHAN LU is Professor of English at the University of Louisville, where she teaches courses in composition, life writing, critical theory, and the pedagogical uses of cultural dissonance. Her most recent book is *Shanghai Quartet: The Crossings of Four Women of China*. She is recipient of the Mina P. Shaughnessy Award for Best Article Published in the *Journal of Basic Writing* for her essay "Redefining the Legacy of Mina Shaughnessy," and her essay "An Essay on the Work of Composition: Composing English Against the Order of Fast Capitalism" won the 2004 Richard Braddock Award.

JAMES R. OTTERY is an assistant professor of English at the University of Illinois at Springfield. Besides his work in composition and rhetoric, he also teaches American Indian literature and the writing of poetry. Maritza is graduating from Dennison University in May 2006.

TARA PAULINY earned her PhD in rhetoric and composition from The Ohio State University in 2002. Her work focuses dually on feminist and queer rhetorics and writing center and writing program administration studies. She is currently an assistant professor at the University of Wisconsin–Oshkosh where she also directs the university's writing center.

LYNN WORSHAM is a professor of English at Illinois State University, where she teaches undergraduate and graduate courses in postcolonial literature, rhetorical theory, cultural studies, and feminism. She is currently working on a monograph on trauma and rhetoric. She serves as editor of *JAC*, an interdisciplinary journal devoted to the study of rhetoric, culture, and politics.

JAMES T. ZEBROSKI, professor of English at Capital University in Columbus, Ohio, has published widely on composition theory. His book *Thinking Through Theory*, popularized the ideas of Lev Vygotsky for college teachers. His current research focuses on social class in composition and rhetoric.

INDEX